As a working security architect, I have three questions of any Does it track my own understanding of my work? Does it cover the problem space comprehensively and well? Does it give insights that are new to me? To all three questions this book gets a resounding 'yes' – it's earned its place on my shelf.

Ben Banks, CEO, Additive Security

Security Architecture is yet another indispensable and comprehensive resource for the cybersecurity community. This insightful book is a must-have, deserving pride of place on every professional's bookshelf for designing proactive and resilient cyber protection.

Philip Blake, Managing Director, Disruptive Cyber Group

The principle of 'Secure by Design' is vital; security must be built into IT systems right from the start. It isn't something that can be successfully retrofitted later! This book will give readers a solid understanding of many key principles and considerations when designing secure systems. I'm sure it will be an essential read for many security architects and will also become a valuable reference guide.

Steve Sands CITP FBCS, Chair of the Information Security
Specialist Group (ISSG) at BCS, The Chartered Institute for IT

This book deftly balances theoretical foundations with practical implementation. This invaluable resource provides security professionals with methodical frameworks and actionable strategies/best practices for effectively building robust organisational security architectures.

Ashish Kirtikar, President, Europe and UK, ControlCase Ltd

Security Architecture clearly describes an integrated approach to governing, designing and implementing architectural practices to proactively mitigate against breach. For aspiring professionals to established practitioners, the book serves as both a learning resource and a valuable reference on-the-job. A must read.

John Burns LL.M CEng MBCS,
Information Security Risk Analyst

'The ability to balance security and usability is important, ensuring that security solutions do not hinder performance or user experience.' This quote really resonated with me. Balancing usability with security is a challenge we face daily, and Green addresses it with clarity and practical advice. Definitely worth a read for anyone working in cybersecurity.

John Fernandes CISSP, Technical Security and
Infrastructure Manager, Saltgate Limited

A valuable guide for those looking to progress into security architecture or develop further in the role. It brings together technical insight with the communication and leadership skills that truly support long term success.

Jacqui Maw, Curriculum Team Leader (Computing and
Emerging Technologies), Burton and South Derbyshire College

An authoritative and lucid masterclass that brilliantly bridges the chasm between abstract theory and tangible security outcomes. It masterfully distils complex frameworks into a definitive, actionable blueprint that empowers architects to engineer proactive and adaptive security defences against tomorrow's sophisticated threats. An indispensable resource.

Dr Sherif Elgendy ChCSP CEng CITP FBCS MCIIS CISM C|CISO,
Cybersecurity Executive

An essential and timely resource for both emerging and established security professionals committed to making a tangible impact within their organisations and across the global cybersecurity landscape. This comprehensive, insight-rich guide combines practical expertise with data-driven analysis, particularly relevant for organisations leveraging AI, machine learning, deep learning, and large language models. A powerful and highly recommended reference.

Thomas Balogun MBCS CITP CEng CSyP,
CEO, Secured Zones

For the security professional or someone who is just starting in the industry this is the first book you need. Filled with case studies which explain the intricacies of how, when and why we need to be aware. It also gives you a 'toolkit' that can allow you to be the SME for the whole organisation. Highly recommended.

Jeff Stone MCSE MCP CNA MBCS CC,
IT Technical Architect, Liverpool Hope University

Security Architecture is a timely addition to the field, arriving at a critical moment for organisations navigating the complexities of an evolving cyber threat landscape. It provides a clear and pragmatic framework for enhancing an organisation's cyber resilience.

Steve Watt CITP FBCS CISSP,
Chief Information Officer, University of St Andrews

A must read for everyone in cybersecurity. It's clear, practical, and insightful, with the standout chapter on system security offering exceptional depth and detail for both early-career and seasoned professionals.

Matt Mason CISSP CCSP CGRC CITP MBCS,
Deputy Head of Information Security,
University of Birmingham

For those who have benefited from the insights offered in *Information Security Management Principles*, *Security Architecture* represents a timely and essential next step. This commendable work equips both seasoned professionals and newcomers with accessible reference material, seamlessly interwoven with practical, real-world examples. Drawing on the author's extensive experience and expertise, it covers a broad spectrum of topics, making it an indispensable guide for anyone looking to excel in this ever-evolving technical field.

Phil Cobley MSc CITP,
Digital Forensics and Security Specialist

A crucial read for any cyber professional, this book provides the essential blueprint to design resilient, proactive cyber defences to protect IT and business assets from cyber threats.

Nigel V Thomas CITP MBCS,
Senior Software Engineer 2, Sophos

Security Architecture is a vital resource for security architects seeking to align technical leadership with inclusive and equitable practice. It bridges the often-overlooked gap between system architecture and organisational culture, offering a compelling, evidence-led framework for embedding equity into the design and governance of secure, resilient systems. A must-read for those shaping the future of security through both technology and values.

Gary Cocklin, CITP CISSP ISSAP,
Security Architect, UK Royal Air Force

SECURITY ARCHITECTURE

BCS, THE CHARTERED INSTITUTE FOR IT

BCS, The Chartered Institute for IT, is committed to making IT good for society. We use the power of our network to bring about positive, tangible change. We champion the global IT profession and the interests of individuals, engaged in that profession, for the benefit of all.

Exchanging IT expertise and knowledge
The Institute fosters links between experts from industry, academia and business to promote new thinking, education and knowledge sharing.

Supporting practitioners
Through continuing professional development and a series of respected IT qualifications, the Institute seeks to promote professional practice tuned to the demands of business. It provides practical support and information services to its members and volunteer communities around the world.

Setting standards and frameworks
The Institute collaborates with government, industry and relevant bodies to establish good working practices, codes of conduct, skills frameworks and common standards. It also offers a range of consultancy services to employers to help them adopt best practice.

Become a member
Over 70,000 people including students, teachers, professionals and practitioners enjoy the benefits of BCS membership. These include access to an international community, invitations to a roster of local and national events, career development tools and a quarterly thought-leadership magazine. Visit www.bcs.org to find out more.

Further information
BCS, The Chartered Institute for IT,
3 Newbridge Square,
Swindon, SN1 1BY, United Kingdom.
T +44 (0) 1793 417 417
(Monday to Friday, 09:00 to 17:00 UK time)
bcs.org/contact

shop.bcs.org/
publishing@bcs.uk

bcs.org/qualifications-and-certifications/certifications-for-professionals/

SECURITY ARCHITECTURE
A practical guide to designing proactive and resilient cyber protection

Jeremy Green

Published by BCS Learning and Development Ltd, a wholly owned subsidiary of BCS, The Chartered Institute for IT, 3 Newbridge Square, Swindon, SN1 1BY, UK.
www.bcs.org

EU GPSR Authorised Representative: LOGOS EUROPE, 9 Rue Nicolas Poussin, 17000 La Rochelle, France.
Contact@logoseurope.eu

Paperback ISBN: 978-1-78017-7144
PDF ISBN: 978-1-78017-7151
ePUB ISBN: 978-1-78017-7168

British Cataloguing in Publication Data.
A CIP catalogue record for this book is available at the British Library.

Disclaimer:
The views expressed in this book are of the author and do not necessarily reflect the views of the Institute or BCS Learning and Development Ltd except where explicitly stated as such. Although every care has been taken by the author and BCS Learning and Development Ltd in the preparation of the publication, no warranty is given by the author or BCS Learning and Development Ltd as publisher as to the accuracy or completeness of the information contained within it and neither the author nor BCS Learning and Development Ltd shall be responsible or liable for any loss or damage whatsoever arising by virtue of such information or any instructions or advice contained within this publication or by any of the aforementioned.

All URLs were correct at the time of publication.

Publisher's acknowledgements
Reviewers: Mark Wolden, Tim Williams
Publisher: Ian Borthwick
Commissioning editor: Heather Wood
Production manager: Florence Leroy
Project manager: Sunrise Setting Ltd
Copy-editor: Mary Hobbins
Proofreader: Barbara Eastman
Indexer: David Gaskell
Cover design: Alex Wright
Cover image: iStock/paulacobleigh
Sales director: Charles Rumball
Typeset by Lapiz Digital Services, Chennai, India

CONTENTS

LIST OF FIGURES AND TABLES

AUTHOR

Jeremy Green is a skilled and experienced security professional with more than 20 certifications across platform, security and DevSecOps including CISSP, CISM, CEH, ECDE and CHFI. He is also an official instructor for ISACA and EC Council and the author of *Information Security Management Principles*, fourth edition.

Jeremy has worked across diverse industries including education, consultancy, telecoms, police and military. He started his career in further education (FE), teaching computer science, before moving into police IT training, including cybercrime and OSINT. After a short period as a full-time police officer, Jeremy dropped back into FE, setting up one of the first cyber security courses in FE. He then transitioned into the world of certification training as a Firebrand instructor across Europe for CompTIA and EC Council. From there, Jeremy joined BT as a cyber security manager working within cyber defence on platforms such as Splunk, MS Sentinel and CrowdStrike, before joining Vodafone as a cyber security advisory manager, initially supporting cyber security of African and Asian markets, before moving into global governance risk and compliance, working with frameworks and controls.

Jeremy is currently a security architect with Leidos. He has served with the Army Reserves and is now serving with the RAF Cyber Reserves as well remaining a long-time serving special constable with the police. He also supports University College Dublin, BCS, IT Governance and Burton and South Derbyshire College with delivery of degree, diploma and certification training and course development. Jeremy is currently undertaking a PhD in computer science, researching quantum computing and its impact on security.

FOREWORD

In the ever-evolving digital landscape where technology permeates every aspect of our lives, security can no longer be considered as an optional enhancement, continuing to be treated as an afterthought. Instead, it must be at the very heart of an organisation's digitally connected ecosystem as new technologies are embraced, and with it so too does the potential attack surface expand exponentially. This is where the discipline of security architecture comes into its own, underpinning the security strategies of an organisation.

Security architecture is not just about selecting the right tools or deploying reactive measures; it is about the intentional creation and implementation of layered and resilient security designs that anticipate threats, mitigate risks and can adapt to change.

This book, which builds upon the knowledge gained from reading *Information Security Management Principles* published by BCS, provides a pragmatic guide to navigating the complex nature of security architecture, offering not only frameworks and models that define modern security architecture, but also including practical insights born from real-world experience.

I commend the author for not only providing clarity to the complex nature of modern security architecture but also for his vision and insight into the future with the advent of quantum computing.

May this book serve as both a compass and a catalyst in your quest to ensure your organisation has both a secure and a resilient digital footprint.

Mark Wolden MSc FBCS
Security Consultant
Semper Fi Consulting

ACKNOWLEDGEMENTS

For this title, I would like to thank my family, especially my amazing wife, my mother and late father who have always offered inspiration, support and guidance throughout my many endeavours, and my three children, Oliver, Charlotte and Ben. I would also like to thank my colleagues across my various employers past and present, including Phil Larner, a true 'Cyber Megamind', Philip Blake for his continuous support, guidance and advocacy over the years, Jacqui Maw of Burton and South Derbyshire College, who has always given unwavering support as both a friend and colleague, Mark Wolden MSc for a great technical review, helpful pointers and expert advice, and Ian Borthwick and Heather Wood of BCS for their help in getting this title into print.

I am also lucky to have been exposed to such a wide variety of experience and knowledge from so many talented individuals I have worked with and taught over the years. None more so than my RAF and Leidos colleagues, who have been a source of so much inspiration and knowledge over the years. We can all learn so much from each other, especially working in security.

ABBREVIATIONS

3DES	triple data encryption standard
5 Ds	deny, degrade, disrupt, deceive and destroy
ABAC	attribute-based access control
ACL	access control list
ADA	application decomposition and analysis
ADM	Architecture Development Method (TOGAF)
AES	Advanced Encryption Standard
AGI	artificial general intelligence
AH	authentication header
AI	artificial intelligence
AKS	Azure Kubernetes Service
AMS	attack modelling and simulation
ANI	artificial narrow intelligence
API	application program interface
APT	advanced persistent threat
AR	augmented reality
AS	authentication server
ASCII	American Standard Code for Information Interchange
ASI	artificial superintelligence
ASVS	Application Security Verification Standard (OWASP)
ATS	App Transport Security
ATT&CK®	adversarial tactics, techniques and common knowledge (MITRE Corp.)
AWS	Amazon Web Services
BCS	British Computer Society, The Chartered Institute for IT
BIA	business impact analysis
BYOD	bring your own device
CASB	cloud access security broker
CCTV	closed-circuit television
CD	continuous development
CEH	Certified Ethical Hacker (certification)
CERT	computer emergency response team

CI	continuous integration
CIA	confidentiality, integrity and availability
CIIP	Critical Information Infrastructure Protection (ENISA)
CIS	Center for Internet Security
CIS-CAT	Center for Internet Security Configuration Assessment Tool
CISM	Certified Information Security Manager (certification)
CISO	chief information security officer
CISSP	Certified Information Systems Security Professional (certification)
COBIT	Control Objectives for Information and Related Technologies
CPU	central processing unit
CRSF	cross-site request forgery
CRUD	create, read, update and delete
CSA	Cloud Security Alliance
CSF	Cybersecurity Framework (NIST)
CVE	Common Vulnerabilities and Exposures database
DAST	dynamic application security testing
DCMS	Department for Culture, Media and Sport
DDoS	distributed denial of service
DevOps	development operations
DevSecOps	development, security and operations
DFD	data flow diagram
DLP	data loss prevention
DMZ	demilitarised zone
DNS	domain name system
DO	definition of the objectives
DORA	Digital Operational Resilience Act
DoS	denial of service
DPA	Data Protection Act
DR	disaster recovery
DREAD	damage, reproducibility, exploitability, affected, discoverability
DTS	definition of the technical scope
EC2	Elastic Compute Cloud
ECS	Elastic Container Service (Amazon)
EDR	endpoint detection and response
EKS	Elastic Kubernetes Service
ENISA	European Union Agency for Network and Information Security
ESP	Encapsulating Security Protocol
EU	European Union
FHE	fully homomorphic encryption
FIPS	Federal Information Processing Standards

FSA	Financial Services Act
FTP	File Transfer Protocol
GCHQ	Government Communications Headquarters
GCM	Galois/Counter Mode
GDPR	General Data Protection Regulation
GKE	Google Kubernetes Engine
GPS	global positioning system
GPU	graphics processing unit
GRC	governance, risk and compliance
HIDS	host intrusion detection system
HIP	host intrusion prevention
HIPAA	Health Insurance Portability and Accountability Act (USA)
HLD	high-level diagram
HTTP(S)	Hypertext Transfer Protocol (Secure)
IA	information assurance
IaaS	infrastructure as a service
IAM	identity and access management
IAST	interactive application security testing
I&T	integration and testing
ICO	Information Commissioner's Office
ICS	industrial control system
ICT	information communications and technology
IDPS	intrusion detection and prevention system
IDS	intrusion detection system
IEC	International Electrotechnical Commission
IETF	Internet Engineering Task Force
III-RM	Integrated Information Infrastructure Reference Model (TOGAF)
IIoT	industrial IoT
IKE	Internet Key Exchange protocol
InfoOps	information operations
IoC	indicator of compromise
IoT	Internet of Things
IP	intellectual property
IPS	intrusion prevention system
IPSec	Internet Protocol Security
IR	incident response
ISACA	Information Systems Audit and Control Association
ISC²	International Information System Security Certification Consortium
ISMS	information security management system
ISO	International Organization for Standardization

IT	information technology
ITIL	Information Technology Infrastructure Library
JIT	just-in-time
KDC	key distribution centre
KPI	key performance indicator
KRI	key risk indicator
LAN	local area network
LiDAR	light detection and ranging
LLM	large language model
LWE	learning with errors
MAC	message authentication code
MFA	multi-factor authentication
MIC	Message Integrity code
ML	machine learning
ML-DSA	Module-Lattice-Based Digital Signature Algorithm (NIST)
ML-KEM	Module-Lattice-Based Key Encapsulation Mechanism (NIST)
MO	modus operandi
MTTD	mean time to detect
MTTR	mean time to respond
NAC	network access control
NCSC	National Cyber Security Centre (part of GCHQ)
NGFW	next-generation firewall
NIDS	network intrusion detection system
NIP	network intrusion prevention
NIS	Network and Information Systems
NISQ	noisy intermediate scale quantum
NIST	National Institute of Standards and Technology
NTFS	New Technology File System
NTLM	New Technology LAN Manager (Microsoft)
OAuth	Open Authorisation
OS	operating system
OSA	Open Security Architecture (framework)
OSINT	open-source intelligence
OT	operational technology
OWASP	Open Web Application Security Project
PaaS	platform as a service
PAM	privileged access management
PASTA	process for attack simulation and threat analysis
PCI DSS	Payment Card Industry Data Security Standard

Pentest	penetration test
PHE	partially homomorphic encryption
PII	personally identifiable information
PKI	public key infrastructure
PSK	PreShared Key
PsyOps	psychological operations
RADIUS	remote authentication dial-in user service
RaMP	Rapid Modernisation Plan
RBAC	role-based access control
RDBMS	Relational Database Management System
RFI	radio frequency interference
RIA	risk and impact analysis
RSA	Rivest–Shamir–Adleman (cryptography)
RTO	recovery time objective
SA	security association
SaaS	software as a service
SABSA	Sherwood Applied Business Security Architecture
SAML	Security Assertion Markup Language
SAST	static application security testing
SBD	Secure by Design
SCADA	supervisory control and data acquisition
SDL	Security Development Lifecycle (Microsoft)
SDLC	software development lifecycle
SFTP	SSH File Transfer Protocol
SHA	secure hash algorithm (hashing)
SHE	somewhat homomorphic encryption
SIEM	security information and event management
SIP	session initiation protocol
SLH-DSA	Stateless Hash-Based Digital Signature Algorithm (NIST)
SOA	service-oriented architecture
SOAR	security orchestration, automation and response
SOC	security operations centre
SOX	Sarbanes–Oxley Act 2002 (USA)
SPL	Search Processing Language (Splunk)
SQL	Structured Query Language
SQLi	SQL injection
SS7	Signalling System 7
SSH	Secure Shell (network communication protocol)
SSL	Secure Sockets Layer

SSO	single sign-on
STRIDE	spoofing, tampering, repudiation, information disclosure, DoS and elevation of privilege
SVP	shortest vector problem
SWIFT	Society for Worldwide Interbank Financial Telecommunication
SWOT	strengths, weaknesses, opportunities and threats
TA	threat analysis
TDE	transparent data encryption
TGS	ticket granting server
TGT	ticket granting ticket
TLS	Transport Layer Security
TOGAF	The Open Group Architecture Framework
TPM	trusted platform module
TRIKE	threat risk identification and knowledge exchange
TRM	Technical Reference Model (TOGAF)
TTPs	tactics, techniques and procedures
UBA	user behaviour analytics
UEBA	user and entity behaviour analytics
URL	uniform resource locator
UTM	unified threat management
VAST	visual, agile and simple threat
VLAN	virtual local area network
VM	virtual machine
VoIP	Voice over Internet Protocol
VPN	virtual private network
VR	virtual reality
WAF	web application firewall
WIDPS	wireless intrusion detection and prevention system
WIDS	wireless intrusion detection system
Wi-Fi	Wireless Fidelity
WIP	wireless intrusion prevention
WLAN	wireless local area network
WORM	write-once-read-many
WPA	Wi-Fi protected access
WVA	weakness and vulnerability analysis
XDR	extended detection and response
XOR	exclusive OR (maths operator)
XSS	cross-site scripting
ZTA	zero trust architecture
ZTNA	zero trust network access

GLOSSARY

ACL (access control list)   A set of rules that control access to resources in a computer environment, specifying which users or system processes are granted or denied access.

AES (Advanced Encryption Standard)   A symmetric key encryption standard widely used to secure data; considered secure against most classical attacks.

APT (advanced persistent threat)   A prolonged and targeted cyberattack in which an intruder gains unauthorised access to a network and remains undetected for an extended period.

CIA (confidentiality, integrity and availability)   A foundational model for information security that ensures sensitive data is protected from unauthorised access, remains accurate and is available when needed.

CISO (chief information security officer)   An executive role responsible for the organisation's information and cyber security strategy, risk management and governance.

CISSP (Certified Information Systems Security Professional)   A globally recognised certification for information security professionals, validating expertise in designing and managing security programmes.

DLP (data loss prevention)   Technologies and strategies that detect and prevent unauthorised data transmission or leakage outside an organisation.

DMZ (demilitarised zone)   A network segment that acts as a buffer between an internal network and untrusted external networks, often used to host public-facing services.

EDR (endpoint detection and response)   Security solutions focused on detecting, investigating and responding to suspicious activity and threats at endpoints.

IAM (identity and access management)   A framework for managing digital identities and controlling user access to systems and information within an organisation.

ISO/IEC 27001   An international standard that defines requirements for establishing, implementing, maintaining and continually improving an information security management system (ISMS).

MITRE ATT&CK   A knowledge base of adversary tactics and techniques based on real-world observations, used for threat modelling and defence strategy development.

NIST (National Institute of Standards and Technology)   A US federal agency that develops standards, including frameworks and cryptographic guidance, for cyber security.

PAM (privileged access management)   A set of technologies and practices that control, monitor and secure access to critical systems and sensitive information by privileged users.

PKI (public key infrastructure)   A framework that manages digital certificates and public-key encryption to secure electronic communications and verify identity.

SABSA (Sherwood Applied Business Security Architecture)   A layered methodology for developing risk-driven enterprise security architectures aligned with business objectives.

SIEM (security information and event management)   A security solution that provides real-time analysis of security alerts and events generated by network hardware and applications.

SOC (security operations centre)   A centralised function within an organisation responsible for monitoring, detecting, responding to and mitigating security incidents.

STRIDE   A threat modelling framework developed by Microsoft to identify security threats using six categories: spoofing, tampering, repudiation, information disclosure, denial of service and elevation of privilege.

TLS (transport layer security)   A protocol that provides end-to-end security for data sent over the internet; used to secure web traffic and email.

VPN (virtual private network)   A secure tunnel between devices and networks over the internet, providing encrypted communication to protect data in transit.

PREFACE

Security architecture is a cornerstone of modern enterprise resilience and an area that demands a strategic and multidisciplinary approach. As technology continues to evolve, so do the threats that seek to exploit vulnerabilities and cause harm. The role of a security architect is not merely about erecting barriers for defence and protection, it is also about creating intelligent, adaptive solutions that balance security with usability, business continuity and technological advancement while supporting organisational objectives. The final element is demonstratable value to the organisation and alignment with organisational strategy. This book aims to equip you with the foundational and advanced knowledge required in a security architecture role and to appreciate the broader context within which security architecture operates. It can also be used as a reference book in the thought process and rationale when considering security architecture. The book looks at a wide range of technologies and tools to aid in the decision-making process. However, this must always fit with the organisation's strategy, mission and goals. Technology should enhance, not detract from, security. Any new implementation should be thoroughly assessed and the risk of its use fully identified as part of the cost–benefit analysis and business impact assessment.

A security architect often holds a senior role requiring key leadership skills, including stakeholder management and effective communication, understanding how security architecture impacts on stakeholders, fragility of the environment, strategies for incident response and security posture. Communication skills are also a key requirement, with the appropriate use of technical language, written and oral communication methods and active listening to engage both technical and non-technical audiences effectively.

This book is designed for aspiring and current security architects, cyber engineers or information security specialists who wish to deepen their understanding of security architecture, develop their ability to apply concepts in practice and enhance their leadership skills. It blends theoretical foundations with practical applications to ensure you can address the complex and ever-changing landscape of security. *Information Security Management Principles* fourth edition is recommended reading for its underpinning knowledge, which this book directly builds on. This book also assumes that you have a solid technical understanding of IT, including networks and basics of IT security.

1 SECURITY ARCHITECTURE

In this chapter, we will explore the fundamentals of security architecture. What it is, why it matters and how it influences an organisation's overall security posture.

We will examine how security architecture not only mitigates risk but also delivers strategic value, supporting business objectives whilst protecting the organisation. Security architecture should aid in the protection and control of the environment, which includes alerting to threats. Also, remember security is something we do with the organisation by building good stakeholder relationships and advising on the required protection whilst ensuring they have accountability for it.

We will then delve into the role of a security architect, outlining their responsibilities, skill set and strategic influence within an organisation. A key focus will be on structured design methodologies, demonstrating how a security-driven approach can be applied to the implementation of new systems whilst adding value to the organisation. Finally, we will introduce the concepts of defence in depth and breadth, exploring how layered security measures contribute to a resilient security posture.

CASE STUDY

DeepSeek

DeepSeek an artificial intelligence (AI)-driven search and data analysis tool was initially seen as revolutionary due to its advanced AI-driven capabilities, which promised to transform data analysis, search efficiency and decision-making across various domains. It was also much more efficient, with a 95% reduction in graphics processing unit (GPU) usage and faster training at significantly lower costs without losing accuracy. However, concerns were quickly raised with DeepSeek around data privacy and leakage. Researchers found that DeepSeek was transmitting sensitive user data unencrypted to servers controlled by ByteDance, the Chinese company behind TikTok. This flaw is made worse due to DeepSeek disabling iOS's App Transport Security (ATS), a built-in protection designed to enforce encrypted communications. Data was also being sent with weak encryption such as the use of triple data encryption standard (3DES). This meant DeepSeek, if not properly controlled, could expose unintended data, leading to privacy breaches. Additionally, inference attacks, especially interception of unencrypted or weakly encrypted data, could allow adversaries to extract confidential insights, even from anonymised datasets. This poses a significant challenge for compliance with regulations such as the General Data Protection Regulation (GDPR) and the Health Insurance Portability and Accountability Act (HIPAA), where organisations must ensure proper data handling to avoid legal and financial repercussions.

Another major threat is model manipulation and data poisoning. As DeepSeek relies on large datasets to function effectively, attackers may attempt to manipulate these sources to introduce biases or misinformation. Poisoned data can lead to incorrect or misleading outputs, potentially affecting business decisions, security monitoring and automated responses. Additionally, backdoors in AI models could be exploited by malicious actors to exfiltrate sensitive data or disrupt operations.

The rise of AI-augmented cyber threats is another concern. DeepSeek can enhance cyber security by improving threat intelligence – the same capabilities can be weaponised by attackers. AI-assisted reconnaissance enables adversaries to map an organisation's attack surface more efficiently. Furthermore, AI-powered phishing and social engineering campaigns can be more convincing using contextual analysis to craft highly targeted attacks. Attackers could also automate vulnerability discovery, making it easier to identify weaknesses in software and infrastructure.

Security vulnerabilities in AI models and application program interface (API) exposure create additional risks. DeepSeek systems often rely on API endpoints for data access and query handling, which introduces potential attack vectors. API abuse, adversarial queries and denial of service (DoS) attacks could degrade service availability or manipulate AI responses. Without proper security measures, these interfaces could become entry points for attackers to extract confidential information or disrupt operations.

Finally, dependency on external and third-party data sources introduces integrity risks. Many AI models rely on third-party datasets, which may be compromised or manipulated. This raises concerns about supply chain attacks, where vulnerabilities inherited from external sources affect the AI system's reliability and security. Organisations must ensure that external data is vetted and continuously monitored for risks.

Not long after DeepSeek went live, concerns were quickly raised such as surveillance risks, data being stored in China and data exposure. This led to the US Navy prohibiting its members from using DeepSeek, citing security and ethical concerns. The National Security Council also initiated a national security review of the application. The Australian federal government, along with several state governments, has banned DeepSeek from all government devices and systems due to potential security risks. Taiwan's digital ministry has advised government departments against using DeepSeek to prevent information security risks. The South Korean government has blocked DeepSeek on official devices, following similar actions by Australia and Taiwan. Several organisations, with more following, have also prohibited and blocked its use on all corporate devices, including mobile devices.

Impact on security architecture

From a security architecture perspective, the use of DeepSeek may well fall outside risk tolerance for some organisations, though it may be an acceptable risk for another organisation. Risk acceptance is down to the organisation to decide after a full risk assessment has been undertaken for its use with risks mitigated and the overall risk deemed acceptable by the organisation. To address security concerns, robust security strategies must be implemented and controls tailored to AI-driven systems. Data governance and access controls should be a top priority. Implementing strict data classification and segregation ensures that DeepSeek can only access authorised information. Role-based and attribute-based access controls (RBAC and ABAC) ensure that only approved users and systems can interact with AI models. Additionally, data masking and anonymisation techniques help to mitigate inference attacks by limiting the exposure of sensitive details.

Securing AI models is equally critical. Organisations must conduct continuous model monitoring and validation to detect anomalies or biases in DeepSeek's outputs. Adversarial training should be implemented to harden AI models against poisoning and evasion attacks. Applying zero trust principles to AI interactions ensures that all queries and responses undergo verification before being processed.

A strong threat detection and incident response framework is essential to mitigate AI-related risks. AI-driven security analytics can help to identify anomalies in DeepSeek's behaviour, while maintaining comprehensive logging and audit trails enables security teams to trace suspicious activity. Integrating DeepSeek with security orchestration, automation and response (SOAR) platforms allows for real-time incident detection and mitigation.

Securing API endpoints and query handling is another critical aspect of AI security. Implementing rate limiting and anomaly detection mechanisms can help to prevent excessive or malicious queries. Input validation and sanitisation should be enforced to defend against adversarial inputs designed to exploit AI vulnerabilities. Encryption and strong authentication protocols, such as Transport Layer Security (TLS) 1.3 and API gateways, should be implemented to protect AI communications.

Given the reliance on external datasets, supply chain and third-party risk management must be prioritised. Continuous risk assessments should be conducted to evaluate the integrity of external data sources. Regular security testing, including red teaming exercises, can help to identify vulnerabilities in AI models before they are exploited. Furthermore, organisations should establish contractual security requirements to ensure that third-party vendors adhere to strict security standards.

Any data being put into DeepSeek must not be of a confidential or sensitive nature or attributable to the business or organisation. This must be strictly adhered to. This, and concerns around potential state listening in China, has meant its use is an unacceptable risk to many. Recommend the use of other services/providers if AI tools are permitted and properly risk assessed in an organisation.

SECURITY ARCHITECTURE

Security architecture is a set of models, methods and security principles that align with organisation objectives. It serves as a blueprint for ensuring the protection of data, systems and networks against threats, and can entail access management and encryption authentication. These requirements can come from legislation, compliance, standards and customer or third-party requirements. Essentially, strong security architecture leads to fewer security breaches, which also has the knock-on effect of helping to build customer confidence both internally and externally. Security architecture can be considered an extended information technology (IT) discipline as it requires underpinning IT and network knowledge to be able to fully understand the impact of applying IT security to a system or service.

The scope of security within any organisation can be categorised into three core responsibilities of: protection; monitoring and response; and advisory. Protection involves implementing measures to prevent security incidents, which includes recommending security solutions containing controls. Monitoring and response cover the ongoing observation of systems for potential threats and the capability to act swiftly and effectively when incidents occur. This includes the right coverage of monitoring within organisational boundaries. Finally, the advisory role entails guiding the business and technical teams on emerging risk, risk assessments, any compliance requirements and secure design principles. This ensures that advice is always 'what is best for the organisation' to meet its mission and profitability and to reduce harm that would prevent the organisation functioning properly.

Anything outside these domains typically falls beyond the remit of the security function. However, in many organisations, this boundary is often misunderstood or blurred. As a result, security teams frequently find themselves pulled into tasks that do not truly belong to them. This includes general IT operations, system administration, hardening, patching or even areas such as physical security and procurement. While collaboration is important, assuming responsibility for these non-security activities can dilute focus, drain resources and ultimately compromise the security architecture's ability to deliver on its primary objectives.

This misalignment often stems from a lack of clarity across the organisation about what 'security' entails. When responsibilities are not clearly defined and communicated, it becomes easy for teams to assign tasks to security simply because they involve systems or data. To address this, organisations must establish and enforce a well-defined security charter, supported by clear boundaries and engagement models with other departments. Doing so enables the security function to remain focused, efficient and strategically aligned with the organisation's actual risk landscape.

NIST 800-37 Rev 2 references security architecture as a set of physical and logical security-relevant representations (i.e. views) of system architecture that conveys information about how the system is partitioned into security domains, and makes use of security-relevant elements to enforce security policies within and between security domains based on how data and information must be protected. Security architecture reflects security domains, the placement of security-relevant elements within the security domains, the interconnections and trust relationships between the security-relevant elements, and the behaviour and interaction between the security-relevant elements. Security architecture, similar to system architecture, may be expressed at different levels of abstraction and with different scopes.

Security architecture is the strategic design of systems, policies and technologies to protect IT and business assets from cyberthreats. A well-designed security architecture aligns cybersecurity with the unique business goals and risk management profile of the organisation (Palo Alto Networks, n.d.).

IT security domains cover network security, which includes measures to protect the confidentiality, integrity and availability (CIA) of network resources. Application security involves securing software applications by identifying, fixing and preventing security vulnerabilities. Endpoint security involves protecting endpoint devices such as computers, mobile devices and multi-function devices. Data security involves ensuring data privacy and protecting data from loss or unauthorised access. Finally, identity and access management (IAM) involves managing user identities and their access to resources.

I think it's useful to recognise that different stakeholders have different viewpoints. As an example, imagine you are standing on a hill: in front of you there is a valley and mountains to the east and west. Multiple people in that same setting will have a different viewpoint depending on where they are standing and the direction they look. This is similar to enterprise architecture: different disciplines, users and stakeholders have a different view depending on their focus. The security architect needs to be able to see all these views at the same time. This is because security is a cross-cutting architectural concept that can't be singled out and put into its own, separate box. Instead, it needs to cut across the whole organisation and take these different viewpoints into account (John Sherwood, chief architect and co-founder of The SABSA Institute, quoted in Moyle and Kelley, 2020).

Security architecture provides strategic and practical benefits to an organisation, aligning security measures with business goals. Strategic alignment integrates security initiatives with the organisation's objectives by ensuring it supports and protects business operations without adding unnecessary costs. It also ensures effective governance and compliance, meeting regulatory requirements efficiently and reducing the risk of fines. However, it is a business and ethical decision whether the organisation chooses to be compliant, as the cost of the fine may be less than the cost of compliance. It may not be an ethical decision, but one a business may choose at a senior management level.

Another key value of security architecture lies in risk reduction. Security architecture should proactively identify and mitigate potential vulnerabilities and threats, lowering the risk of harm including data loss or service disruptions by ensuring critical data is secured via the use of encryption and access controls. Ultimately it is about protecting the organisation from loss, which can be costly – especially personal or sensitive data loss that is reportable to an authority such as the Information Commissioner's Office (ICO), which could result in a fine or even civil or criminal proceedings. There is also reputational damage, which can impact share prices as well as causing a loss of customers.

Good security architecture should help to optimise investments in technology and processes, prioritising those that offer the best cost and benefit, hopefully preventing unnecessary expenditure on redundant tools and being resource-efficient whilst adding value. Additionally, it can lower costs associated with incident management by reducing the likelihood and impact of security incidents, which often involve data loss, recovery expenses, regulatory penalties and reputational harm. Incidents can be very costly, reduce output and quickly use up limited resources.

Enhanced agility and scalability are achieved through effective security architecture. It is there to support secure adoption of newer technologies, such as containers, quantum computing and AI tools, although any new technology should be thoroughly risk assessed with use cases to ensure it is of use to the organisation and not a vanity project or the organisation has been misled by a vendor or consultant. It must add value and have a demonstratable benefit to the organisation.

Improved resilience is another benefit, as security architecture contributes to business continuity and disaster recovery (DR) planning, enabling the organisation to maintain operations even during adverse events. It also helps to ensure efficient crisis management, allowing for swift and effective responses to incidents, which minimises downtime, cost and damage.

Trust and reputation are crucial both internally and externally. Security architecture can help to build stakeholder confidence and give a level of assurance. Clients, partners and regulators are more likely to trust an organisation that demonstrates a strong commitment to security, potentially creating competitive advantages and stronger partnerships.

Finally, security architecture can facilitate better security culture and awareness within the organisation. It often involves raising awareness and training employees, making security a shared and embedded responsibility across all areas or business units, including senior management understanding the value of security. When designed well, security should integrate seamlessly into business processes, promoting secure behaviour without compromising productivity and thereby adding value to the organisation.

Security layers

Security layers include: physical security, which involves protecting hardware, software, data and employees from physical threats; perimeter security, which involves defending the outermost layer of the network, typically with firewalls and intrusion detection systems (IDSs); internal network security, which involves safeguarding internal network communications and assets; host security, which involves protecting individual systems and servers within the network; application security, which involves securing applications and ensuring they are free from vulnerabilities during design and on release; and. finally, data security, which involves protecting stored and transmitted data.

Core components of security architecture

Security architecture is a blend of principles, policies, models and components designed to deliver a robust, layered and comprehensive security posture.

- **Policies and standards:** These are high-level requirements and rules that guide how security is to be managed. They set the foundation for the security framework and ensure compliance with laws and regulations. Examples include password policies, access control policy, data handling standards, encryption standards, logging and monitoring and access control guidelines.

- **Enterprise information security architecture:** This is a structured approach to integrating security into an organisation's overall enterprise architecture. It aligns security policies, controls and technologies with business objectives, ensuring a consistent and scalable security posture across the organisation.

- **Threat modelling and risk assessment:** Security architecture incorporates methodologies to identify, assess and model threats and vulnerabilities. This process is used to understand potential attack vectors, prioritise risk and apply appropriate controls.

Security controls and mechanisms

Controls often influence user or system behaviours to mitigate risks. For example, implementing multi-factor authentication (MFA) affects user behaviour by requiring additional verification steps, while network segmentation, such as using virtual local area network (VLAN), affects system behaviour by restricting traffic flows. Analysing behaviour change helps to assess the control's effectiveness and user adoption challenges. Controls should be clearly documented in a control register to ensure accountability, support audits and provide a clear overview of the organisation's security and compliance. The control register should be reviewed and updated on a regular basis.

A controls register is a structured document or database used to track, manage and monitor security or compliance controls within an organisation and typically includes:

- **Control ID:** A unique identifier for each control.
- **Description:** A brief explanation of the control and its purpose.
- **Objective:** The goal the control is intended to achieve (e.g. mitigate a specific risk or comply with a standard).
- **Category:** The control type (e.g. administrative, technical, physical).
- **Owner**: The individual or team responsible for implementing and maintaining the control.
- **Status:** The implementation or operational status (e.g. in progress, implemented, under review).
- **Reference**: The links to relevant policies, procedures or other documentation.
- **Testing/monitoring frequency:** The specification for how often the control is reviewed or tested.
- **Effectiveness:** The metrics or observations indicating how well the control achieves its objectives. When designing a control, incorporate real-time and automated metrics to monitor the control.

Endpoint security

Endpoint security refers to the protection of endpoints, such as desktop computers, laptops, mobile devices, printers and servers, from threats. It involves implementing security measures such as anti-virus software, endpoint detection and response (EDR), encryption, firewalls and access controls to prevent malware, ransomware, phishing attacks and unauthorised access. Modern endpoint security solutions often use AI-driven threat detection, behavioural analysis and zero trust principles to enhance protection. Effective endpoint security is crucial in preventing breaches, especially in remote work and bring your own device (BYOD) environments.

Below are some points to think about when considering controls. This will link up with risk management and asset identification that we will cover in Chapter 4.

Think about what the specific asset, process or system is that the control is designed to safeguard. It could involve sensitive data, physical infrastructure, intellectual property or operational processes. Clearly defining what the control is protecting ensures that efforts are aligned with organisational priorities and clarifies its role within the security system.

If there is already a control in place, consider the current condition of the control, such as whether it is operational, partially implemented or in development. Evaluating the state helps in identifying gaps, understanding potential risks and planning improvements.

Assess the broader implications of the asset being compromised. Significance might include legal obligations, reputational risks, financial impacts or national security concerns. For example, a breach of customer financial data could lead to regulatory fines and a loss of public trust, amplifying the importance of the control. A breach of a government or military control could mean the leak of highly sensitive data that impacts national security.

Think about the control's ability to reduce risk, either by preventing incidents, detecting anomalies or minimising impact. A high-value control might mitigate severe risks or provide critical early warning, whereas a low-value control may have limited effectiveness or redundancy in the environment.

Also, consider the cumulative effectiveness of the control within the larger security environment. Controls rarely operate in isolation; their value often depends on how well they complement other measures. An aggregate evaluation determines whether the control contributes significantly to reducing overall organisational risk.

Finally, think about the total cost of implementing, maintaining and monitoring the control over a year. Costs can include financial investment, resource allocation and operational overhead. Comparing protective costs against the control's value helps in determining cost-effectiveness and prioritisation within the budget.

Control classification

Controls can be classified in various ways, such as administrative (e.g. policies), technical (e.g. firewalls) or physical (e.g. door locks). Classification informs the type of threats it addresses and the skill sets required for its implementation and management, helping to align with organisational security layers that cover people, process and technology. Control types include (Figure 1.1):

- **Preventive controls:** These are measures to stop security incidents before they occur (e.g. firewalls, anti-malware, encryption).

- **Detective controls:** These are tools to identify and monitor malicious activity (e.g. IDSs, security information and event management (SIEM) solutions, SOAR).

- **Corrective controls:** These are steps to mitigate damage and recover from incidents (e.g. backup systems, incident response procedures).

- **Compensating controls:** These are used to compensate for a deficiency of a main control, or system that cannot use a main control, often due to being end of life (add an extra firewall, virtual private network (VPN), network segmentation, disk encryption).

- **Deterrent control:** In cyber security, this is a measure designed to discourage potential attackers from attempting to breach systems or data by instilling fear of consequences or making attacks seem futile.

Figure 1.1 Control type and effect

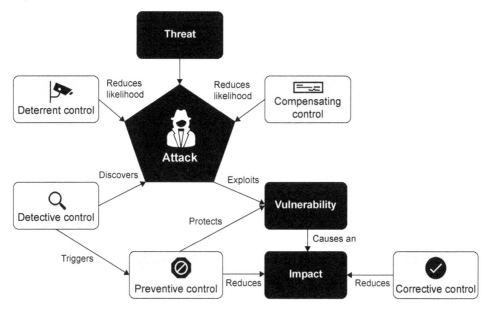

Architecture layers and their security considerations

Network security architecture

- **Perimeter security:** This involves firewalls, intrusion prevention systems (IPSs) and network access controls (NACs) to secure the external boundaries.

- **Internal segmentation:** Segmentation divides the network into zones using VLANs and micro-segmentation to contain a compromise and to limit lateral movement.
- **Secure remote access:** These are VPNs, zero trust network access (ZTNA) and secure configurations for remote and hybrid work models.

Endpoint and device security

- **Device hardening:** These are configuration baselines to reduce vulnerabilities on servers, workstations and mobile devices. They follow guidelines from the Center for Internet Security (CIS), Microsoft, the National Institute of Standards and Technology (NIST) and the National Cyber Security Centre (NCSC) as well as vendor guidance.
- **EDR:** Continuous monitoring and analysis of endpoint activity to detect and respond to advanced threats can also be extended detection and response (XDR).

Application security architecture

- **Integrating security practices:** These are software development lifecycle (SDLC) practices such as code reviews, static and dynamic analysis and secure coding principles for development, security and operations (DevSecOps).
- **Application layer defences:** These use web application firewalls (WAFs), secure APIs and proper authentication mechanisms such as Open Authorisation (OAuth) or Security Assertion Markup Language (SAML).

Data security architecture

- **Data classification and protection:** These define the sensitivity of data and apply appropriate protection mechanisms such as encryption and tokenisation masking.
- **Data loss prevention (DLP) policies and tools:** These monitor and prevent unauthorised data exfiltration.

Identity and access management

- **Authentication and authorisation:** This uses MFA and RBAC to ensure that only authorised users can access specific resources.
- **Privileged access management (PAM):** This is used to secure administrative accounts and implement just-in-time (JIT) access controls to reduce the attack surface.

Security architecture frameworks

Several frameworks guide the development of a security architecture, which we will cover in more detail in Chapter 2:

- **The Open Group Architecture Framework (TOGAF)** provides a comprehensive approach to designing, implementing and managing enterprise architecture.
- **Sherwood Applied Business Security Architecture (SABSA)** is a risk-driven framework that focuses on linking security architecture to business requirements.

- **OSA** (Open Security Architecture) is a framework used for designing and implementing security systems.
- **Zachman Framework**, though not security-specific, helps to structure an enterprise architecture, including security aspects.
- **Control Objectives for Information and Related Technologies (COBIT)** is a framework for governance and management of enterprise IT, developed by the Information Systems Audit and Control Association (ISACA).

Zero trust architecture (ZTA)

Zero trust has become an important strategy in security architecture. It operates under the principle of 'never trust, always verify', assuming that any attempt to access resources should be treated as potentially malicious. Key elements of ZTA include:

- **Micro-segmentation:** This is dividing networks into smaller segments and applying strict access controls.
- **Continuous monitoring and analytics:** This is tracking user and device behaviour to detect anomalies.
- **Strong identity verification:** This is relying heavily on IAM to authenticate and authorise users and devices rigorously.

Security architecture in the cloud

Cloud environments introduce unique security challenges. A well-designed cloud security architecture should include:

- **Shared responsibility model:** This is understanding what security controls are managed by the cloud service provider and what remains the responsibility of the customer.
- **Cloud access security brokers (CASBs):** These are tools that provide visibility, compliance, data security and threat protection for cloud services.
- **Secure configuration management:** This is ensuring cloud resources are securely configured, with ongoing assessments to identify misconfigurations.

Wireless security architecture

Wireless security architecture is concerned with the design and implementation security mechanisms for wireless networks. It refers to the framework of technologies, policies and controls designed to protect wireless networks from cyber threats such as unauthorised access, eavesdropping and data breaches.

- **Encryption and authentication:** This uses protocols such as Wi-Fi protected access 3 (WPA3), 802.1X authentication and TLS to secure communications and verify users.
- **Network segmentation:** Segmentation separates guest, corporate and Internet of Things (IoT) networks to minimise attack surfaces.

- **Intrusion detection and prevention systems (WIDS/WIDPS):** These monitor for rogue access points and malicious activities.
- **Zero trust and access control:** This enforces least privilege using message authentication code (MAC) filtering, remote authentication dial-in user service (RADIUS) and NAC.

Governance, risk and compliance (GRC)

Security architecture incorporates GRC to ensure that all processes align with organisational goals and regulatory requirements. This includes:

- risk management frameworks for continuous risk assessment and management practices to adapt to evolving threats;
- compliance monitoring to ensure that security controls and processes comply with regulations such as GDPR, HIPAA or the Payment Card Industry Data Security Standard (PCI DSS).

Continuous improvement and evolution

Security architecture is not static. It requires ongoing assessment, updates and adaptations to address new threats and technological advancements. This may include:

- red teaming and penetration testing for simulating attacks to identify weaknesses;
- threat intelligence integration to deploy threat intelligence to pre-emptively address emerging threats.
- SOAR, using tools to automate incident response and improve efficiency;
- indicators of compromise (IoCs) to help pick up either an attack in progress or precursor to an attack;
- digital forensics to investigate and gather evidence from the incident for either internal or external use, such as law enforcement investigation.

WHAT IS SECURITY ARCHITECTURE?

A security architect plays an important role in designing, developing and implementing security solutions to protect an organisation's IT systems and data from harm. The role encompasses a broad spectrum of responsibilities, from high-level strategic planning to detailed technical execution, with a focus on establishing a comprehensive security posture to safeguard critical assets. Security architects are responsible for creating a cohesive security architecture by designing security frameworks that integrate with an organisation's existing IT infrastructure. This involves developing detailed high-level and low-level designs and documentation to map out the placement and interaction of security controls, ensuring that every component of the IT ecosystem is adequately secured. They may work in tandem with a solution architect to ensure appropriate security is included in the design. They will most certainly engage with stakeholders across the organisation, educating stakeholders as well as helping them to understand security requirements. A security architect is a senior technical role within an organisation with a lot of responsibility and, whilst they don't normally line-manage personnel, they do require leadership skills.

Risk assessment and threat modelling are also fundamental aspects of a security architect's work. They continuously analyse potential threats and vulnerabilities, employing methods to identify and prioritise risks that could impact the organisation's assets. Depending on the size of the organisation, this may come from information security, threat intelligence or cyber defence teams. In a smaller organisation, they may be the one looking at incidents and threat reports to inform their architecture and defence strategy.

Based on these assessments, a security architect will then develop risk mitigation strategies that balance security needs with business and security operations, often conducting cost–benefit analyses to propose feasible and effective security measures – as they must demonstrate the value to the organisation to ensure any decision can be funded and is supported by senior management. Security architects also play a key role in establishing and maintaining security policies and standards, collaborating with governance teams to ensure these align with industry best practices and regulatory requirements. They are also responsible for fostering security awareness across the organisation, providing guidance and training to internal teams to maintain a secure environment.

In terms of technology, security architects are tasked with evaluating, selecting and implementing security solutions that meet the organisation's specific needs. This involves researching and testing new security technologies, assessing their effectiveness and determining how they can be integrated into the existing infrastructure. They often oversee or directly participate in the deployment of security tools such as firewalls, IDSs, endpoint security platforms and identity management systems. Their work extends beyond technology to collaboration, as they work alongside solution architects, software developers, network engineers, cyber engineers and business stakeholders to ensure security requirements are integrated into every phase of project development. Communication is a critical skill, as they must be able to articulate security risks and strategies to both technical teams and non-technical individuals at all levels of the organisation.

Incident response and management is another responsibility for security architects. They design and implement systems for quick detection and response to security incidents, ensuring the organisation is prepared for worst-case scenarios. This includes developing and rehearsing incident response plans to contain and mitigate incidents effectively. Post-incident, they conduct thorough analysis to determine the root causes, which should be used to enhance future defences and prevent incident reoccurrence. Compliance and governance are also integral to the role, with security architects ensuring that all security measures align with regulatory and compliance requirements such as GDPR, Data Protection Act (DPA), Digital Operational Resilience Act (DORA) or PCI DSS. They perform regular audits and work with legal teams to understand and implement necessary security measures.

A successful security architect must have a diverse set of skills. Technical knowledge is crucial, particularly in areas such as network security, cloud security, operating system (OS) hardening and cryptography, which is why security architects should have a background in or knowledge of IT, including networks, and security experience along with relevant certifications, education or experience that support this. International Information System Security Certification Consortium (ISC²), Certified Information

Systems Security Professional (CISSP) or ISACA Certified Information Security Manager (CISM) are often required certifications for a security architect role. Analytical and problem-solving skills are necessary for conducting risk analyses and incident investigations, while strategic thinking is required to align security initiatives with long-term business goals. The ability to balance security and usability is important, ensuring that security solutions do not hinder performance or user experience – there is something called 'too much security' where a user will either avoid using the system or find ways to bypass security, as the security is too complex or difficult to use. Strong communication and leadership skills enable security architects to effectively lead teams, mentor staff and convey complex security concepts in a clear and understandable manner to both technical and non-technical audiences.

Security architects often work on critical projects such as overhauling security architecture to meet modern standards, implementing cloud security measures or rolling out zero trust strategy. Their projects may also involve automating threat detection and response or designing comprehensive defence-in-depth strategies. Projects will often use a variety of tools and technologies, including SIEM, endpoint detection platforms, IAM solutions and threat intelligence platforms. They also need to understand not only what these are, but how best to implement and use them. Security architects typically have a background in roles such as security analyst or engineer and often pursue certifications such as Certified Ethical Hacker (CEH), CISM, CISSP, TOGAF or specialised cloud security certifications to advance their careers.

Despite the rewarding nature of the role, security architects face several challenges, and it can at times be a very demanding role if there are multiple priorities or time constraints. They may have to push back on a decision that is inherently insecure but considered a good idea elsewhere in the business. The ever-evolving threat landscape requires them to stay ahead of sophisticated cyberattacks, vulnerabilities and new attack vectors. They must balance rigorous security requirements with the organisation's mission and operational and financial requirements, often working within budget constraints while implementing effective measures.

Trying to work around legacy or end of life equipment without a quick or easy solution can be particularly challenging, as can be managing the security of increasingly complex IT environments that may include a mix of on-premises, cloud, operational technology (OT) and mobile components. They may join an organisation that places little value on security or does not understand security, meaning a long, upward battle to introduce security, often in conflict with IT and other stakeholders. In these scenarios, fully understanding the organisation and slowly trying to align stakeholders to security is one approach, by demonstrating its protective and defensive nature to reduce loss and add value to the organisation, at the same time pointing out accountability to senior management, and, finally, providing an insightful and holistic view of security to ensure the organisation is protected from harm and well defended.

STRUCTURED DESIGN APPROACH

When tasked with creating a new design, a security architect should follow a structured approach to ensure the solution is secure, scalable and aligned with the organisation's objectives. Below is one example of a structured approach that could be undertaken. The security architect may need to create the high-level diagram (HLD) on open free software such as ArchiMate to help visualise the proposal. ArchiMate is an open and standardised enterprise architecture modelling language developed by The Open Group. It provides a structured way to visualise, analyse and describe business processes, organisational structures, information flows, IT systems and infrastructure within an enterprise. ArchiMate is designed to align with frameworks such as TOGAF, and offers a layered approach (business, application and technology) to support decision-making and improve communication between stakeholders.

Understand business requirements

The security architect begins by collaborating with stakeholders to gather a comprehensive understanding of the organisation's goals, operational requirements and the purpose of the new system or design. It is crucial to fully understand the context before moving towards the design phase.

Key activities

- Identify functional and non-functional requirements (e.g. performance, availability, scalability).
- Understand regulatory and compliance obligations (e.g. GDPR, PCI DSS, Sarbanes–Oxley Act 2002 (SOX).
- Assess business risks, including financial, operational and reputational considerations.
- Map out critical assets and data flows.

Perform a threat and risk assessment

A thorough threat and risk assessment is conducted to identify potential vulnerabilities and threats that could affect the design.

Key activities

- Use several methodologies such as spoofing, tampering, repudiation, information disclosure, DoS and elevation of privilege (STRIDE), process for attack simulation and threat analysis (PASTA) or MITRE adversarial tactics, techniques and common knowledge (ATT&CK) (see Chapter 3) to identify threats.
- Classify assets by their criticality and sensitivity.
- Evaluate the likelihood and impact of threats.
- Prioritise risks to address in the design phase.

Define security requirements

Based on the risks identified, the security architect establishes security requirements that the design must meet. These requirements align with the organisation's policies, industry best practices and compliance mandates.

Key activities

- Define access control requirements (role-based or attribute-based access).
- Specify encryption and data protection measures.
- Establish logging and monitoring needs.
- Define incident detection and response capabilities.
- Determine secure development and deployment practices.

Develop the security architecture

Using the gathered requirements, the security architect designs the system architecture, incorporating security by design.

Key activities

- Create a high-level architecture diagram showing components, data flows and integration points.
- Incorporate defence-in-depth principles by layering security controls (e.g. network segmentation, firewalls and endpoint protection).
- Design for scalability, resilience and redundancy to handle future growth and potential disruptions.
- Use secure-by-default technologies and approaches, such as least privilege and zero trust models.
- Ensure interoperability with existing systems and infrastructure.

Select technologies and vendors

The security architect evaluates and selects appropriate technologies, tools and vendors to implement the design.

Key activities

- Research solutions that align with the architecture, considering factors such as cost, compatibility, vendor reputation and previous contracts.
- Conduct proof of concept tests to validate solutions.
- Ensure selected technologies comply with organisational standards and frameworks.

Validate the design

Before implementation, the security architect validates the design through reviews and testing to ensure it meets security, business and technical requirements.

Key activities

- Conduct design reviews with technical teams and stakeholders.
- Simulate threat scenarios to identify potential weaknesses.
- Perform a gap analysis against established security frameworks (e.g. NIST Cybersecurity Framework (CSF), ISO 27001).
- Adjust the design based on feedback and findings.

Implementation planning

Once the design is finalised, the security architect collaborates with implementation teams to plan the deployment.

Key activities

- Define a phased implementation approach to reduce risk.
- Develop detailed security control configurations.
- Plan for secure integration with existing systems.
- Coordinate with development operations (DevOps) teams to integrate security into continuous integration and continuous development (CI/CD) pipelines.

Monitor and iterate post-implementation

After deployment, the security architect ensures that the design operates as intended and remains effective against evolving threats.

Key activities

- Monitor for security incidents using tools such as SIEM, SOAR, EDR and XDR.
- Conduct periodic security assessments, such as penetration testing and vulnerability scanning.
- Update the architecture as new technologies and threats emerge.
- Provide feedback to improve future designs and processes.

Documentation and knowledge sharing

Throughout the process, the security architect documents the design, rationale and decisions to support ongoing operations and future updates.

Key activities

- Create comprehensive design documentation, including diagrams and risk assessments.
- Develop runbooks and playbooks for incident response.
- Provide training and knowledge transfer to operations teams.

DEFENCE IN DEPTH

Defence in depth involves having multiple layers of defence, similar to a castle with its moat, portcullis and outer and inner walls (Figure 1.2). Each layer is a barrier to access the next, slowing down or stopping an intrusion. It often starts with policy, physical security measures, access control and encryption of data at rest and in motion. Defence in depth should also look inwards as well as outwards to protect against the insider threat.

Figure 1.2 Defence in depth

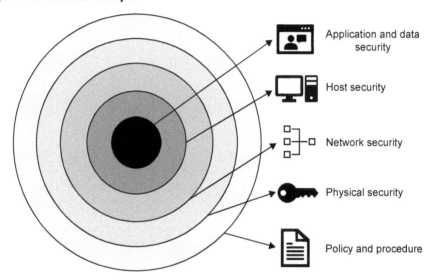

Even when systems are running, they require ongoing monitoring and maintenance, as they will require updates and patches as well as continuous logging, monitoring and auditing to ensure they remain secure and stay within the risk tolerance of the organisation. Threats and technology changes along with incidents highlight security issues that may need to be addressed. Examples could be a control that may have failed during an incident, or a severe vulnerability that has been found in a system and needs addressing urgently.

Defence in depth and breadth

These principles are a critical instrument that must be fully appreciated and, where appropriate, implemented if security is to be established and maintained effectively.

The principle of defence in depth is that there are layers of security that build on one another. Today it is virtually impossible for any organisation, large or small, to protect all their information assets to the highest degree possible. One reason is that of cost, but there is also a more practical reason: whereas some information assets need to be freely available to staff members in order for them to undertake their routine daily work activities, other information is far more critical and sensitive and so must be afforded a high level of protection, thereby almost certainly making it more difficult to access and use.

Defence in breadth is a more recently coined phrase that has come about due to the need to consider all the connections to any networked system. The complexity of the networks now in place in many organisations is staggering and, when connections to suppliers, customers, different physical locations around the world, homeworkers and many more are considered, they become ever more difficult to manage. The concept of understanding the breadth of the network and its connectivity is critical since, as the old adage says, the weakest link of a chain is where it will break. The part of the complex network that has the lowest level of security will be where the criminal or other intruder will find their way. Malware is now very sophisticated software, and it has the capacity to find ways of traversing a network to find holes or legitimate portals into other areas that, because it is already inside the network, might, for example, allow the intruder to be seen as a trusted user.

2 SECURITY ARCHITECTURE FRAMEWORKS

In this chapter, we will begin by exploring the concept of security architecture frameworks, their purpose and how they can be effectively utilised. We will then examine several widely recognised frameworks, including TOGAF, SABSA, OSA, Zachman and COBIT.

The selection of a security architecture framework is a strategic decision influenced by organisational needs, existing documentation and prior experience. There is no single correct choice; choice should be based on the framework that best aligns with the organisation's requirements, governance structure and strategic objectives.

ARCHITECTURE FRAMEWORK

A security architecture framework is a structured and strategic approach used to design and implement an organisation's IT security. It serves as a blueprint to ensure security measures are effectively integrated, consistent and aligned with the enterprise architecture. The primary purpose of such a framework is to protect information systems and data from harm by using an organised, repeatable and holistic approach. Architectures should always be used to fit with organisational strategy and, if the architecture does not work, either adapt the framework or choose a different model. A framework is there to provide guiding principles, but they must be customised to the organisational context.

A framework typically comprises several key components. At the foundation are policies and standards that establish the expectations for managing and enforcing security practices across the organisation. These should have been derived from the overall governance and strategy aligning with the organisation's mission and goals. Policy and standards are used to dictate security behaviours and provide a basis for designing secure systems. Principles such as defence in depth, least privilege, zero trust and Secure by Design (SBD) should guide the overall design philosophy, while controls and safeguards should cover both technical and administrative elements. Controls can include firewalls, encryption, authentication, security training, swipe cards and incident response plans. Security architecture often divides into layers (such as network, host and application layers) and zones (trusted, semi-trusted and untrusted) to ensure that the right measures are applied to each component of the system. A crucial part of the framework also involves threat modelling and risk assessment, which are covered in Chapters 3 and 4. There are several established frameworks that organisations use to create and implement security architecture, which is covered later on in this chapter.

The amount of security to be applied should directly relate to the level of protection required for the assets. This will be driven by the sensitivity and value of the data being transmitted, stored and processed.

When designing security architecture, it is essential to consider several factors. The architecture must align with the organisation's business objectives, ensuring that security supports organisational objectives and strategy, and offer acceptable protection within budget. It needs to be scalable and flexible, accommodating growth and adaptive to meet emerging threats and new technologies. Interoperability is a key factor, as security measures must integrate smoothly with other enterprise systems and not just business operations. Security measures should not operate in silos but rather integrate seamlessly with enterprise architecture, IT infrastructure and business processes. Poor interoperability can lead to inefficiencies, increased attack surfaces and operational bottlenecks.

For instance, IAM solutions should integrate with human resources systems for automated provisioning and deprovisioning. Similarly, SIEM platforms must correlate logs across disparate sources for meaningful threat intelligence. The same applies to quantum-resistant cryptographic solutions in the future, as their adoption will be hindered despite their security benefits without proper interoperability.

The implementation of a security architecture framework involves a multi-step approach. It begins with a comprehensive assessment of the current security posture, followed by identifying gaps and areas for improvement. The next phase involves designing and modelling a security architecture that outlines how security will be applied across various components, including logical and physical aspects. Once designed, the security measures are deployed and integrated into the existing infrastructure. Security testing and verification is critical to ensure the effectiveness of security measures put in place and that they work as designed. Controls should not hinder or slow down business process but keep them secure and available as required, and also prevent theft, disclosure, tampering or destruction of data. Continuous monitoring and maintenance are necessary to adapt to new threats and ensure ongoing resilience.

Utilising a security architecture framework provides consistency in applying security measures across the organisation, reducing the likelihood of gaps and inconsistencies. It is a structured approach that should make security processes more efficient and less resource-intensive. It also enhances the organisation's resilience to cyberattacks, making it better equipped to detect, respond and recover from incidents.

By improving risk management, a framework helps to prioritise security requirements effectively and to simplify compliance with regulatory requirements. However, organisations must also navigate challenges when implementing a security architecture framework. The process can be complex and resource-intensive, requiring skilled personnel along with significant investment. The architecture must also remain adaptable to the changing threat landscape as well as organisational changing requirements. Finding the right balance between security and performance is also critical, as security measures can sometimes impact system efficiency. Finally, there may be cultural resistance within the organisation, with employees, management and stakeholders potentially resistant to new security processes that seem disruptive or inconvenient. This can be especially true of IT, who want availability and efficiency and are not always concerned with security – especially on a project where they see security as the 'no department' and will try and push things through by bypassing security simply to hit a project milestone, often due to conflicting targets and goals. The other big issue is a lack of understanding of what security actually is, and ensuring everyone understands that it is protective and defensive to reduce harm and therefore loss should the worst happen.

TOGAF

TOGAF is a widely recognised framework used for developing and managing enterprise architecture (Figure 2.1). It provides a comprehensive approach for designing, planning, implementing and governing an enterprise IT architecture in a structured and organised manner. TOGAF is designed to help organisations align their IT infrastructure with their overarching business goals, ensuring that technology investments deliver maximum value. This alignment is particularly crucial for security architecture, as it ensures that security initiatives and solutions are seamlessly integrated into the broader enterprise strategy.

Figure 2.1 TOGAF architecture principles

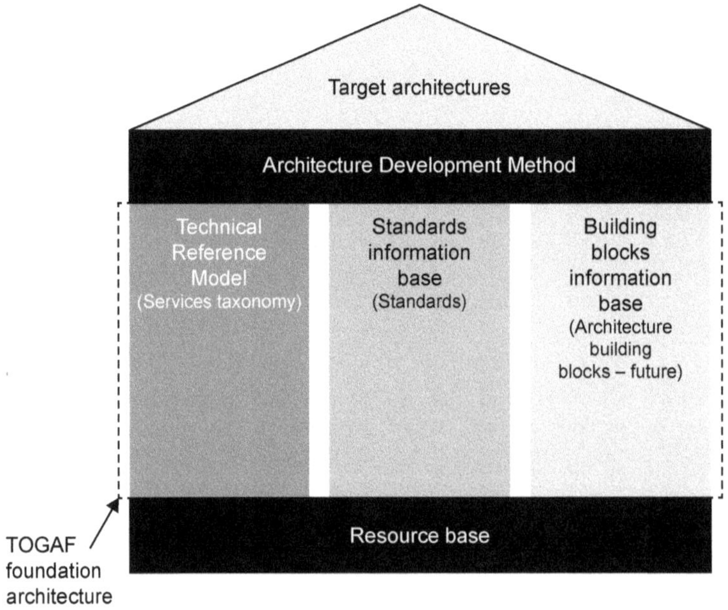

Core components of TOGAF

Architecture Development Method (ADM)
The ADM is the heart of TOGAF, offering a step-by-step approach to developing enterprise architecture. It consists of a series of iterative phases that guide architects through the planning, design and implementation of architecture projects.

Preliminary phase   This initial phase establishes the architecture capability within the organisation. It involves defining the scope, stakeholders and governance structure for the architecture project. The focus is on preparing the organisation for architecture work, including setting up the necessary tools, processes and resources.

Architecture vision   This phase creates a high-level vision of the architecture project that aligns with the organisation's strategic goals. It involves defining the objectives, key drivers and requirements for the architecture effort. Stakeholder engagement is crucial here and the vision serves as a guiding reference throughout the project.

Business architecture   This phase develops a detailed understanding of the organisation's business processes, goals and requirements. It focuses on how the business operates and it identifies areas where IT can drive improvements or support strategic objectives. Security architects, for example, would ensure that business operations are protected from threats.

Information systems architectures   This includes developing the data architecture and the application architecture. The data architecture defines how data is stored, managed and used across the organisation, while the application architecture outlines how applications interact to meet business needs. Security is integrated here by specifying access controls, encryption data and privacy measures.

Technology architecture   This phase defines the technical infrastructure needed to support the business, data and application architectures. It includes specifying networks, hardware and software. Security architects work in this phase to ensure that firewalls, IDSs and secure configurations are part of the technology blueprint.

Opportunities and solutions   This phase identifies potential solutions and opportunities for implementing the target architecture. It involves gap analysis to compare the current architecture with the target architecture, followed by selecting and prioritising projects. Security-related projects, such as enhancing identity management systems or upgrading encryption protocols, are proposed here.

Migration planning   Here, architects create a detailed plan for transitioning from the current architecture to the target architecture. This includes defining the sequence of activities, timelines and resource allocation. Security architects ensure that data and systems remain protected during the migration process, addressing any transitional vulnerabilities.

Implementation governance   This phase involves overseeing the implementation of the architecture, ensuring that projects are executed according to the defined architecture vision and principles. Security governance is a crucial aspect, with continuous monitoring and auditing to confirm compliance with security standards.

Architecture change management   The final phase addresses the ongoing management of the architecture. It involves assessing and implementing changes as new business needs or technological advancements arise. Security architects play a role in ensuring that changes do not introduce new risks and that the architecture remains secure.

ADM guidelines and techniques

The ADM is supported by a set of guidelines and techniques that help to tailor the methodology to an organisation's specific needs. These resources provide best practices for adapting the ADM to various scenarios, including different architectural styles such as service-oriented architecture (SOA), layered architecture, microservices architecture, ZTA, cloud-native architecture or blockchain-based architecture. For example, if an organisation is heavily focused on security, these guidelines would offer tailored approaches for integrating security measures throughout each phase of the ADM. Techniques for stakeholder management, risk analysis and capability assessment are also provided to ensure a holistic approach to architecture development.

Architecture Content Framework

The Architecture Content Framework provides a detailed model for creating architecture artefacts and deliverables and the relationships between them. It defines a structured approach for documenting and organising architecture components, making it easier for architects to manage complex projects. The framework includes the architecture content metamodel, which outlines the structure of key elements such as business processes, data entities and technology components. Security architecture artefacts are also included, such as security policies, risk assessments and compliance documentation. This framework ensures that all architecture components are documented in a standardised way, improving communication and understanding among stakeholders.

Enterprise Continuum and tools

TOGAF introduces the Enterprise Continuum, a classification mechanism for organising and managing architecture and solution artefacts. It is divided into two main parts: the Architecture Continuum and the Solutions Continuum. The Architecture Continuum describes a progression from generic, foundational architectures to more specific, tailored architectures, while the Solutions Continuum focuses on practical, implementable solutions. This structure allows organisations to reuse architecture artefacts and streamline their architecture development process. Tools and repositories are often used to manage these artefacts, making it easier to access and utilise previous work. Security architects can use the Enterprise Continuum to store and reuse security components, such as encryption models or compliance templates, for future projects.

TOGAF reference models

TOGAF provides reference models to help organisations establish a solid foundation for their enterprise architecture. These models include the TOGAF Foundation Architecture, also known as the Technical Reference Model (TRM), which outlines basic infrastructure services and the Integrated Information Infrastructure Reference Model (III-RM), which focuses on the information infrastructure needed to support business operations. Security architects can use these reference models to identify common security services and standards, such as authentication mechanisms, audit trails and secure communication protocols. These models provide a standardised approach to implementing security measures across the organisation.

Architecture Capability Framework

The Architecture Capability Framework focuses on establishing and sustaining an architecture practice within an organisation. It addresses governance, roles, responsibilities and skills required for effective architecture management. This framework ensures that the architecture function is well-integrated into the organisation's operations and that there is a continuous focus on improvement. Security architects, for instance, are identified as key roles within the architecture team, with specific responsibilities for ensuring that security is a core component of all architectural decisions. The framework also outlines governance mechanisms to manage security risks and ensure compliance with regulatory requirements.

Integrating security architecture with TOGAF

Security architecture within the TOGAF framework must be carefully aligned with the organisation's goals and objectives. This alignment ensures that security measures are not just technical solutions but are also strategic components that support business operations. For instance, when designing a security architecture, architects must consider the organisation's risk tolerance, regulatory requirements and strategic priorities. Documentation is crucial; every phase of the ADM should include detailed records of security requirements, risk assessments and compliance measures. Effective communication with stakeholders, including business leaders and technical teams, is essential to ensure that everyone understands the security posture and the rationale behind security decisions.

Risk management is another key aspect. Security architects use TOGAF's risk management techniques to identify potential threats and vulnerabilities, assess their impact and develop mitigation strategies. This proactive approach ensures that the architecture is resilient and adaptable to evolving threats. Furthermore, TOGAF encourages the use of security standards and best practices, such as encryption protocols, secure software development practices and identity management frameworks, to enhance the overall security of the architecture.

SABSA FRAMEWORK

The SABSA is a robust and comprehensive framework designed to build risk-driven enterprise security and information assurance architectures. Developed in 1995 by John Sherwood, Andy Clark and David Lynas, SABSA provides a methodical approach to aligning business goals with security strategies, ensuring that security architecture is not only effective but also tightly integrated with the overall business objectives of the organisation. The SABSA methodology focuses on delivering security services that are crafted to meet specific business needs, starting from high-level business requirements and cascading down to technical implementations. This top-down approach ensures that security becomes an enabler for business operations rather than an afterthought.

SABSA is built on a layered architecture model, which divides the development of security architecture into six distinct layers. Each layer addresses a specific aspect of security, from understanding the business environment to deploying and managing security technologies. This multi-layered approach ensures that all dimensions of security are considered, with a continuous focus on risk management and the alignment of security strategies with business goals (Figure 2.2).

Figure 2.2 SABSA matrix

	Assets (What)	Motivation (Why)	Process (How)	People (Who)	Location (Where)	Time (When)
Contextual	Business decisions	Business risk	Business processes	Business governance	Business geography	Business time dependence
Conceptual	Business knowledge and risk strategy	Risk management objectives	Strategies for process assurance	Roles and responsibilities	Domain framework	Time management framework
Logical	Information assets	Risk management policies	Process maps and services	Entry and trust framework	Domain maps	Calander and timetable
Physical	Data assets	Risk management practices	Process mechanisms	Human interface	ICT infrastructure	Processing schedule
Component	ICT components	Risk management tools and standards	Process tools and standards	Personnel management tools and standards	Locator tools and standards	Step timing and sequence tools
Service management	Service delivery management	Operational risk management	Process delivery management	Personnel management	Management of environment	Time and performance management

SABSA layers explained

Contextual layer: requirements and environment
The contextual layer establishes the foundation for the entire security architecture by defining the organisation's context, vision, goals and objectives. This layer identifies who the key stakeholders are and what their security needs entail. It considers the organisation's operational environment, including industry-specific regulations, business models and strategic priorities. The main purpose of the contextual layer is to ensure that the security architecture is designed to support the overarching business objectives. In this phase, architects conduct stakeholder analysis to determine the business requirements that security must fulfil, such as protecting intellectual property, ensuring customer trust or maintaining regulatory compliance. The output of this layer is a clear and detailed understanding of the organisation's security requirements, framed in business terms.

Conceptual layer: high-level security concepts
Building on the contextual layer, the conceptual layer develops a high-level view of the security requirements that have been derived from the organisation's business goals. It articulates the key security concepts, principles and services needed to support these goals. This layer focuses on translating business requirements into security objectives and conceptual models. For example, if the business requirement is to protect customer data, the conceptual security model might outline the need for data privacy, secure access controls and encryption mechanisms. The goal here is to abstract security into fundamental concepts without yet deciding on specific technologies or solutions. The output includes a set of security principles, such as least privilege or defence in depth, which will guide the development of more detailed security models.

Logical layer: security architecture and models
The logical layer translates high-level security concepts into detailed security models and architectures. This layer defines what needs to be done to meet the security requirements identified in the conceptual layer. It outlines specific security services, functions and policies, such as IAM, threat detection mechanisms and data encryption standards. Importantly, the logical layer focuses on functionality and relationships rather than on the implementation specifics. For instance, it may specify the need for RBAC without specifying which software or platform to use. This ensures that the architecture remains flexible and can adapt to changing technologies. The output from this phase includes security models, detailed risk assessments and logical representations of how security measures will function within the business environment.

Physical layer: technology-specific solutions
The physical layer takes the logical security models and translates them into technology-specific solutions. Here, architects choose the technologies and products that will implement the security services defined in the logical layer. This layer defines the physical and technical controls needed to secure the organisation's assets, such as firewalls, encryption hardware, authentication systems and IDSs. It is in this layer that practical decisions are made about how to implement security measures. Architects select vendors, design the network topology and define technical specifications for hardware and software. This phase also includes designing the security infrastructure to be robust, scalable and aligned with the organisation's performance requirements.

The output is a detailed description of the security technologies and how they will be used to mitigate risks and protect the organisation.

Component layer: configuration and implementation

The component layer focuses on the detailed design, configuration and implementation of the components identified in the physical layer. This includes specific settings, software configurations and integration details necessary for deploying the chosen security technologies. It addresses questions such as how firewall rules should be configured, how encryption keys should be managed and how systems should be integrated to provide seamless security coverage. Security architects work closely with implementation teams to ensure that every component is configured according to best practices and the overall security strategy. This layer also includes the development of installation scripts, configuration guide and integration plans. The emphasis is on translating theoretical models into practical implementations that function effectively within the organisation's IT environment.

Service management: day-to-day security operations

The final layer, the operational layer, deals with the ongoing management and maintenance of the security architecture. This includes the policies, procedures and practices required to ensure that security measures are effective and remain up to date. It covers areas such as security monitoring, incident response, change management and continuous improvement. Security teams establish operational guidelines to maintain the architecture's integrity and to adapt to emerging threats and changes in the business environment. This layer ensures that there are mechanisms in place for auditing, reporting and compliance monitoring. It also focuses on training staff, maintaining security awareness and refining security practices as needed. The operational layer makes sure that the security architecture is not static but evolves to meet new challenges and supports the organisation's long-term security strategy.

Key concepts of SABSA

The SABSA framework has a focus on risk management using a holistic approach to security. It ensures that security is not just about technology but is also about aligning with the strategic and operational requirements of the business. One of the best practices in using SABSA is to continuously consider the context in which the organisation operates. This involves understanding the business environment, potential partners and the evolving threat landscape. SABSA emphasises the importance of ongoing stakeholder communication to ensure that security measures are always aligned with business priorities.

Risk management is embedded throughout the SABSA layers. Security architects use a risk-driven approach to prioritise security investments and ensure that resources are allocated to the areas of greatest impact. For example, in the contextual and conceptual layers, architects assess risks to the organisation and develop high-level security requirements. As they move to the logical, physical and component layers, these risks are addressed with specific security controls and technologies. By the time the architecture reaches the operational layer, mechanisms for monitoring, responding to and mitigating risks are fully in place.

Another strength of SABSA is its adaptability. It provides a flexible framework that can be tailored to the unique requirements of different organisations and industries. For instance, a financial institution might focus heavily on data encryption and regulatory compliance, while a healthcare organisation might prioritise patient privacy and secure medical records. The SABSA framework allows for this level of customisation while maintaining a structured approach to security architecture development.

OSA FRAMEWORK

The OSA framework is a versatile framework used for the design and implementation of security systems across diverse organisational environments (Figure 2.3). The framework's primary aim is to provide adaptable and reusable security solutions that can be easily tailored to an organisation's unique requirements. OSA recognises that security architecture is not a one-size-fits-all endeavour; it must be flexible enough to integrate with an organisation's existing processes, technologies and strategic goals. It is particularly effective when used alongside other established security frameworks, such as SABSA, to provide a holistic approach to security management. Additionally, the OSA framework can be supported further by incorporating elements or recommendations from frameworks such as ISO/IEC 27001 and NIST CSF, ensuring security measures are both effective and compliant.

Figure 2.3 OSA design principles

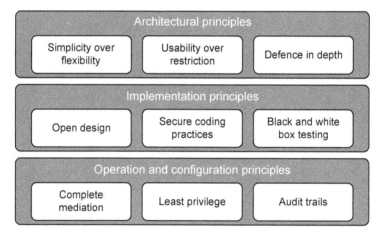

Foundational elements of the Open Security Architecture

One of the defining features of OSA is its pattern-based approach. Rather than prescribing rigid security controls, OSA offers a collection of reusable security patterns designed to address common security challenges. These patterns represent proven strategies that have been refined through real-world applications and serve as templates that security architects can customise to fit their specific context. Each security pattern within OSA includes detailed descriptions of the security issue it addresses, the architectural solution, the necessary security controls and the implementation considerations; for instance, there are patterns for IAM, data encryption, secure software development and network segmentation. By using these patterns, organisations can accelerate the design of their security systems whilst ensuring consistency and reliability. The reusable nature of these patterns also promotes efficiency and knowledge sharing within and across organisations, reducing the risk of implementing ineffective or incomplete security solutions.

The community-driven nature of OSA is another critical aspect that sets it apart from traditional, top-down security frameworks. The framework is developed and continuously updated by a global community of security professionals, which ensures that it reflects the latest security trends, technologies and threat landscapes. This collaborative approach brings together a wide range of expertise and insights, enabling OSA to remain relevant and robust in the face of evolving cyber threats. Community contributions include not only new security patterns but also updates to existing ones, as well as the sharing of real-world use cases and implementation guidance. This continuous evolution of OSA makes it a dynamic and ever-improving resource for organisations seeking to build or enhance their security architectures. Furthermore, this global collaboration fosters innovation and knowledge exchange, encouraging the development of innovative security strategies and best practices.

Documentation and guidance are central to the effectiveness of the OSA framework. It provides architects and developers with resources to support successful implementation of security controls. These resources include detailed documentation, visual diagrams and illustrative examples that help to explain complex security concepts and design principles. The documentation is designed to be user-friendly, making it accessible to those without an extensive background in security architecture. For instance, OSA provides step-by-step guides for implementing specific security patterns, complete with explanations of the underlying risks and the expected outcomes of the security measures. Diagrams are used extensively to visualise how different security components interact within a system, aiding in the understanding of architectural dependencies and potential points of failure. This wealth of resources ensures that security architects, developers and stakeholders have the information they need to make informed decisions and implement effective security strategies.

The technology-agnostic design of OSA is another of its key strengths. Unlike frameworks that are tied to specific technologies or platforms, OSA has been deliberately created to be applicable across a wide range of environments and technologies. This flexibility promotes interoperability, enabling organisations to implement OSA-based security controls in both traditional and modern IT systems, including cloud environments, on-premises data centres and hybrid configurations. The framework's adaptability also supports the integration of emerging technologies, such as IoT, AI, OT and blockchain. By being technology-agnostic, OSA ensures that security measures remain relevant and effective as organisations evolve and adopt new technologies. Additionally, this flexibility allows for scalable security solutions that can grow with the organisation, accommodating increasing complexity and scope without requiring a complete overhaul of the security architecture.

Integrating OSA with other security frameworks

The OSA framework is highly effective when integrated with other security frameworks, providing a complementary approach that enhances the overall security posture of an organisation. For example, when used alongside the SABSA framework, OSA can provide the detailed, pattern-based security solutions needed to address the strategic security requirements defined in SABSA's layered architecture. SABSA focuses on aligning security measures with business goals and risk management, while OSA provides the practical, implementation-level guidance necessary to realise those measures. This synergy allows organisations to create security architectures that are both strategically aligned and technically robust. Aligning OSA implementations with ISO/IEC 27001, NIST CSF and CIS Critical Security Controls (CIS 18) can help organisations to ensure that their security architecture meets requirements. It does not have to be just one framework, as several can help to identify gaps. It also helps to incorporate a continuous improvement cycle for monitoring and updating controls.

Ongoing monitoring and continuous improvement

Effective security architecture is not static, and the OSA framework recognises the importance of ongoing monitoring and continuous improvement. Once security measures are implemented using OSA patterns, they must be regularly tested and monitored to ensure they remain effective and responsive to new threats. This involves deploying SIEM systems, conducting regular security assessments and performing vulnerability scans to identify potential weaknesses. Additionally, incident response procedures should be in place to swiftly address any security breaches or anomalies. OSA provides guidance on setting up these monitoring and response mechanisms, ensuring that organisations can proactively manage their security posture.

The framework also advocates for continuous improvement by incorporating feedback loops into the security architecture lifecycle. Lessons learned from security incidents, audits and assessments are used to refine and enhance existing security patterns and controls. This iterative process ensures that the security architecture evolves alongside the organisation's changing risk landscape and business requirements. By maintaining a proactive and adaptive approach, organisations can build a resilient security infrastructure that is capable of mitigating both current and emerging threats.

When combined with other security frameworks and standards, OSA provides a holistic and risk-driven approach to protecting organisational assets, ensuring that security measures are both strategically aligned and technically sound. The emphasis on continuous monitoring and improvement further enhances the framework's effectiveness, enabling organisations to stay ahead of the evolving threat landscape.

ZACHMAN FRAMEWORK

The Zachman Framework for Enterprise Architecture was developed by John Zachman in the 1980s as a pioneering and comprehensive approach to structuring and understanding complex enterprise systems. It serves as a classification schema for organising and analysing an organisation's architecture, providing a logical structure for enterprise documentation that reflects multiple perspectives and various dimensions of enterprise systems. The framework does not prescribe how to develop an architecture but rather serves as a blueprint that outlines all the necessary components and relationships in a way that ensures alignment between business and technology. The Zachman Framework is particularly useful for large, complex organisations that need a structured way to manage the exchange between business processes, data, systems and technology infrastructure.

At its core, the Zachman Framework is a two-dimensional matrix that defines how an organisation can be described from multiple perspectives, using a comprehensive taxonomy that ensures no critical elements of the enterprise are overlooked (Figure 2.4). The rows of the matrix represent the different perspectives or viewpoints within an enterprise, ranging from the high-level vision of executives to the more detailed views of implementers. These rows include the Planner, Owner, Designer, Builder, Subcontractor and the final row, which reflects the Functioning Enterprise. Meanwhile, the columns of the matrix represent the interrogatives or aspects of the enterprise architecture that need to be considered: What (Data), How (Function), Where (Location), Who (People), When (Time) and Why (Motivation). Together, these perspectives and aspects create a comprehensive and holistic view of the enterprise, ensuring that both business and IT concerns are addressed cohesively.

Rows: perspectives in the Zachman Framework

The rows of the Zachman Framework outline the different perspectives of an enterprise system, each providing a unique view that contributes to a holistic understanding of the organisation.

Planner (scope contexts)
The Planner's perspective, at the topmost level, defines the overall scope and strategic vision of the enterprise. It answers fundamental questions about the organisation's goals, mission and strategic direction. The outputs from this level include high-level descriptions and models, such as lists of key business processes, the organisation's core data entities, strategic objectives and major organisational functions. This perspective is akin to an architect's initial sketch of a building, giving a broad overview without diving into intricate details. The goal is to establish a strategic context and provide guidance for further architectural development.

Owner (business concepts)
The Owner's perspective translates the Planner's scope into detailed business models that reflect the requirements and needs of the organisation. This level focuses on the business view, detailing the processes, organisational structures and information that support business activities. It provides business process models, information models and business objectives that guide the design of IT systems. This perspective ensures that the architecture reflects the needs and desires of the business stakeholders, essentially forming the blueprint of how the enterprise should operate to fulfil its strategic goals. Key outputs include process maps, data entity-relationship models and business event models.

Figure 2.4 Zachmann Framework

	What Data	How Function	Where Location	Who People	When Time	Why Motivation
Planner	Business data	High-level business process	Business location	Organisation chart	Business events	Business motivation
Owner	Data map	Process analysis	Business logistics	BPNM	Event schedule	Strategy map
Designer	Class – platform independent model	Activity	Data distribution architecture	Use case	State transition	Business role model
Builder	Physical data model	Class – platform specific model component	Deployment	User interface	Interaction communication	Role design
Subcontractor	Data definition		Network architecture	Security architecture	Timing	Role specification
Functioning enterprise	Usable data	Working function	Usable network	Functioning organisation	Implemented schedule	Working strategy

Designer (system logic)

The Designer's perspective deals with the logical representation of the system. This level translates the business requirements into logical system models, defining the structure and behaviour of the IT systems without being tied to specific technologies or platforms. It includes detailed specifications of data structures, software functions and system interfaces. This perspective focuses on what the system must do to support the business processes outlined in the Owner's perspective. Examples of artefacts produced at this level include logical data models, detailed functional specifications and system architecture diagrams.

Builder (technology physics)

The Builder's perspective takes the logical models created by the Designer and translates them into technology-specific models. This level specifies how the system will be implemented using particular technologies, platforms and infrastructure components. It involves selecting software solutions, configuring hardware and designing network topologies. The focus is on defining the physical implementation details necessary to make the logical models operational. Outputs include database schemas, software design specifications and network infrastructure layouts. This layer provides the technical blueprints needed to build the enterprise systems.

Subcontractor (detailed representations)

The Subcontractor's perspective represents the detailed specifications and configurations necessary for the system's implementation. This level is where the actual coding, hardware assembly and system integration occurs. It provides the granular details required by developers, engineers and vendors to create and deploy the system components. This perspective focuses on individual components and modules, covering aspects like programming code, server configuration and security settings. Deliverables at this level include source code, detailed network configuration files and deployment scripts. The focus is on ensuring that all components work together as intended and meet the business requirements specified in higher layers.

Functioning enterprise

The final row represents the fully implemented and operational system. This perspective shows how the system is functioning in the real world, including monitoring, performance analysis and continuous improvement. It provides a feedback loop to ensure that the system is meeting its intended business objectives and is capable of adapting to changing requirements. Artefacts at this level include operational dashboards, performance reports and documentation of issues and resolutions. This perspective highlights the importance of monitoring and maintaining the architecture over time to ensure ongoing effectiveness and efficiency.

Columns: aspects of the Zachman Framework

The columns of the Zachman Framework represent the six interrogatives that provide a comprehensive view of the enterprise architecture. Each column addresses a specific aspect of the system and is explored from each of the six perspectives described above.

What (data/information)

This aspect focuses on the data and information critical to the organisation. It explores questions such as what data is needed, how it is structured and how it flows through the enterprise. Models in this column range from high-level lists of data concepts in the

Planner's perspective to detailed data models and database schemas in the Builder's and Subcontractor's perspectives. The goal is to ensure that information is effectively managed and supports the organisation's objectives.

How (function/process)

The Function aspect addresses how the organisation operates and how it performs its business processes. It describes the actions, processes and workflows that transform inputs into outputs. Models here include business process maps, system functionality specifications and software design models. The focus is on understanding and documenting how business and system processes should be executed to achieve desired outcomes.

Where (network/location)

The Location aspect examines the geographical and technological distribution of the organisation's resources. It explores questions about where data is stored, where business activities occur and how different locations are connected. Models range from high-level maps of organisational facilities to detailed network diagrams that specify communication protocols and data flows between systems. This aspect ensures that location-based requirements and constraints are accounted for in the architecture.

Who (people/organisation)

This aspect addresses the roles and responsibilities of people within the organisation. It defines who is involved in different processes, what their responsibilities are and how they interact with the system. Models include organisational charts, RBAC matrices and descriptions of user interactions with IT systems. The goal is to ensure that human factors are considered in the architecture, including security, usability and organisational dynamics.

When (time/event)

The Time aspect explores the temporal aspects of the organisation, including business events, scheduling and project timelines. It examines when processes occur, how often they are executed and how time-based constraints affect system performance. Models include business event sequences, process timelines and system performance schedules. This column ensures that timing and scheduling requirements are incorporated into the architecture, enabling effective coordination and management of resources.

Why (motivation/strategy)

The Motivation aspect focuses on the business drivers, goals and objectives that underpin the enterprise architecture. It explores why certain decisions are made, what the strategic priorities are and how success is measured. Models include business goal hierarchies, strategy maps and decision-making frameworks. This aspect ensures that the architecture is aligned with the strategic intent of the organisation and that every component of the system contributes to achieving business objectives.

The benefits and applications of the Zachman Framework

The Zachman Framework is invaluable for organisations that need a systematic and structured approach to managing complexity. It provides a comprehensive taxonomy and ensures that all critical aspects of the enterprise are addressed, reducing the risk of oversights that could lead to operational inefficiencies or security vulnerabilities.

The framework promotes alignment between business and IT by providing a common language and structure that both business executives and technical teams can use to understand and communicate architectural requirements.

One of the key benefits of the Zachman Framework is its flexibility and adaptability. While it provides a rigorous structure, it does not dictate a specific development methodology or sequence, allowing organisations to adapt it to their existing processes and frameworks. For example, organisations can use the Zachman Framework alongside Agile or DevSecOps methodologies, using it as a guide for architectural documentation and governance. The framework is also highly scalable, making it suitable for both small projects and large, enterprise-wide initiatives.

COBIT 2019

ISACA's Control Objectives for Information and Related Technologies is a globally recognised framework for governance and management of enterprise IT. It provides a structured approach to ensuring that IT is aligned with business objectives, delivers value and effectively manages risks. The latest version, COBIT 2019, builds on COBIT 5 with greater flexibility. It provides a customisable governance system and aligns IT goals with business strategies. It helps organisations to align IT with business objectives while ensuring compliance, risk management and performance improvement. The framework is structured around six governance system principles and three governance framework principles, ensuring a balanced approach to value delivery, risk optimisation and resource efficiency.

To use COBIT 2019, start by understanding the organisational context and identifying key stakeholders. Conduct a gap analysis to assess the current state of IT governance against COBIT's governance and management objectives. This helps in prioritising areas that need improvement based on business needs, risk appetite and compliance requirements.

Next, define tailored governance and management objectives using COBIT's 40 objectives mapped to key business functions. Each objective includes processes, activities, capability levels and performance metrics. Organisations should establish a governance system that integrates with existing frameworks (e.g. Information Technology Infrastructure Library (ITIL), ISO 27001, NIST CSF) to ensure consistency and avoid duplication.

Implementation should follow a structured approach, using the COBIT Design Guide to customise governance based on enterprise goals, industry and regulatory requirements. The COBIT Implementation Guide provides a step-by-step methodology, from planning and execution to continuous monitoring and improvement. Regular assessments should be conducted to measure performance, address gaps and adapt governance to evolving business and technological changes.

The three framework principles identify the underlying principles for a governance framework that can be used to build a governance system for the enterprise (Figure 2.5).

1. A governance framework should be based on a conceptual model, identifying the key components and relationships among components, to maximise consistency and allow automation.

2. A governance framework should be open and flexible. It should allow the addition of new content and the ability to address new issues in the most flexible way, while maintaining integrity and consistency.

3. A governance framework should align to relevant major related standards, frameworks and regulations.

Figure 2.5 COBIT framework principles

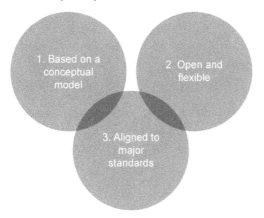

The six COBIT principles are the core requirements for a governance system for enterprise information and technology (Figure 2.6).

1. Each enterprise needs a governance system to satisfy stakeholder needs and to generate value from the use of integration and testing (I&T).

2. A governance system for enterprise I&T is built from a number of components that can be of different types and that work together in a holistic way.

3. A governance system should be dynamic. This means that each time one or more of the design factors are changed, the impact of these changes on the enterprise governance of IT system must be considered.

4. A governance system should clearly distinguish between governance and management activities and structures.

5. A governance system should be tailored to the enterprise's needs, using a set of design factors as parameters to customise and prioritise the governance system components.

6. A governance system should cover the enterprise from end to end, focusing not only on the IT function but on all technology and information processing the enterprise puts in place to achieve its goals.

Figure 2.6 COBIT principles

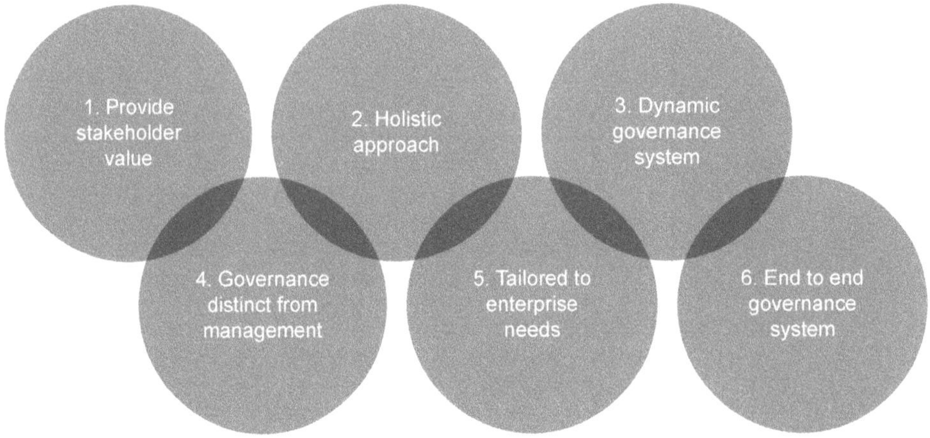

CASE STUDY

Zero trust architecture implementation in a global financial institution

Scenario
A leading multinational bank, with operations spanning over 50 countries, faced an increase in cyber threats, particularly targeted phishing campaigns and advanced persistent threats. Additionally, the rapid adoption of hybrid and remote working practices strained the existing perimeter-based security model. Recognising that traditional 'trust but verify' principles no longer provided sufficient protection, the organisation made the strategic decision to adopt a ZTA. This approach is aimed at enhancing security while maintaining business agility and compliance with financial regulatory frameworks such as the Financial Services Act (FSA), GDPR, PCI DSS and local banking regulations.

Focus areas

Micro-segmentation strategy
The bank implemented a micro-segmentation approach to minimise lateral movement within its network. Core data assets, such as payment processing systems and customer data repositories, were segmented into isolated zones. Communication between zones required strict policy enforcement through software-defined network controllers. For example, access to Society for Worldwide Interbank Financial Telecommunication (SWIFT) messaging systems was segmented, limiting the potential impact of a breach.

IAM integration
Advanced IAM solutions, including MFA and PAM, were deployed to establish strong identity verification mechanisms. RBAC was defined based on job functions, and

ZTNA solutions replaced legacy VPN systems, ensuring that access to critical systems was granted only on a 'need-to-know' basis.

Least privilege access
The bank shifted its policies towards enforcing least privilege access across all systems. Users and devices were granted access only to specific resources required for their roles, significantly reducing exposure to insider threats and compromised credentials. Automated tools were introduced to review and revoke unnecessary permissions – to reduce privilege creep or no longer require accounts to remain active.

Continuous monitoring
Having SIEM and EDR tools in place, the bank implemented continuous monitoring to ensure real-time anomaly detection. A centralised Security Operations Centre (SOC) used AI-powered threat analytics to proactively identify and mitigate threats across global branches. Continuous trust evaluation was applied to both users and devices, dynamically adjusting access permissions based on risk scores.

Challenges

Migration from legacy systems
Many of the bank's core systems relied on outdated technologies that were incompatible with modern zero trust principles. Legacy authentication methods, flat network designs and hard-coded credentials posed significant migration hurdles. The IT teams faced challenges in mapping legacy dependencies and retrofitting security measures without disrupting critical financial operations.

Cultural resistance to change
Employees and middle management initially resisted the changes due to perceived complexities in accessing systems and concerns about productivity impact. Front-line staff were particularly concerned about multi-step authentication processes and regular policy reviews, requiring intensive communication campaigns to support buy-in by ensuring the positives, and the 'why' was addressed to ensure users and stakeholders were fully informed and updated.

Extensive training needs
To ensure successful adoption, the organisation rolled out training programmes tailored to different user groups. Security hygiene workshops for employees, technical training for IT teams and executive briefings for leadership were conducted to align all stakeholders with zero trust principles.

Balancing compliance and security
Financial institutions operate under stringent regulatory requirements. The bank had to carefully balance the implementation of zero trust policies with maintaining compliance across jurisdictions, ensuring no operational or legal gaps were introduced during the transition.

Outcomes

Increased visibility
The bank achieved end-to-end visibility of network activities, allowing it to monitor and audit all interactions between users, devices and applications. This heightened situational awareness enabled quicker responses to potential threats.

Improved threat detection
Continuous monitoring and the use of AI-enabled tools led to a significant improvement in the detection of anomalous behaviours, with mean time to detect (MTTD) and mean time to respond (MTTR) reduced by 45%.

Reduced attack surface
By implementing micro-segmentation and least privilege access, the organisation effectively minimised the pathways attackers could exploit. Critical systems were isolated, ensuring that any breach was contained to a small segment.

Challenges faced during rollout
Despite the successes, the rollout encountered delays due to the complexity of retrofitting zero trust principles onto legacy systems. Employee feedback highlighted that initial user experiences were hindered by MFA and access policy configurations, necessitating further refinement and user experience optimisation.

Key learnings

- Early stakeholder engagement and change management are essential to overcoming cultural resistance.

- Phased implementation of zero trust principles, starting with high-risk areas, can help to demonstrate value, build momentum and identify issues for the next phase.

- Automation tools for access management and threat detection can significantly enhance scalability and operational efficiency.

- Ongoing education and iterative improvements ensure sustained success and alignment with evolving regulatory and security landscapes.

These case studies are placed throughout the book; they are used to help support the design and thought process of security architecture. Use the case studies to tailor or add to, using your own using critical thinking. After the theory contained within this book, the next step is practical application of security architecture, be it a real-world project as an individual or team or a desktop exercise.

3   THREAT MODELLING

In this chapter, we explore the concept of threat modelling. What it is, why it matters and how it can be effectively applied. We examine its critical role in the design process and its significance as a fundamental component of SBD principles.

We will delve into several established threat modelling methodologies, including STRIDE, PASTA, threat risk identification and knowledge exchange (TRIKE), visual, agile and simple threat (VAST), MITRE ATT&CK® and deny, degrade, disrupt, deceive and destroy (5 Ds), using practical examples to illustrate their application. Finally, we will discuss the role of threat intelligence in refining and enhancing the threat modelling process.

THREAT MODELLING

Threat modelling is a structured approach used to identify, evaluate and mitigate potential security threats to a system. It is an essential practice within security and software development, aiming to anticipate and address vulnerabilities before adversaries can exploit them. The goal is to ensure that security considerations are integrated into the design, development and operational phases of a system. With 'shift left' and Secure by Design, security should be considered at the start and then at each and every stage of development of a system or software. Shift left is a software development and security approach that involves integrating testing, quality assurance and security earlier in the development lifecycle to identify and resolve issues sooner and more efficiently. Security could be the reason not to do something or add additional costs not considered, making further development uneconomic. Threat modelling is an essential element of SBD because it enables a proactive approach to identifying and mitigating potential security risks during the design and development phases of a system, application or process.

SBD is a proactive security approach where security is integrated into the design and development of systems, software, and infrastructure from the outset, rather than being added as a later consideration. One of the key principles of SBD is threat modelling. We will delve deeper into SBD in Chapter 7.

Purpose of threat modelling

The primary objective of threat modelling is to provide a systematic framework to:

- **Identify:** Uncover potential threats, vulnerabilities and weaknesses within a system or application.
- **Understand:** Comprehend how these threats could impact the system, including the attacker's motivations, capabilities and possible attack vectors.

- **Prioritise:** Assess and rank the identified threats based on their severity, likelihood of occurrence and potential impact.

- **Mitigate:** Develop and implement strategies to reduce or eliminate these threats. This can involve redesigning parts of the system, strengthening defences or implementing monitoring and response measures.

When to perform threat modelling

Threat modelling should ideally be an integral part of the SDLC. Conducting threat modelling early in the development process during the design or requirement phases allows for the identification of potential security issues before they become costly to fix or could mean the project is not viable in the first place. However, it can also be beneficial to revisit and update the threat model periodically, especially when:

- significant changes are made to the system's architecture or functionality;

- new threats or attack techniques are discovered;

- the system's environment changes, such as being deployed in a different infrastructure.

Core elements of threat modelling

Threat modelling encompasses several key components:

- **Assets** represent the valuable elements of the system that need protection, such as sensitive data, intellectual property, system functionality or user privacy. Understanding the importance and sensitivity of each asset is crucial for prioritising threats.

- **Attackers** or threat actors are individuals or groups that may attempt to exploit vulnerabilities in the system. Threat actors can range from cybercriminals and hacktivists to nation-state actors and insider threats. Modelling attackers involves understanding their motivations, skill levels and potential attack vectors.

- **Threats** are a potentially negative action or event that could lead to the compromise of an asset. Threats are typically categorised based on the methods an attacker might use, such as malware infections, data breaches, DoS attacks or phishing campaigns.

- **Vulnerabilities** are weaknesses or gaps in the system's design, implementation or configuration that could be exploited by an attacker. Vulnerabilities can include unpatched software, misconfigured permissions or a lack of input validation.

- **Attack vectors** represent the paths or methods an attacker uses to gain access to a system or exploit a vulnerability. Examples include phishing emails, social engineering, open ports or compromised third-party libraries.

- **Countermeasures** are security measures or controls put in place to mitigate or eliminate the threats identified. Countermeasures can be technical (firewalls, encryption, access controls), procedural (security policies, user training) or physical (restricted access to data centres).

THREAT MODELLING FRAMEWORKS

Attack Trees

Attack Trees is a method for analysing and understanding potential security threats in a structured and systematic way. They are used extensively in cybersecurity, risk assessment and threat modelling to identify how an attacker might compromise a system and to determine the most effective mitigation strategies.

> Attack Trees provide a formal, methodical way of describing the security of systems, based on varying attacks. Basically, you represent attacks against a system in a tree structure, with the goal as the root node and different ways of achieving that goal as leaf nodes (Schneier, 1999).

Overview of Attack Trees

An Attack Tree is essentially a hierarchical, tree-like diagram that represents the different ways an adversary could achieve a specific malicious goal. The root or trunk of the tree represents the ultimate objective of the attacker, such as 'Gain access to confidential data' or 'Disrupt system operations'. From this trunk, various branches spread out, representing different attack vectors or methods an attacker could use to reach that goal. The branches are further broken down into sub-branches and leaves, each depicting increasingly detailed and specific attack steps or actions. The structure provides a comprehensive and visual representation of the potential threats, helping security professionals to understand and address the full spectrum of attack possibilities.

Hierarchical structure

The hierarchical nature of Attack Trees makes them an efficient tool for threat modelling. The root node, which symbolises the attacker's primary objective, serves as the starting point of the analysis. As you move down the tree, the branches represent different avenues or strategies an attacker might employ. These branches can be further decomposed into sub-branches, breaking down complex attacks into smaller, more manageable components. Each node in the tree represents a potential threat or a step in the attack process and the leaves represent the most granular attack actions.

For example, if the root goal is to 'Steal sensitive customer data', the primary branches could include 'Exploit software vulnerability', 'Conduct phishing attack' or 'Use physical intrusion'. These branches can then be decomposed into more detailed actions, such as 'Identify software vulnerability', 'Craft malicious email' or 'Bypass physical security measures'.

Threat decomposition

Threat decomposition is a critical part of the Attack Tree methodology. It involves breaking down complex threats into simpler, more specific sub-threats or attack vectors. This decomposition process helps security teams to gain a deeper understanding of how each threat can be realised and the different steps an attacker might take.

Figure 3.1 Attack Tree malware

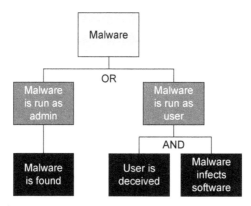

The decomposition continues until each branch of the tree represents a distinct and actionable threat scenario, making it easier to analyse and develop targeted defences.

Visual representation
The visual nature of Attack Trees makes it easy to understand (Figure 3.1). The tree-like diagram makes it easy for stakeholders, including non-technical decision-makers, to understand the security challenges faced by an organisation. The graphical format clarifies how different attack vectors are related and which paths are most critical to the attacker's success. This visual representation facilitates effective communication and collaboration among security teams, management and other stakeholders, ensuring that everyone has a shared understanding of the threat landscape.

Systematic approach
Attack Trees employ a systematic approach to threat modelling, which consists of several key steps.

Define the asset or goal   The first step is to clearly identify the asset that needs protection or the security goal to be achieved. This could be anything from protecting sensitive data to ensuring the availability of critical infrastructure. The asset or goal becomes the root node of the Attack Tree.

Identify threats   Next, potential threats to the asset or goal are identified. These are represented as the first set of branches extending from the root. Threat identification should be comprehensive, considering a wide range of attack vectors, including technical, human and physical threats.

Decompose threats   Each identified threat is broken down into sub-threats or attack vectors. This step involves thinking like an attacker and mapping out all possible methods that could be used to achieve the malicious goal. The decomposition continues until all attack steps are represented at a sufficient level of detail.

Analyse and prioritise   Once the tree is complete, each threat and sub-threat is assessed based on factors such as likelihood and impact. This analysis helps to prioritise which threats require the most urgent attention and resources for mitigation.

It also enables the identification of critical paths – those branches of the tree that are most likely to be exploited or have the most severe consequences.

AND/OR logic

Attack Trees use Boolean AND/OR logic to represent the relationships between different threats and attack vectors.

- **AND nodes:** These nodes indicate that all sub-threats must occur for the parent threat to be realised. For instance, an attack might require both 'Access to the building' and 'Bypassing internal security' to be successful. In this case, both conditions need to be met and the AND node signifies this dependency.

- **OR nodes:** These nodes indicate that any one of the sub-threats can lead to the parent threat being realised. For example, if an attacker can either 'Exploit a software vulnerability' or 'Steal an admin password' to gain access to a system, the OR node shows that fulfilling any one of these conditions is sufficient.

This logical structure allows for a clear understanding of how different attack steps interact and helps to identify the weakest links in the security chain.

Risk assessment

Risk assessment is a crucial aspect of working with Attack Trees. Each threat and sub-threat is evaluated for its risk level, which typically involves estimating the likelihood of the threat occurring and the potential impact if it does. Factors to consider might include the attacker's motivation, resources and technical capabilities, as well as the existing security controls. By assigning risk levels to each node, security teams can prioritise their efforts and focus on mitigating the most critical threats.

Mitigation strategies

For each identified threat, security professionals develop mitigation strategies aimed at reducing the likelihood or impact of the attack. These strategies might include implementing technical controls, such as firewalls and IDSs, or administrative measures, such as security policies and user training. The tree structure allows for an organised approach to mapping these defences directly to the threats they are designed to counter. Additionally, by visualising the attack paths, teams can ensure that there are no gaps in the security measures and that critical paths are well protected.

Benefits and applications

The benefits of using Attack Trees are numerous. They provide a clear and methodical way to understand the different attack strategies an adversary might use, allowing organisations to make informed decisions about where to allocate security resources. Attack Trees are highly versatile and can be used for a wide range of scenarios, from analysing the security of physical facilities to assessing vulnerabilities in complex IT systems. They also support collaborative threat analysis, enabling cross-functional teams to work together in identifying and addressing potential risks.

Attack Trees can be used as a post-incident analysis tool as well. By mapping out the attack paths that were exploited, security teams can better understand how an incident occurred and what changes are needed to prevent future occurrences.

STRIDE

The STRIDE threat modelling framework was developed by Microsoft in the late 1990s. It still serves as a reliable and simple method for identifying and addressing potential security threats in systems. This model was created as part of Microsoft's Trustworthy Computing initiative, which aimed to significantly improve the security, privacy and reliability of their software products. The initiative was launched in response to the growing need for comprehensive security measures with the rapid expansion of interconnected systems and increase of sophisticated cyber threats. Damage, reproducibility, exploitability, affected, discoverability (DREAD) was originally developed by Microsoft as part of the STRIDE framework but is now less commonly used due to subjectivity in scoring. DREAD is a qualitative risk assessment model and was used in threat modelling to evaluate and prioritise security threats.

Origin and development of STRIDE

STRIDE was developed by Loren Kohn Felder and Praerit Garg, members of Microsoft's security team. Their work emerged from the realisation that software products, particularly OSs such as Windows, were becoming critical to both personal and enterprise environments. As the digital landscape evolved, so did the complexity of security challenges, prompting the need for a robust threat modelling framework. STRIDE was designed to be integrated into Microsoft's Security Development Lifecycle (SDL), a structured process ensuring that security considerations are addressed throughout the software development lifecycle, from design to deployment and beyond.

The SDL mandates threat modelling as a key component, ensuring that security is proactively considered and embedded into the architecture rather than being treated as an afterthought. STRIDE, therefore, became an important methodology within this process. Offering a simple yet comprehensive approach to categorise and analyse threats, its structured nature made it accessible not only to security experts but also to software developers and engineers, promoting a culture of security awareness across different teams.

STRIDE framework components

STRIDE is an acronym representing six distinct types of threats: spoofing, tampering, repudiation, information disclosure, DoS and elevation of privilege. Each component addresses a different aspect of security and provides guidance on what to look for when evaluating a system's security posture.

Spoofing   This threat occurs when an attacker pretends to be someone or something they are not to gain unauthorised access to resources. In simpler terms, spoofing targets the authentication mechanisms of a system. Common examples include stealing login credentials to impersonate a legitimate user or creating a fake website that tricks people into entering their sensitive information. To mitigate spoofing threats, it is essential to implement strong authentication methods such as MFA and the use of digital certificates.

Tampering   Tampering refers to the unauthorised modification of data, either in transit or at rest. This threat compromises the integrity of the information, meaning that attackers can alter data, which can lead to devastating consequences. For example, tampering can occur when a malicious actor intercepts and modifies communications between systems or alters stored files. To prevent tampering, the use of data encryption, hash files or data and robust access controls ensure that data remains unchanged and trustworthy.

Repudiation   Repudiation threats involve situations where a user denies performing an action and the system lacks the capability to prove otherwise. This aspect of STRIDE targets the non-repudiation requirement, which ensures that actions taken by users can be traced back to them definitively. For example, if a user denies making an online transaction, the system should have appropriate logging and auditing mechanisms to verify the claim. Digital signatures and comprehensive logging frameworks are commonly employed to counter repudiation threats.

Information disclosure   Also known as a breach of confidentiality, information disclosure refers to the unauthorised exposure of sensitive data. This type of threat can manifest when attackers eavesdrop on network communications, access unsecured files or exploit vulnerabilities to gain unauthorised access to data. To defend against information disclosure, security architects use data encryption, strict access control mechanisms and proper data classification and handling procedures to ensure that sensitive information remains confidential.

Denial of service   DoS attacks aim to make a system or service unavailable to its intended users by overwhelming it with excessive traffic or exploiting vulnerabilities to crash it. The availability of a system is crucial, especially for services that need to be operational 24/7. Common strategies to mitigate DoS attacks include implementing rate limiting, using WAFs and designing systems with redundancy and failover capabilities to maintain service continuity.

Elevation of privilege   This threat occurs when an attacker gains higher permissions than those initially granted, enabling them to perform unauthorised actions within a system. Elevation of privilege compromises the authorisation controls and can lead to severe security breaches. For instance, a user exploiting a vulnerability to gain administrative privileges could have unrestricted access to sensitive data or critical system functions. Mitigating this threat involves implementing the principle of least privilege (ensuring users have only the permissions they need), regular privilege audits and patching software vulnerabilities promptly.

Practical application of STRIDE
One of the significant advantages of the STRIDE model is its simplicity and versatility, making it applicable across a variety of systems and services. Security teams and developers can use STRIDE to perform systematic threat analyses during the design phase, helping them to understand and anticipate potential risks. By categorising threats using STRIDE, security architects can ensure a holistic evaluation of security concerns, addressing everything from authentication mechanisms to data integrity and availability.

Using STRIDE in threat modelling
In practice, threat modelling using STRIDE typically begins with understanding the architecture of the system being analysed. Security professionals create data flow diagrams (DFDs) to visualise how data moves through the system, identifying key components such as data stores, processes and communication links. Each element

of the DFD is then evaluated using the STRIDE model to identify possible threats. For example, a data store might be analysed for tampering or information disclosure risks, while a communication channel might be scrutinised for potential spoofing or DoS vulnerabilities.

Integrating STRIDE with other frameworks

Although STRIDE is a robust framework in its own right, it is often used in conjunction with other security models and standards, such as Open Web Application Security Project (OWASP) for web application security, ISO/IEC 27001 for information security management or NIST for comprehensive risk management. By combining STRIDE with these frameworks, organisations can ensure a well-rounded approach to security, addressing both software-specific and broader organisational threats.

STRIDE remains a useful tool for identifying evolving threats and because of its simplicity of use its emphasis on systematically breaking down potential attack vectors has proven helpful in understanding and mitigating complex threats. The framework's adaptability makes it relevant even as new technologies emerge, such as containers, AI, OT and the IoT.

The effectiveness of STRIDE lies in its methodical approach and its ability to foster a security-first mindset among development teams. By integrating STRIDE into the SDL, organisations can better protect their assets and maintain the trust and security of their systems in an ever-changing threat landscape. This proactive approach ensures that security is an integral part of software design, reducing the risk of vulnerabilities being exploited in production environments.

Example STRIDE use case: web application

Context: A healthcare web application that allows patients to schedule appointments, view medical records and communicate with their healthcare providers. The application includes a web interface, a back-end server, a database and third-party integrations (e.g. payment processing).

Spoofing

Threat: An attacker impersonates a legitimate user to gain unauthorised access.

Example scenario: An attacker uses stolen credentials to log in as a patient.

Mitigation strategies:

- Implement MFA.
- Use strong password policies and encourage regular password changes.
- Monitor for unusual login patterns and alert users of suspicious activity.

Tampering

Threat: An attacker modifies data in transit or at rest.

Example scenario: An attacker intercepts and alters prescription information between the client and server.

Mitigation strategies:

- Use TLS 1.2/1.3 to encrypt data in transit.
- Implement data integrity checks (e.g. digital signatures).
- Store sensitive data in an encrypted format in the database.
- Use hashing and salting for passwords.

Repudiation

Threat: A user denies performing an action without a way for the system to prove otherwise.

Example scenario: A patient denies having requested a medication refill, claiming it was a system error.

Mitigation strategies:

- Implement comprehensive logging for all user actions.
- Use non-repudiation techniques such as digital signatures.
- Ensure logs are tamper-proof and securely stored.
- Ensure information disclosure.

Information disclosure

Threat: Sensitive information is exposed to unauthorised individuals.

Example scenario: A vulnerability in the application allows an attacker to access other patients' medical records.

Mitigation strategies:

- Enforce strict access control policies.
- Use data encryption both in transit and at rest.
- Perform regular security audits and vulnerability assessments.
- Implement least privilege principles for database access.

DoS

Threat: An attacker disrupts the service, making it unavailable to legitimate users.

Example scenario: An attacker floods the server with requests, causing it to crash and become unavailable.

Mitigation strategies:

- Implement rate limiting and throttling to control request rates.
- Use WAFs to detect and block malicious traffic.

- Deploy redundancy and load balancing to handle high traffic volumes.
- Monitor network traffic for unusual patterns.

Elevation of privilege
Threat: An attacker gains higher privileges than intended.

> **Example scenario:** A regular user exploits a vulnerability to gain administrative access.

Mitigation strategies:

- Implement proper RBAC.
- Perform regular security code reviews and penetration testing.
- Apply security patches and updates promptly.
- Use principle of least privilege for all users and services.

PASTA

PASTA is a comprehensive, risk-centric threat modelling methodology developed to assess and manage the security of applications or systems from the perspective of an attacker. PASTA distinguishes itself from other models by its emphasis on simulating real-world attack scenarios to identify potential vulnerabilities and assess the impact of threats on the organisation's assets and processes. By incorporating an attacker's perspective, PASTA enables security teams to better anticipate and mitigate threats that could have a significant impact on the organisation. The methodology was designed to be scalable and adaptable, providing a structured and systematic approach to threat analysis.

Risk-centric approach
At the core of PASTA is its risk-centric approach, which aligns security activities with an organisation's business objectives and risk management framework. This model focuses not only on the identification of potential security threats but also on understanding the potential impact of these threats on critical business processes and assets. By prioritising threats based on their impact on organisational goals, PASTA ensures that security efforts are efficient and aligned with the broader risk management strategy. This alignment is critical for organisations looking to optimise their security investments and focus resources on the most significant threats.

The seven stages of PASTA
PASTA's structured approach is organised into seven distinct stages, each building on the insights gained from the previous stage. This progression allows for a thorough and continuous analysis of the security landscape, leading to the development of a robust threat management strategy.

Stage 1: Definition of the objectives (DO)   The first stage involves defining the organisation's objectives and security goals. Security teams work closely with business stakeholders to identify critical assets, business processes and the potential impact of security breaches. The goal is to establish a clear understanding of what needs to be protected and the security priorities of the organisation. This stage lays the foundation for the entire PASTA process by ensuring that all subsequent activities are aligned with the organisation's strategic goals.

Stage 2: Definition of the technical scope (DTS)   In this stage, the technical environment and scope of the analysis are defined. Security teams document the system architecture, components, communication flows and technologies used. This includes a detailed inventory of hardware, software, data assets and external dependencies. By clearly defining the technical boundaries, the team can focus on understanding how different elements interact and what might be at risk.

Stage 3: Application decomposition and analysis (ADA)   This stage involves breaking down the application or system into its individual components and analysing how they interact. The goal is to understand data flows, trust boundaries and dependencies. Security analysts create DFDs to visualise the movement of data and identify potential points of attack. This detailed analysis helps to uncover how data is processed, stored and transmitted, which is crucial for identifying areas that may be susceptible to attack.

Stage 4: Threat analysis (TA)   The fourth stage focuses on identifying potential threats and attack vectors that could target the application or system. Threat intelligence and historical attack data are used to inform this analysis, ensuring that the model reflects real-world threats. Techniques such as STRIDE can be incorporated to categorise and understand the nature of potential threats. The goal is to develop a comprehensive threat library that includes both known and emerging threats relevant to the system.

Stage 5: Weakness and vulnerability analysis (WVA)   In this stage, security teams conduct a detailed analysis of the system's weaknesses and vulnerabilities. This involves reviewing the codebase, configuration settings and architecture to identify points of failure or potential exploit paths. Vulnerability scanning tools, manual code reviews and security assessments are commonly used to uncover vulnerabilities. The focus is on understanding how an attacker might exploit these weaknesses and the potential damage they could cause.

Stage 6: Attack modelling and simulation (AMS)   The sixth stage involves simulating real-world attacks to model potential threat scenarios. Using penetration testing, red team exercises or attack simulation software, security professionals evaluate the feasibility of the identified threats. The objective is to understand how an attack could be carried out, and the potential consequences of a successful breach. This hands-on testing helps to validate the theoretical analysis and provides a clearer picture of the security posture. The simulation results are used to refine the threat model and inform risk assessments.

Stage 7: Risk and impact analysis (RIA)   The final stage focuses on assessing the risk and impact of the identified threats and vulnerabilities. Security analysts evaluate the likelihood and potential impact of each threat, prioritising them based on the risk they pose to the organisation. Risk assessments consider factors such as threat actor capabilities, exploitability of vulnerabilities and the business value of targeted assets. The outcome of this stage is a prioritised list of threats and corresponding mitigation strategies, which inform the development of a comprehensive security plan.

Attack simulation and real-world threat modelling

One of PASTA's unique features is its emphasis on attack simulation, which models real-world threat scenarios to uncover potential weaknesses. This dynamic approach helps organisations to understand how an attacker might exploit a vulnerability and the broader impact of such an attack on business operations. The use of attack simulations also aids in assessing the effectiveness of existing security controls and identifying areas that require additional protection. By simulating attacks, organisations can develop a deeper understanding of the threat landscape and take proactive measures to strengthen their defences.

Organisation impact focus

PASTA places a strong emphasis on understanding the impact of threats on the organisation's processes and assets. This ensures that security measures are prioritised based on their significance to the business, rather than purely technical considerations. By aligning security efforts with business priorities, PASTA helps organisations to allocate resources more effectively and respond to threats in a way that minimises operational disruption. This business-driven approach is particularly valuable in environments where security must be balanced with performance, usability and cost considerations.

Iterative and continuous improvement

PASTA is designed to be iterative and adaptable, recognising that the threat landscape is constantly evolving. Security or threat teams are encouraged to revisit and update the threat model regularly, especially when there are significant changes to the system or new threats emerge. This continuous improvement process ensures that the organisation's security posture remains robust and responsive to evolving risks. The iterative nature of PASTA allows for ongoing refinement of the threat model, making it a living document that evolves alongside the organisation's needs and technological advancements.

By following a structured seven-stage process, organisations can gain understanding of potential threats and vulnerabilities, prioritise risks based on their impact and implement effective security measures. This framework's adaptability and emphasis on real-world scenarios make it particularly well-suited for modern, dynamic environments where security threats are always evolving.

Example PASTA use case: e-commerce website

Stage 1: Definition of objectives (DO)

> **Organisation objectives:** Provide a secure platform for online shopping, ensure customer trust and protect sensitive data.

> **Security objectives:** Prevent unauthorised access, safeguard customer data, ensure transaction integrity and comply with data protection regulations.

Stage 2: Definition of the technical scope (DTS)

> **Application scope:** e-commerce website, including the web server, database, payment gateway and third-party integrations.

Technologies used: web server (e.g. Apache), database (e.g. MySQL), front-end framework (e.g. React), back-end language (e.g. Node.js), payment processors (e.g. PayPal, Stripe).

Network infrastructure: load balancers, firewalls, TLS for secure communication.

Stage 3: Application decomposition and analysis (ADA)

Components: user authentication module, product catalogue, shopping cart, payment processing, order management, user profile management.

Data flows: user inputs credentials, searches for products, adds items to the cart, proceeds to checkout, enters payment details, confirms order, receives order confirmation.

Entry points: user login page, product search, add to cart, checkout page, payment gateway, API for third-party services.

Trust boundaries: user device, web server, application server, database server, third-party payment processors.

Stage 4: Threat analysis (TA)

Threats:

- **unauthorised access:** brute force attacks, credential stuffing;
- **data breaches:** SQL injection (SQLi), exposed APIs;
- **financial fraud:** credit card fraud, unauthorised transactions;
- **DoS/distributed denial of service (DDoS) attacks:** overloading the server to disrupt service;
- **cross-site scripting (XSS):** injecting malicious scripts via input fields;
- **cross-site request forgery (CSRF):** unauthorised actions on behalf of authenticated users.

Stage 5 Weakness and vulnerability analysis (WVA)

Vulnerabilities:

- **weak password policies:** allowing easily guessable passwords;
- **unpatched software:** outdated libraries or frameworks;
- **misconfigured security settings:** improperly configured TLS;
- **lack of input validation:** no sanitisation of user inputs;
- **exposed APIs:** publicly accessible without proper authentication.

Tools for analysis: vulnerability scanners (e.g. Burp, Qualys, Nessus), code review, penetration testing.

Stage 6 Attack modelling and simulation (AMS)

Attack scenarios:

- **SQL injection attack:** An attacker exploits a vulnerability in the login form to access the database.
- **Brute force attack:** An attacker attempts to gain access by trying numerous username–password combinations.
- **DDoS attack:** Attackers overwhelm the server with traffic, causing downtime.

Simulation: Conduct penetration tests simulating these attacks to understand their impact and likelihood.

Stage 7 Risk and impact analysis (RIA)

Risk assessment: Evaluate the likelihood and impact of identified threats.

- **SQL injection:** high impact, high likelihood without proper sanitisation;
- **Brute force:** medium impact, medium likelihood mitigated by account lockout mechanisms;
- **DDoS:** high impact, varying likelihood depending on mitigation measures like content delivery networks.

Risk mitigation: prioritise remediation efforts based on risk assessment.

Mitigations:

- Implement strong password policies and MFA.
- Regularly update and patch software.
- Configure security settings correctly.
- Validate and sanitise all user inputs.
- Secure APIs with proper authentication and authorisation mechanisms.
- Use WAFs and DDoS protection services.

TRIKE

TRIKE stands out in security auditing as an open-source framework designed with a distinct focus on risk management. Unlike traditional models that seek to eliminate all risk, TRIKE embraces the reality that risk cannot always be entirely eradicated. At some point residual risk must be accepted. Instead, it emphasises the management and prioritisation of risk, defining acceptable thresholds that organisations can tolerate based on their risk appetite. This pragmatic approach makes TRIKE particularly valuable in environments where resources for risk mitigation are limited and prioritisation becomes essential.

Core concepts and risk management perspective

At its heart, TRIKE revolves around the principle that effective risk management should guide security decisions. It integrates the generation of threat models into the risk management process, facilitating a structured approach to assessing and addressing security concerns. By using threat models not as a means to eliminate risk entirely but to manage and reduce it to acceptable levels, TRIKE shifts the focus to achieving a balanced security posture. It achieves this by delineating acceptable levels of risk for different system assets, providing clarity on what is critical and where mitigating efforts should be concentrated.

System asset and user breakdown

A fundamental aspect of TRIKE is how it decomposes the system into two essential elements: system assets and system users. For each asset, the framework examines the user's access level and the permissions associated with specific actions. These actions typically include the create, read, update and delete (CRUD) operations, which are crucial in understanding how data and resources can be manipulated or exposed. By mapping out these interactions, TRIKE provides a detailed view of the system's security posture, highlighting where permissions may introduce unnecessary risk.

For instance, if a user has broad permissions to delete critical data, but should only require read access, TRIKE's analysis would flag this as an area needing attention. This fine-grained approach ensures that the organisation has a detailed understanding of potential vulnerabilities linked to user permissions and asset accessibility.

Risk management principles for threat prioritisation

TRIKE integrates risk management principles to ensure that threats are evaluated not only by their existence but by their potential impact and likelihood of occurrence. This is a crucial aspect, as it helps organisations to make informed decisions about which threats require immediate attention and which can be deprioritised or accepted based on their risk levels. The framework assigns a risk value to each identified threat, allowing teams to allocate resources efficiently and focus on mitigating risks that pose the highest danger to the organisation.

Components of TRIKE's threat modelling process

TRIKE's method for modelling threats is structured around three main components, each playing a critical role in creating a comprehensive security overview:

- **Requirements model** defines the security requirements of the system, which are often derived from the organisation's security goals and the assets needing protection. It lays the groundwork for understanding what must be secured and what constitutes acceptable security outcomes. For example, if an asset is highly sensitive, the model might specify strict access controls as a requirement.

- **Implementation model** describes the system design, detailing the data flow and interactions within the environment. This model identifies critical elements such as entry points, where external data or users can interface with the system and trust boundaries that separate different security domains. By mapping out how data moves through the system, it becomes possible to spot weak points, such as unsecured entry points or inadequate boundary protection.

- **Threat model** is based on the requirements and implementation models. It maps threats to the system, illustrating where and how potential attacks could occur. This mapping process highlights vulnerabilities and visualises possible attack vectors, enabling a thorough assessment of how an adversary might compromise the system. By considering the specific architecture and security requirements, the threat model becomes a tool for visualising the system's threat landscape comprehensively.

Role-based approach

TRIKE's effectiveness is enhanced through a role-based approach that engages various participants in the threat modelling process. Each role brings a unique perspective, ensuring a holistic and well-rounded model. Stakeholders may define what assets are critical based on business value, while analysts focus on technical vulnerabilities and risk assessment. Meanwhile, developers provide insights into the system's architecture and can suggest practical mitigation measures. This collaboration fosters a shared understanding of security concerns across the organisation and helps to ensure that no crucial detail is overlooked.

Structured and systematic process

The TRIKE framework follows a well-defined process to build threat models. The steps typically include:

- **Identifying and cataloguing assets** by establishing an inventory of assets to determine what needs protection.

- **Defining security requirements** by specifying what security outcomes are needed to protect those assets effectively.

- **Mapping out the system architecture** by describing how data flows, identifying entry points, trust boundaries and actors.

- **Identifying and classifying threats** by analysing how adversaries could compromise the system, based on the gathered information.

- **Assessing risks and prioritising them** by evaluating the potential impact and likelihood of each threat to prioritise mitigation strategies.

- **Developing mitigation strategies** by creating actionable plans to address the highest-priority risks and protect the system.

Iterative and adaptive approach

TRIKE is not a static framework; it is designed to be iterative, meaning that the threat modelling process can and should be revisited as the system evolves or new threats emerge. This flexibility ensures that the threat model remains relevant and up to date throughout the system's lifecycle. The model can be refined as changes are made to the architecture or new information becomes available, providing an evolving and responsive approach to risk management.

VAST

VAST modelling stands as a methodology designed to streamline the process of identifying and mitigating security threats. Built to accommodate the speed and flexibility required in modern software development, VAST focuses on three main principles: visual representation, agility and simplicity. By providing a structured yet efficient way of incorporating threat modelling into development cycles, VAST addresses the challenge of balancing security needs with development agility.

Principles of VAST: visual, agile and simple

Visual representation   At the core of VAST is the use of visual diagrams and charts to convey the security landscape of a system. This visual aspect is crucial because it transforms complex security concepts into intuitive and easily digestible formats. VAST maps out:

- **System architecture:** Detailed diagrams illustrate how different components of the system interact, revealing how data moves and where potential security weaknesses may exist.

- **Data flows:** Visually representing how data flows within and across the system boundaries, VAST helps to identify potential vulnerabilities in how data is transmitted or processed. These diagrams highlight where encryption or other security controls might be necessary.

- **Trust boundaries:** Clear demarcations show areas of varying levels of trust, such as where internal networks interface with the internet or third-party services. Understanding these boundaries is essential for applying appropriate security measures.

- **Potential attack vectors:** VAST diagrams illustrate where threats could potentially breach the system, helping to visualise attack paths. This might include points where malicious actors could inject data, compromise user authentication or exploit misconfigurations.

This visual approach not only makes threat modelling accessible to non-security stakeholders, such as developers and project managers, but also enhances communication between security and development teams. When everyone can see the same diagram and understand the risks, it should increase productive collaboration and ensure that security remains a shared responsibility.

Agile approach   VAST is designed to align seamlessly with Agile development practices. In today's software development world, Agile has now become the dominant methodology, characterised by short development cycles, continuous integration and regular feedback loops. VAST integrates threat modelling into these cycles, ensuring that security considerations are not an afterthought but are embedded throughout the development process.

The key benefits of this Agile integration include:

- **Iterative threat modelling:** Threat models are not created once and then left static. Instead, they evolve with the system, being revisited and refined during each development sprint. This ensures that, as new features are developed or system changes are made, the security model remains current.

- **Continuous security feedback:** Just as Agile encourages continuous feedback on code quality and functionality, VAST supports continuous feedback on security posture. Security teams can assess and communicate threats rapidly, allowing developers to make security improvements without disrupting the development flow.

- **Flexibility:** VAST allows for quick adjustments. If a new vulnerability is discovered or a change in architecture introduces new risks, the methodology makes it easy to update the threat model and reprioritise mitigation strategies accordingly.

By embracing Agile principles, VAST ensures that security does not slow down development but instead becomes a natural and integrated part of the process.

Simplicity   VAST places a strong emphasis on simplicity. Security can often be overwhelming, with numerous threats and complex models. VAST simplifies threat modelling by focusing on what is most critical. This means prioritising the most significant threats and vulnerabilities rather than trying to address every possible risk.

Key elements of this simplified approach include:

- **Actionable insights:** VAST generates practical and easily understandable recommendations that developers and security teams can implement without requiring extensive background knowledge in security.
- **Focused efforts:** By narrowing down the focus to the most impactful risks, VAST ensures that security efforts yield tangible improvements in the system's security posture. This means avoiding analysis paralysis and enabling teams to make meaningful progress.

Structured methodology of VAST

Despite prioritising simplicity, VAST maintains a structured and rigorous methodology to ensure that threat modelling is both effective and comprehensive. The key steps in this methodology are asset identification, threat identification, risk assessment and mitigation strategies.

Asset identification   The first step involves identifying and categorising assets that need protection. Assets may include data (e.g. sensitive customer information), systems (e.g. critical servers) and other components vital to business operations. Understanding what needs protection sets the stage for evaluating potential threats.

Threat identification   Next, VAST identifies threats and attack vectors that could exploit vulnerabilities in the system. This involves analysing how a threat could materialise and what it would target. Potential threats could include common attack types like XSS, SQL injection or unauthorised access attempts.

Risk assessment   Once threats are identified, VAST performs a risk assessment to determine the likelihood and impact of each threat. This helps to prioritise threats, ensuring that the most severe risks are addressed first. For example, a threat with a high likelihood and severe impact would receive immediate attention, while low-impact threats may be deprioritised.

Mitigation strategies   VAST then develops strategies to mitigate identified risks. These strategies may include technical controls (e.g. implementing MFA, encrypting data at rest) and procedural controls (e.g. updating incident response plans or conducting regular security training for employees). The focus is on practical, effective measures that align with the system's design and the organisation's capabilities.

Integration with the development process

One of VAST's key strengths is its seamless integration into the development workflow. Security cannot exist in an island; VAST promotes collaboration between security teams, developers, product managers and other stakeholders. By embedding threat modelling into the development lifecycle, VAST ensures that security is considered at every stage, from initial design to deployment and beyond.

This integration offers several advantages:

- **Early security involvement:** Security considerations are addressed early in the development cycle, reducing the likelihood of expensive and time-consuming fixes later.

- **Improved communication**: Visual diagrams and simplified models make it easier for all team members to understand and contribute to the security discussions, creating a shared understanding of the system's security posture.

- **Proactive threat mitigation:** By regularly revisiting and updating the threat model, VAST enables teams to proactively address security issues before they can be exploited, enhancing the system's overall resilience.

MITRE ATT&CK

The MITRE ATT&CK framework is a widely adopted and influential resource in the cyber security community. It serves as a comprehensive and systematic matrix of tactics, techniques and procedures (TTPs) used by adversaries, providing a robust structure to analyse and enhance an organisation's defensive strategies against cyber threats. Consider it as an encyclopaedic framework that enables security teams to both understand how real-world attacks unfold and to better design, assess and improve their security postures.

> MITRE ATT&CK® is a knowledge base that helps model cyber adversaries' tactics and techniques—and then shows how to detect or stop them (Mitre, n.d.).

Purpose and utility of MITRE ATT&CK

MITRE ATT&CK's primary purpose is to catalogue adversary behaviours in a structured way that allows organisations to learn from past attacks and be better prepared for future ones. By using detailed threat intelligence and understanding how attackers operate, defenders can anticipate adversary actions and strengthen their defences. The framework is used to bridge the gap between threat intelligence and practical defence measures, helping both security professionals and organisations to align their security efforts with real-world attack patterns.

The ATT&CK framework's utility extends across multiple domains of cyber security, including:

- **Threat intelligence:** By providing a detailed analysis of TTPs, the framework aids security teams in understanding threat actor behaviours. This understanding enhances the context of threat intelligence, making it more actionable and relevant for defensive operations.

- **Incident detection and response:** By mapping security incidents to specific TTPs within the framework, organisations can identify gaps in their current detection and response capabilities. This mapping helps to prioritise and refine security controls and incident response processes.

- **Adversary emulation:** ATT&CK serves as a foundation for red teaming, penetration testing and adversary emulation exercises. Security teams can simulate realistic attack scenarios to evaluate how well an organisation can withstand and respond to actual threats.

- **Security operations and monitoring:** SOCs use ATT&CK to enhance threat detection, monitoring and alerting. By understanding the techniques attackers are likely to use, SOC analysts can create more effective detection rules and response playbooks.

- **Security control assessment and improvement:** Organisations can use ATT&CK to perform a gap analysis of their security controls. By identifying techniques that are not well defended, security teams can prioritise investments in new tools or processes to improve their overall security posture.

- **Training and awareness:** ATT&CK is an invaluable educational resource for security professionals. It helps in training employees to recognise and respond to various attack vectors and to understand the importance of specific security measures.

Structure of MITRE ATT&CK

The framework is organised into three primary components: TTPs, which outline the adversary's goals, methods and specific steps taken to achieve those goals.

Tactics Tactics represent the overarching technical objectives or goals that an adversary is trying to achieve. They are the 'what' behind an attack and provide a high-level context of the adversary's intent. Each tactic encompasses a range of techniques used to fulfil these goals. Here are some of the core tactics described in ATT&CK:

- **Initial access:** Methods attackers use to gain their first foothold in a system, such as phishing or exploiting vulnerabilities.

- **Execution:** Tactics that result in adversary-controlled code execution on a system, including running malicious scripts or exploiting applications.

- **Persistence:** Strategies attackers use to maintain their access over time, such as creating new user accounts or modifying startup files.

- **Privilege escalation:** Methods used to gain higher-level permissions, often necessary for full control of a target system, like exploiting vulnerabilities in software to become an administrator.

- **Defence evasion:** Tactics to avoid detection by security systems, such as disabling anti-virus software or using obfuscation methods.

- **Credential access:** Tactics aimed at stealing sensitive information like usernames and passwords. This includes keylogging, credential dumping and password spraying.

- **Discovery:** Tactics to gather information about the network, systems and resources, such as scanning for open ports or listing active accounts.

- **Lateral movement:** Methods to move through a network from one system to another, often to gain access to more sensitive resources. Examples include using remote desktop protocols or pass-the-hash attacks.

- **Collection:** Methods to gather data of interest to the attacker, such as copying documents or recording keystrokes.

- **Exfiltration:** Tactics used to move stolen data out of a compromised environment, like compressing and encrypting files before sending them to an external server.

- **Command and control:** Strategies to maintain communication with compromised systems, which might include setting up a secure channel to receive instructions from the attacker.

Techniques   Techniques describe the specific methods attackers use to achieve a tactic. They represent the 'how' and provide a detailed breakdown of the actions an adversary may take. Each technique is further subdivided into sub-techniques to offer even more granularity. For example:

- **Phishing (under initial access):** A widely used method of tricking individuals into providing sensitive information or downloading malicious attachments. Sub-techniques include:

  - **Spear phishing:** targeted attacks on specific individuals or organisations.

- **Phishing links:** This is directing victims to malicious websites.

- **PowerShell (under execution):** A scripting language commonly used in attacks to automate tasks. Attackers use it to download payloads, execute scripts or evade detection.

- **Registry Run keys/Startup folder (under persistence):** Techniques that allow malware to execute automatically when the system starts.

- **Credential dumping (under credential access):** Techniques to extract password hashes and sensitive information from memory to impersonate legitimate users.

- **Pass the hash (under lateral movement):** This using a captured hash of a password to authenticate without needing the plaintext (readable data) password.

- **Data encrypted (under Exfiltration):** This is encrypting data before exfiltration to avoid detection during transmission.

Procedures   Procedures describe the specific ways threat actors implement the tactics and techniques. These are the detailed, actionable steps attackers have used in real-world scenarios. Procedures provide concrete examples of how techniques have been observed and are crucial for understanding how a theoretical attack manifests in practice. For example:

- An adversary might execute a spear phishing campaign targeting the finance department of an organisation, including malicious attachments crafted to look like invoices.

- Using PowerShell scripts, attackers may automate the download of additional payloads from command-and-control servers.
- In a pass-the-hash attack, the adversary could use stolen credentials to move laterally within the network, gaining access to higher-value targets.

Applications of MITRE ATT&CK
The framework has a wide range of applications across various security disciplines, with some of those listed below.

Threat intelligence   By mapping adversary behaviours to ATT&CK, security teams gain valuable insights into how attacks unfold and what techniques are commonly used by specific threat groups. This information is used to enhance threat intelligence reports, enabling organisations to anticipate and counteract future attacks effectively. Understanding an attacker's modus operandi (MO) allows defenders to predict the attacker's next steps and implement proactive measures.

Detection and response   MITRE ATT&CK provides a valuable reference for SOC analysts when developing detection strategies. By understanding which techniques attackers use, analysts can create more effective rules and alerts. For example, if credential dumping is identified as a common threat, a SOC can deploy monitoring tools to detect unusual access to sensitive credential stores.

Additionally, ATT&CK assists in post-incident analysis. By mapping the actions of an attacker to ATT&CK techniques, security teams can understand the full scope of an incident, identify gaps in defences and implement measures to prevent similar attacks.

Adversary emulation and red teaming   Red team exercises often use MITRE ATT&CK to create a simulation of a real-world attack scenario. By emulating the TTPs of known threat actors, red teams can test the effectiveness of an organisation's security measures and highlight areas of weakness. ATT&CK provides a structured approach for designing these simulations, ensuring they are realistic and comprehensive.

Security control assessment and improvement
Organisations use ATT&CK to assess their security controls systematically. By identifying techniques that are not adequately defended, security teams can prioritise improvements. This assessment can guide investments in new technologies, such as EDR solutions, or inform updates to security policies and procedures.

Training and awareness
ATT&CK serves as an excellent training tool for security professionals. It provides a clear and organised way to learn about different attack techniques and how to defend against them. Security teams can use ATT&CK to educate employees on specific threats relevant to their roles, fostering a deeper understanding of how attacks happen and what can be done to prevent them.

Implementation of MITRE ATT&CK
To implement the MITRE ATT&CK framework effectively, organisations must take a structured and strategic approach:

- **Mapping incidents to ATT&CK:** When a security incident occurs, mapping it to specific tactics and techniques in the ATT&CK matrix helps the security team to understand the attack path and the adversary's methods. This insight informs incident response and future prevention measures.

- **Developing and enhancing controls:** Using the framework to analyse attack techniques allows organisations to implement targeted defences. For example, if PowerShell misuse is a recurring threat, security teams can implement stricter policies and monitoring for PowerShell use.

- **Creating threat detection rules:** By understanding the techniques attackers are likely to use, organisations can develop detection rules for their security monitoring tools, such as SIEM systems. These rules should trigger alerts for suspicious activities that match known ATT&CK techniques.

- **Conducting gap analysis:** Regularly reviewing security posture against the ATT&CK matrix helps to identify areas where defences are lacking. This analysis guides investments in security measures and helps to prioritise security initiatives.

- **Facilitating red team and blue team collaboration:** Using ATT&CK as a common language fosters collaboration between red (offensive) and blue (defensive) teams. Red teams can simulate attacks using specific ATT&CK techniques, while blue teams can develop and refine their defences based on these simulations.

- **Informing security strategy:** ATT&CK helps in aligning security strategy with real-world threats. By understanding the most commonly used attack techniques, organisations can prioritise resources and efforts to defend against the highest risks.

Example scenario using MITRE ATT&CK
Consider an organisation that experiences a spear phishing attack. The incident can be analysed using the ATT&CK framework as follows:

- **Tactic:** initial access.

- **Technique:** spear phishing attachment.

- **Procedure:** The adversary sends a targeted email to a finance department employee. The email contains a malicious Excel attachment disguised as an invoice. When opened, the attachment exploits a vulnerability to download malware.

- **Defence measures:** To mitigate such attacks, the organisation could implement email filtering solutions to block malicious attachments, conduct regular security awareness training for employees and deploy endpoint detection systems to monitor for suspicious file execution.

In this example, mapping the attack to ATT&CK helps the organisation to understand the specific techniques used and refine its defences to prevent similar incidents in the future.

Another way to explain Mitre ATT&CK may be with a real-world example from my time as a police officer. One evening, I was sent to investigate two burglaries. Each of these burglaries saw the offender gain entry to the rear of the property by smashing a rear patio door then stealing mainly high-value electrical items and jewellery. A white BMW coupe was also seen in the area on both occasions. A few months later I was working in a different area and attended another two burglaries with the same MO with a white

BMW coupe seen in the area. Therefore, it was highly likely these two sets of burglaries were conducted by the same people due to the TTPs.

MITRE ATT&CK works in a similar fashion by enabling you to overlay TTPs onto a matrix (Figure 3.2). You can choose between Enterprise, Mobile or an industrial control system (ICS) matrix and follow an attack through with either a threat or techniques such as T1566 Phishing, which has four sub-techniques of T1566.001 Spear phishing attachment, T1566.002 Spear phishing link, T1566.003 Spear phishing via service and T1566.004 Spear phishing voice.

Figure 3.2 Extract from the MITRE ATT&CK Enterprise matrix showing APT28 threat group

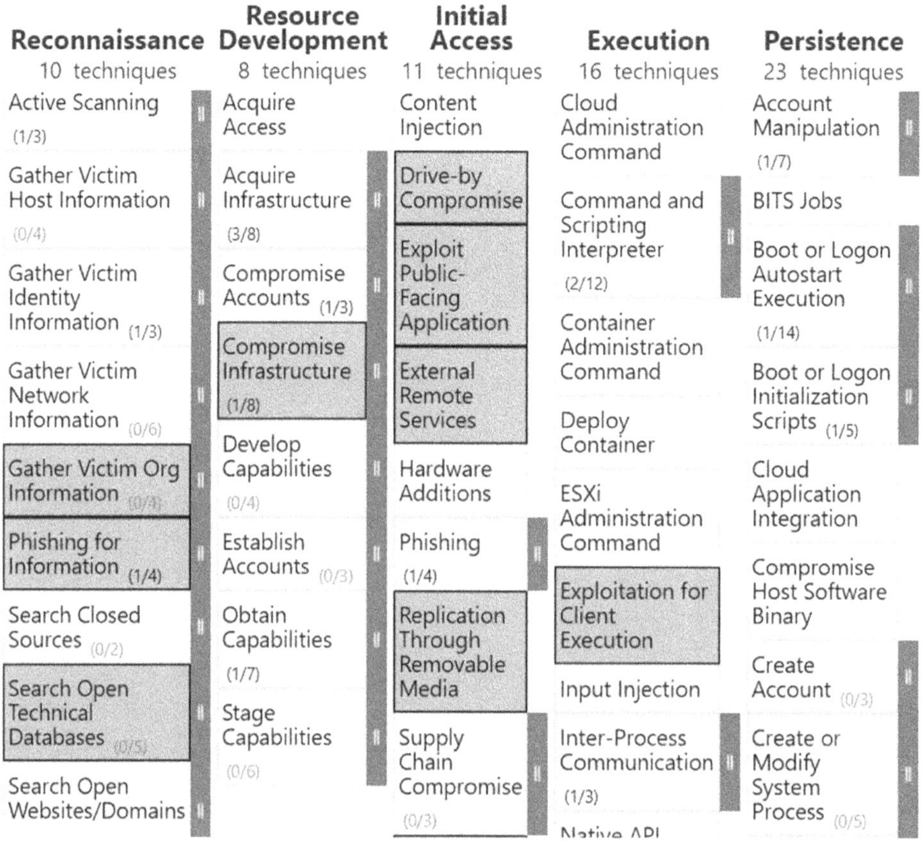

The top 10 most frequently seen techniques are:

1. **T1059**: Command and Scripting Interpreter   52.3%
2. **T1027**: Obfuscated Files or Information   46.5%
3. **T1083**: File and Directory Discovery   38.6%
4. **T1021**: Remote Services   37.3%
5. **T1082**: System Information Discovery   37.1%
6. **T1070**: Indicator Removal   35.1%
7. **T1071**: Application Layer Protocol   34.0%
8. **T1033**: System Owner/User Discovery   31.7%
9. **T1140**: Deobfuscate/Decode Files or Information   31.5%
10. **T1190**: Exploit Public-Facing Application   28.7%

5 Ds FRAMEWORK

The 5 Ds Framework is a strategic model commonly used in military and cyber security contexts to describe the spectrum of effects that can be achieved through offensive or defensive cyber operations. It focuses on imposing adverse outcomes on an adversary's information systems, such as reducing operational capability, impairing decision-making or undermining trust in digital infrastructure. While traditionally viewed from the defender's or operator's perspective, the framework is equally useful in understanding how an attacker might apply these effects to compromise or incapacitate systems and data. The 5 Ds can be used in threat modelling and scenario planning to anticipate attacker behaviour, identify security gaps and define protection requirements.

Deny
Deny refers to preventing access to systems, services or information. This can be achieved through traditional cyber security mechanisms such as access controls, firewalls or authentication restrictions. In an offensive context, denial might be enacted through DDoS attacks or by locking an adversary out of their own systems, effectively obstructing their ability to operate.

Degrade
Degrade means reducing the performance or effectiveness of a system without completely disabling it. For example, a cyber operation may introduce delays, reduce throughput or impair functionality in a way that hampers mission-critical activities. This can be subtle and may go unnoticed initially, which makes it useful in prolonged operations where persistent interference is more desirable than overt damage.

Disrupt
Disrupt is the deliberate interruption of normal system functionality, usually for a limited duration. This can involve crashing services, interfering with communications or introducing malware that causes erratic behaviour. While disruption is often temporary,

it can be strategically timed to coincide with critical events, such as elections, military operations or financial transactions.

Deceive
Deceive involves deliberately misleading an adversary by feeding false information, impersonating systems or users or setting up honeypots to detect or misdirect intrusions. This tactic aims to erode trust in the information environment and can lead an attacker to waste resources, make flawed decisions or reveal their tactics.

Destroy
Destroy is the most extreme of the five, involving the permanent disabling or elimination of systems, data or hardware. This can be achieved through destructive malware, firmware corruption or even cyber-physical attacks that cause real-world damage (such as Stuxnet's effect on Iranian centrifuges). Destruction is usually reserved for high-stakes scenarios due to its irreversible nature and potential escalation.

CASE STUDY

Resilience and disaster recovery for a national infrastructure provider

Scenario
A national infrastructure provider responsible for critical services such as energy distribution, water supply or transportation faced growing risks from cyber threats, such as ransomware and state-sponsored attacks, as well as natural disasters, including flooding and extreme weather. Recognising the devastating impact of potential service disruptions, the organisation embarked on an initiative to design a resilient security and DR framework. The aim was to ensure continuity of operations under all circumstances while complying with national security and regulatory requirements such as the Network and Information Systems (NIS) Directive.

Focus areas

Multi-layered defence-in-depth strategy
The organisation adopted a defence-in-depth model, layering multiple security controls to protect against a broad range of threats:

- **Perimeter defences:** These included firewalls, IDSs and IPS to secure network boundaries.

- **Endpoint protection:** Advanced EDR solutions were deployed to protect OT and IT systems.

- **Data encryption:** Sensitive data in transit and at rest was encrypted to mitigate the risk of interception or theft.

- **Network segmentation:** OT and IT environments were segmented to limit potential attack surfaces and to contain breaches.

- **Incident response playbooks:** Predefined workflows were developed to address threats, ensuring rapid containment and recovery.

Robust backup and DR plans

A three-tiered backup strategy was implemented:

- **Real-time replication:** Core systems were configured to replicate data to geographically distributed data centres in near real-time.

- **Immutable backups:** Backups were stored in a tamper-proof format to safeguard against ransomware.

- **Air-gapped backups:** Physical, offline backups were maintained to provide an additional layer of protection.

DR plans were regularly tested through live simulations of cyber incidents and natural disasters to identify weaknesses and improve response times.

Real-time monitoring for threats

A SOC equipped with AI and machine learning (ML) tools monitored both physical and cyber environments. Threats were detected and analysed using SIEM tools integrated with OT-specific threat intelligence feeds. For example, the SOC continuously monitored for anomalies such as unauthorised access attempts on supervisory control and data acquisition (SCADA) systems or sudden spikes in network traffic, indicative of potential DDoS attacks.

Challenges

Comprehensive risk assessment identifying all potential vulnerabilities across a vast and interconnected infrastructure was a complex task. The risk assessment had to encompass both digital assets (e.g. ICSs) and physical components (e.g. substations, pipelines). Collaboration between IT, OT and risk management teams was essential to develop a unified risk profile.

Maintaining uptime during security upgrades

Implementing security upgrades across critical systems without impacting uptime was a major challenge. Many of the infrastructure systems operated on a 24/7 basis, with limited windows for maintenance. Detailed planning and phased rollouts ensured minimal disruption while applying patches and upgrading defences.

Compliance with national regulations

Compliance requirements often varied, depending on the location and type of infrastructure. The organisation needed to align its resilience and DR plans with standards, such as ISO 27001, NIS Directive and sector-specific regulations, while avoiding operational conflicts.

Outcomes

Improved resilience to cyber and physical incidents
The defence-in-depth strategy reduced the likelihood and impact of successful attacks. For example, in a simulated ransomware attack, segmentation and endpoint defences ensured that only a limited subset of systems was affected, and recovery times were significantly improved due to the availability of immutable backups.

Faster recovery times
The organisation achieved a recovery time objective (RTO) of less than four hours for mission-critical systems, compared to the previous RTO of 12 hours. Recovery drills demonstrated seamless failover to secondary data centres during simulated power outages and cyber incidents.

Coordination between IT and operations teams
The project fostered stronger collaboration between IT and OT teams. Joint training sessions and incident simulations bridged knowledge gaps, ensuring both groups were aligned on security priorities and understood each other's operational constraints.

Key learnings

- Integrating physical and cyber threat monitoring ensures a holistic approach to resilience.

- Regular testing of DR plans under real-world conditions is essential to validate assumptions and refine strategies.

- Coordination between IT and OT teams, supported by shared tools and processes, is critical for protecting hybrid environments.

- Continuous improvement cycles, informed by threat intelligence and post-incident reviews, ensure that resilience plans remain effective against evolving risks.

THREAT INTELLIGENCE

Threat intelligence is a critical component of an organisation's cyber security strategy, focusing on the systematic collection, analysis and dissemination of information about current or emerging threats that pose a risk to the organisation's security posture. This process aims to equip security teams with actionable intelligence that can inform decision-making, strengthen defences and minimise the impact of potential cyber incidents.

The threat intelligence cycle is a structured process involving the direction, collection, processing, analysis, dissemination and action of threat data to inform and support security decision-making (Figure 3.3).

Figure 3.3 Threat intelligence cycle

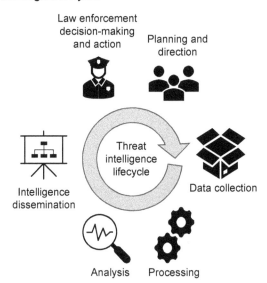

Planning and direction phase

This is the foundational stage where the intelligence requirements are established based on organisational objectives, risk appetite and threat landscape. It involves collaboration between security teams, business units and executives to define what information is required. Effective planning ensures the cycle remains focused, relevant and aligned with strategic or operational needs.

Collection phase

The collection phase of threat intelligence involves gathering data from a wide variety of sources, both internal and external. These sources can include threat feeds, open-source intelligence (OSINT), proprietary data, dark web monitoring, security vendor information, social media monitoring, malware analysis and more. Automation and intelligence platforms often play a significant role in aggregating and processing vast amounts of data efficiently.

Data processing phase

Once data has been collected from various sources – such as OSINT, internal logs, dark web monitoring or threat feeds – it often arrives in unstructured or incompatible formats. Processing transforms this raw data into a standardised, structured and manageable format suitable for analysis. This might include translation, data enrichment, correlation, filtering noise and formatting.

Analysis phase

This phase transforms this raw data into meaningful insights. Threat analysts employ a combination of advanced data analytics, behavioural analysis and expert judgement to identify and characterise threat actors, campaigns and potential vulnerabilities. This stage often focuses on understanding the TTPs used by adversaries, as well as their motives and target selection processes. The MITRE ATT&CK framework is frequently used as a reference model to categorise and study these TTPs, enabling better understanding and comparison across different attack scenarios.

Dissemination phase

This phase ensures that relevant and actionable intelligence is shared with the appropriate teams within the organisation. This can be delivered through detailed reports, timely alerts, structured threat intelligence feeds via APIs and periodic threat briefings. By providing up-to-date intelligence, security teams can prioritise their resources to address the most pressing threats. This intelligence can also feed into other security tools, such as SIEM systems, intrusion detection and prevention systems (IDPSs) and threat-hunting platforms, for automated response and enhanced detection capabilities.

Action phase

This stage ensures that the finished intelligence is shared with the right stakeholders in a timely and actionable format. Depending on the audience, this may take the form of executive summaries, tactical indicators – such as intellectual property (IP) addresses or malware hashes – or strategic assessments of threat actor behaviour. Crucially, dissemination should be tailored to the recipient's role.

Types of threat intelligence

Common categories include:

- **Strategic intelligence:** This is high-level information tailored for senior executives and decision-makers. It provides insights into the overall threat landscape, major trends and potential risks affecting business objectives.

- **Operational intelligence:** This is information focused on specific, imminent threats. This type of intelligence is highly relevant for incident response teams and is used to understand active campaigns and threat actors.

- **Tactical intelligence:** This gives insights into the adversary's TTPs, which are valuable for defenders working to harden the network and identify possible IoCs. This intelligence is granular and often involves technical details, such as attack patterns and malware signatures.

- **Technical intelligence:** This is data about specific threats, including IoCs such as IP addresses, file hashes or URLs associated with malicious activity. This intelligence is generally used for configuring security tools and filtering malicious activity.

The benefits of threat intelligence extend beyond simple threat detection. By understanding the methods and motives of threat actors, organisations can proactively shore up defences and mitigate risks before they materialise into incidents. Effective threat intelligence supports threat hunting, incident response, vulnerability management and strategic planning. Moreover, it fosters collaboration within the wider security community, as shared threat intelligence can benefit multiple organisations in combatting common adversaries.

Threat intelligence platforms and tools help to streamline the management and distribution of threat intelligence. They enable automation in data processing, reduce analysts' workload and facilitate more coordinated threat analysis. Additionally, integration with SOAR systems can enable organisations to respond more swiftly and efficiently to threats. An effective security strategy involves multiple layers, enabling security teams to predict and understand cyber threats targeting an organisation. By anticipating potential attackers and their methods, security teams can prioritise resources and respond effectively to cyberattacks. CrowdStrike Falcon Intelligence™ provides the crucial foresight with timely, comprehensive and contextually rich threat intelligence. This intelligence is delivered in formats that can be used in enterprise systems (API feeds) and security staff (alerts, reports). SOC managers and intelligence analysts can better prioritise and respond to threats using threat intelligence reports. These reports include specific information about threat actors, their TTPs and the industry sectors they target. Falcon Intelligence offers insights and IoCs through an all-source methodology of intelligence gathering, analysis and dissemination. CrowdStrike's global threat intelligence team employs various collection methods (human intelligence, signals intelligence, open-source intelligence, the dark web, etc.) to gather, analyse and report on more than 90 threat actors operating worldwide. Other threat intelligence frameworks include MISP, NormShield, Yeti and ThreatStream.

Threat-informed defence

Threat-informed defence is a strategy that integrates knowledge of potential threats and adversarial behaviours into defensive planning and operations. This approach uses intelligence about specific threats, such as TTPs employed by attackers, to inform and enhance defensive measures. If an organisation understands how adversaries operate, they can then prioritise their defences, anticipate potential attacks and respond more effectively. This strategy can involve the use of frameworks such as MITRE ATT&CK to map out known threats and put in place a response to those threats.

Information warfare

Information warfare refers to the use and management of information to gain a competitive advantage over an adversary. It encompasses a wide range of tactics and strategies that target the information systems and infrastructure of an opponent, including both offensive and defensive measures. Key aspects of information warfare include cyber warfare, which involves attacks on computer networks such as hacking, deploying malware and conducting DoS attacks to disrupt, disable or control the opponent's information systems. Electronic warfare uses the electromagnetic spectrum (radio waves, microwaves, etc.) to intercept, jam or deceive enemy communications and radar systems. Psychological operations (PsyOps) disseminate propaganda, misinformation and psychological tactics to influence the perceptions, emotions and decision-making processes of the adversary and its populace. Information operations (InfoOps) involve coordinated actions to gather, distribute and manage information to disrupt, corrupt or usurp adversarial decision-making while protecting information and information systems.

Intelligence and surveillance are crucial for gathering and analysing information to understand and predict the actions and strategies of opponents, thereby enabling informed decision-making. Social media manipulation involves using social media platforms to spread false information, create fake accounts and influence public opinion to achieve strategic objectives. Information warfare can be conducted by nation-states, non-state actors and individuals, playing a crucial role in modern conflicts and geopolitical strategies by using the interconnected nature of information systems and the widespread availability of digital.

4 RISK MANAGEMENT

In this chapter, we will explore the risk management process, covering key stages from asset identification and risk identification to risk evaluation, risk treatment, risk mitigation and ongoing risk monitoring. Effective risk management is fundamental to an organisation's security strategy, ensuring that threats are proactively identified, assessed and addressed in a structured and repeatable manner so that suitable protection can be put in place to reduce harm. However, at the same time, when an organisation feels protected it can also become complacent – perhaps harbouring a simple risk that is generally overlooked until it is too late.

Building on the foundational principles discussed in *Information Management Security Principles* fourth edition (Green, 2024), we will examine how risk management serves as a protective measure, reducing harm while demonstrating tangible value to stakeholders. However, risk management does not function in silos; risks must be aggregated rather than considered in isolation. Even seemingly minor risks, when combined, can escalate into significant threats with far-reaching consequences.

Threat modelling, which we discussed in Chapter 3, can help to create well-constructed scenarios to enhance risk identification by uncovering vulnerabilities and fragility that might otherwise be overlooked. By applying structured methodologies, organisations can gain a more comprehensive and realistic understanding of their risk landscape, ensuring that security measures are both proactive and proportionate. The end result should be protection of the organisation from harm, and if harmed the impact is reduced.

> To secure effectively, you must first understand the harm your environment can suffer and the fragility that makes it possible.
>
> (Jeremy Green, 2025)

RISK MANAGMENT

At its heart, risk management is the structured response to uncertainty. Every organisation operates in an environment filled with unknowns, from emerging threats and evolving attack techniques to shifting regulatory landscapes and unpredictable business conditions. These uncertainties introduce potential risks that can impact operations, financial stability, compliance and reputation.

> ISACA defines risk management as 'Mitigating risk and reducing potential impacts on information resources to an acceptable level through execution of appropriate measures' (ISACA, 2022).

Risk, by definition, is the possibility of an event occurring that negatively (or positively) affects an organisation's objectives. However, risk would not exist without uncertainty. If you think about it, if we could predict the future with complete accuracy, we could eliminate risk entirely. However, organisations must operate within imperfect knowledge, making decisions based on probabilities, trends and expert analysis rather than absolute certainty.

Managing uncertainty in risk assessment

Uncertainty arises in several key areas of risk management:

- **Threat landscape:** Attackers are constantly evolving their tactics, making it difficult to predict when and how a cyber threat might materialise.
- **Vulnerability discovery:** New vulnerabilities are uncovered daily, and even well-secured systems may contain unknown weaknesses or uncovered bugs.
- **Impact estimation:** The true consequences of a risk materialising are not always clear. Some incidents may have cascading effects that are difficult to foresee.
- **Control effectiveness:** Protection measures are implemented to reduce risk, but their effectiveness can vary due to misconfigurations, emerging attack methods or evolving business processes.

The role of probabilities and aggregated risk

Since absolute certainty is unattainable, risk management relies on probability assessments and scenario analysis to estimate how likely a risk is to occur and what impact it may have. However, organisations must also recognise that risks do not exist in isolation. A series of small, low-impact risks can compound to create a much larger issue. For example:

- A minor software misconfiguration might seem insignificant on its own.
- When combined with a lack of monitoring, an attacker may exploit the risk unnoticed.
- If this leads to unauthorised data access, the organisation now faces a major data breach.

By accounting for uncertainty and interdependencies, organisations can move from a reactive to a proactive risk management approach, continuously identifying, evaluating and mitigating risks before they escalate into critical threats.

Reducing uncertainty through threat intelligence and continuous monitoring

To minimise uncertainty, security teams should make use of threat intelligence, real-time monitoring and historical data to improve risk assessments:

- **Threat modelling:** Identify potential attack paths and weak points before they can be exploited.

- **Continuous risk monitoring:** Use automation and security analytics to detect emerging threats and trends.

- **Incident response testing:** Run simulations to gauge preparedness and refine response strategies.

- **Adaptive security controls:** Implement security measures that evolve based on changing threat conditions.

Risk management can be perceived differently across various roles within an organisation. For senior management, it often focuses on risks that could hinder the achievement of strategic goals. On the other hand, business line managers might prioritise threats that affect their operations and their ability to meet performance targets. Therefore, a risk management programme must be seamlessly integrated into the entire enterprise management system and tailored to address the specific needs of different organisational elements. Often, the biggest issue is getting stakeholders to understand risk and its impact on the organisation. They need to fully understand the context of the business and its risks – never assume leadership fully understands this. Security can be unwanted, completely misunderstood and seen as a financial drain. Business units may look for ways to bypass security or hide risk so that they can reach goals or targets that they perceive security might hinder. The military phrase 'winning the hearts and minds' is especially important for security – especially security leaders – but not by simply doing what the organisation wants, but by doing what is best for the organisation and at times protecting it from itself.

Key themes emerging from the AICPA and CIMA '2024 State Of Risk Oversight Report: 15th edition' (Beasley and Branson, 2024) are:

- Executives perceive the overall volume of risks in the business environment to be complex and increasing.

- While management dashboards highlight key performance indicators, most dashboards do not have robust sets of key risk indicators to monitor changes in risk conditions.

- While organisations have advanced the maturity of their risk management processes, the progress that has been made is relatively slow, with most respondents indicating their risk management processes are not yet mature or robust.

- Over the past 15 years, the percentages of organisations appointing an individual to serve as a chief risk officer or creating a management-level risk committee have steadily increased, with most risk committees meeting monthly or quarterly.

- Organisations continue to struggle to connect their risk management efforts with their strategic planning processes, with only a small percentage of respondents indicating their risk management processes provide significant strategic advantage.

- Most boards are delegating their risk oversight responsibilities to a subcommittee of the board, which is typically the audit committee except for financial services organisations that delegate to risk committees of the board.

- Most organisations engage in formal risk identification processes on an annual basis, focusing on operational, compliance and financial risk issues, with emerging strategic market risks given the least attention.

- Pressure from the board and external parties continues to be placed on senior executives to increase their involvement in risk oversight activities.

- Numeric scales are generally provided to guide executives in their assessment of a risk's likelihood and impact.

- Despite progress in advancing risk management activities over time, barriers continue to exist within organisations that limit such progress.

As a security architect you need to understand the organisation you have either been employed in or brought in to support. Take the time to ask questions about what the business does and how it operates. Is it local or international? Where are its customers located and what sort of data do they handle? What are the long-term strategy and goals of the organisation? How important is security to the organisation? These may seem like basic questions, but they are often overlooked and, if you don't understand the full context, how can you think about what the risks are to the organisation and therefore implement suitable protection? You need to know exactly what you are protecting and defending against before any design considerations.

Risk management also informs strategic planning, allowing business leaders to make more informed decisions based on a clear understanding of potential challenges and opportunities. Compliance with legal and regulatory requirements is another advantage, as robust risk management demonstrates due diligence and commitment to safeguarding stakeholders' interests. Additionally, it helps to build trust and confidence among investors, partners and customers with a level of assurance. Risk management is about achieving an optimal balance between taking calculated risks for potential gains and protecting the organisation from potential harm and loss.

Various frameworks and standards provide structured guidance for risk management, helping organisations to establish consistent and effective processes. One of the most widely recognised is ISO 31000, which offers a set of principles, guidelines and best practices applicable across industries. While it does not prescribe specific controls, it does provide a flexible foundation for managing risk within any organisation.

In the realm of information security, frameworks such as the NIST CSF, CIS 18 and ISO/IEC 27001 are frequently used to identify, assess and mitigate risks. However, no single standard can fully capture the unique risk landscape of every organisation. Rigid adherence to a framework without adaptation may inadvertently introduce gaps, inefficiencies or even new risks. Instead, these frameworks should be viewed as toolkits with different tools for different purposes. Some tools may be useful, others not. The important factor is that they are tailored to an organisation's specific needs rather than strict rulebooks.

A modular approach to frameworks often delivers the most effective results – much like a Lego kit, which provides a structured model when built according to instructions. The kit though, consists of individual components that can be assembled into countless alternative designs; frameworks offer similar flexibility. They can be decomposed, mixed and adapted to suit different organisational needs. Organisations may choose to adopt a framework in its entirety, selectively integrate elements from multiple sources or implement only the most relevant controls. This adaptability ensures that risk management remains practical, effective and aligned with business objectives, rather than becoming a rigid, checkbox-driven compliance exercise.

ASSET IDENTIFICATION

Asset identification is a critical component of risk management and is foundational to effective security, compliance and resource management within an organisation. It involves identifying and categorising an organisation's assets, whether tangible or intangible, to assess their value, ensure they are properly protected and manage associated risks. These assets can range from physical infrastructure, such as hardware and facilities, to intangible items, such as intellectual property, data and organisational knowledge.

For digital and IT assets, this could involve scanning network devices, reviewing software licences and inventorying devices. For physical assets, manual inventories and inspections might be necessary. Tools such as asset management software (e.g. ServiceNow, Lansweeper or Ivanti) can automate this process.

Importance of asset identification

Asset identification helps an organisation to gain visibility over critical resources, enabling effective risk management and decision-making. As asset identification is being undertaken, it should also include a business impact analysis (BIA) to ascertain the impact on the organisation should this asset be unavailable. An organisation needs to have a robust asset identification, tracking and management programme in place.

To aid in the BIA you need to understand the strategic value by recognising the importance of the asset in achieving organisational objectives. For instance, protecting customer data ensures compliance with regulations and maintains trust, while safeguarding critical infrastructure prevents disruptions to essential services. This perspective helps in prioritising investments and resource allocation based on the potential impact on operations and longer term strategies.

The thought process around assets should be to consider if it is tangible or intangible, static or dynamic and whether its value is intrinsic or derived. For instance, intellectual property has intangible value but is crucial for innovation and competitive advantage, whereas physical servers may be tangible but are only valuable because of the data they hold.

How vulnerable is the asset to threats? High-exposure assets may be publicly accessible or subject to frequent interaction with external parties, increasing the risk. Conversely, low-exposure assets may reside in isolated or highly secure environments. Understanding exposure guides the intensity and nature of the control measures required. At the same time, also understand the fragility of the asset and what it could be fragile to, so that adequate protection can be put in place.

Fragility refers to the susceptibility of an asset to damage, disruption or failure when exposed to stress, threats or environmental changes. In an organisational context, assets including systems, data, processes and infrastructure will vary in their levels of fragility based on their ability to withstand intentional or unintentional harm whilst maintaining functionality.

You can assess an asset's potential fragility with some simple questions:

- Could the asset fail easily under stress or pressure?
  - For example, is it vulnerable to DoS attacks, high workloads or electrical issues such as voltage spikes?
- Does the asset lack redundancy or resilience?
  - For example, are there no backups, failover systems or alternative components to maintain service continuity?
- Is the asset highly sensitive to variability?
  - For example, could minor changes in input, demand, configuration or environment cause it to malfunction or fail?
- Does the asset have high dependency on external factors?
  - For example, does it rely on utilities, network connectivity, external data sources or third-party services or vendors?

Protecting critical resources is a fundamental aspect of effective asset management. By identifying and classifying high-value or high-risk assets, organisations can ensure that these receive the appropriate levels of protection and oversight, reducing the likelihood of compromise or loss. Maintaining an up-to-date asset inventory is also essential for compliance. Regulatory frameworks such as GDPR and ISO 27001 explicitly require organisations to keep accurate records of their information assets, ensuring that security controls are applied appropriately and audits can be conducted effectively.

Understanding which assets are most important enables organisations to prioritise their security efforts. By focusing resources on the assets that have the greatest value or pose the highest risk if compromised, security teams can operate more efficiently and effectively. Accurate asset identification also supports better cost management. With clear visibility into what assets exist and their importance, organisations can allocate budgets more strategically, avoid unnecessary expenditure and enhance overall operational efficiency.

Asset types in an organisation

Assets can be broadly classified into several categories:

- **Physical assets:** These include hardware, such as servers, workstations, network devices (routers, firewalls, switches) and storage devices, and physical premises, such as data centres or office buildings.

- **Digital assets:** This category encompasses data (e.g. customer data, intellectual property), software (including OSs, enterprise applications and databases), digital certificates and digital currencies.

- **Human resources:** Employees, contractors and other stakeholders are vital assets. They contribute knowledge, expertise and intellectual capital. Identifying key personnel, their skills and their roles is important for managing operational continuity and security.

- **Intellectual property:** Patents, trademarks, copyrights, proprietary algorithms, source code and research and development outputs are considered invaluable assets, particularly in knowledge-based industries.

- **Financial assets:** These include monetary resources, investment portfolios, accounts receivable and anything with direct financial value to the organisation.

- **Reputation:** While intangible, a company's reputation can be its most valuable asset, influencing customer loyalty, brand strength and market value, including share prices.

- **Legal assets:** This includes any contracts, agreements, licences and legal documents essential for the operation of the business.

Steps for asset identification

To conduct effective asset identification, organisations must follow a structured approach. Some key steps are listed below.

Define the asset identification scope

Before beginning the identification process, determine the scope of the assets to be identified. This may include:

- **Enterprise-wide assets:** These are all assets across the organisation, including departments, divisions, subsidiaries, etc.

- **Functional assets:** These are focused on specific departments (e.g. IT assets, financial systems or intellectual property).

- **Geographical assets:** These are assets identified in different regions or branches.

It's important to engage relevant stakeholders (e.g. department heads, IT managers) in this planning phase to ensure the scope is comprehensive.

Create an asset inventory

An asset register is a comprehensive inventory of an organisation's assets, typically used for management, tracking and risk assessment purposes. In the context of security, it serves as a foundational tool for protecting critical resources. It typically includes:

- **asset identification:** a unique ID for each asset;

- **description:** details about the asset (e.g. name, type, function);

- **classification:** sensitivity level or criticality (e.g. confidential, public);

- **owner:** the individual or team responsible for the asset;

- **location:** physical or digital location of the asset;
- **value:** business or operational importance, including financial impact if compromised;
- **dependencies:** connections to other systems or processes;
- **security controls:** existing measures to protect the asset;
- **status:** current state (e.g. active, deprecated, under review);
- **review date:** when the asset should next be reviewed.

Map asset dependencies and interrelationships

Understanding the interdependencies between assets is essential, especially in complex systems such as enterprise IT infrastructure; for example, a server hosting critical business applications may be linked to other assets such as databases, storage devices or networking equipment. Mapping these relationships helps to identify the critical assets that would have a cascading effect if compromised. Visual tools, such as dependency mapping and network diagrams, can help to illustrate these relationships.

Classify and prioritise assets

Once the assets are identified and mapped, the next step is to classify them based on their criticality to the business. Common classification schemes include:

- **High, medium, low value:** This can be based on factors such as financial value, business importance and legal requirements.
- **Asset value:** Understand the whole-life cost of the asset, not just its replacement cost, but operational cost, design and implementation cost, cost to the organisation of it not functioning and any loss of revenue. Finally, is there any associated reputational cost if it is not operating?

This classification helps in focusing organisational resources on the most critical assets. Once identified, the most critical assets should be subject to the highest levels of protection and monitoring.

Assess asset risk

After identifying and classifying assets, it's important to assess the risks associated with each asset. This involves evaluating the potential threats, vulnerabilities, fragility and possible impact of a risk materialising. An example such as the risk of a cyberattack on a high-value customer database may include data breach, financial loss and reputational damage. By identifying the risks associated with each asset, organisations can implement appropriate mitigation strategies.

Document and maintain the asset inventory

Proper documentation is vital for asset identification. The asset inventory must be continuously updated, especially when new assets are acquired, disposed of and reaching end of life. It's important that asset identification is part of the organisation's overall asset management practices, ensuring that assets are tracked and managed across their entire lifecycle. Regular audits of the asset register against actual assets in the organisation is essential.

Tips for effective asset identification

Effective asset identification requires collaboration across all departments, not just IT. Finance, Legal, HR and Operations should each contribute to identifying their respective assets. This cross-functional approach ensures that no asset is overlooked, and that the organisation gains a complete and accurate picture of its resources. Automation can play a key role in enhancing accuracy and efficiency. By deploying asset management tools, organisations can automate the discovery and tracking of hardware and software assets. This not only reduces manual errors but also provides real-time visibility into the asset landscape, which is essential for informed decision-making.

Clear ownership should be established for every asset. This is especially important for intangible assets such as data and intellectual property, where defined accountability is crucial for ensuring both protection and regulatory compliance. Knowing who is responsible for each asset will support faster issue resolution and more effective risk management. An up-to-date inventory is critical, as assets continually change over time – whether through acquisition, decommissioning, or shifts in value and usage. Maintaining this accuracy requires a regular review cycle to reflect the current state of assets within the organisation.

Integrating the asset inventory with other enterprise management systems, such as incident, change and procurement management, can streamline operations. This integration facilitates more effective asset tracking, enhances risk and compliance oversight and supports overall business continuity planning. Asset management should also consider the full asset lifecycle from procurement to disposal. By tracking assets throughout their lifespan, organisations can ensure secure and compliant use to ensure the optimisation of the resource and reduce waste.

Finally, regular audits and verification is essential. Whether through physical inspections or automated scanning tools, periodic checks validate the accuracy of the asset inventory. This helps to identify discrepancies and detect unauthorised devices or software to ensure data is relevant and up to date when used for security and operational decisions.

RISK IDENTIFICATION

Risk identification is a critical and foundational step in the risk management process. It involves systematically identifying and documenting potential risks that could impact an organisation's operations, assets, objectives or reputation. This process ensures that an organisation is prepared for both expected and unexpected challenges, enabling it to develop strategies to manage and mitigate these risks before they escalate into real threats.

Risk identification is not a one-time exercise but an ongoing effort, requiring continual monitoring of internal and external environments to ensure that emerging risks are recognised and appropriately addressed. Below, we'll explore the importance of risk identification, the types of risks that should be considered, the steps involved in identifying risks and tips for conducting it effectively within an enterprise.

Importance of risk identification

Risk identification is crucial for several reasons:

- **Proactive risk management:** By identifying risks early, organisations can take proactive steps to prevent or mitigate potential negative consequences, rather than reacting after an event occurs.
- **Resource allocation:** Understanding which risks are most critical enables organisations to allocate resources (time, budget, people) more effectively, ensuring that risk mitigation efforts are focused where they are needed most.
- **Compliance:** Many regulatory frameworks and industry standards require organisations to perform regular risk assessments, which include identifying and addressing risks.
- **Business continuity:** Early risk identification helps organisations to plan for potential disruptions and ensures that they have strategies in place for business continuity in case of adverse events.
- **Strategic decision-making:** Identifying risks also helps to inform strategic decisions, allowing organisations to navigate uncertainties and make more informed decisions about investments, acquisitions or new initiatives.

Types of risks to identify

Organisations face a wide variety of risks, which can generally be grouped into several categories to help with the identification and assessment of risk.

- **Strategic risks** are those that affect an organisation's long-term goals and overall direction. These risks often arise from external shifts in market conditions, evolving consumer behaviours or increasing competitive pressures. For example, emerging competitors, disruptive new technologies or changes in regulatory environments can all threaten an organisation's strategic position and require timely adaptation to remain relevant and competitive.
- **Operational risks** stem from the day-to-day functioning of an organisation. These can be linked to internal processes, human factors, systems or external events that disrupt routine operations. Common examples include supply chain disruptions, equipment breakdowns, human error and IT system outages. Such risks can significantly impact service delivery, productivity and customer satisfaction.
- **Financial risks** relate to the organisation's economic health and performance. These include fluctuations in market conditions, issues with liquidity or financial mismanagement. Specific examples include foreign exchange volatility, interest rate changes, credit defaults and fraud. Managing these risks is critical to maintaining financial stability and investor confidence.
- **Compliance risks** arise when an organisation fails to meet the legal, regulatory or industry standards that govern its operations. These risks can lead to significant penalties and reputational damage. Examples include breaches of data protection laws, violations of employment legislation or non-compliance with environmental regulations.

- **Reputational risks** involve the potential for damage to an organisation's public image or brand value. These risks often emerge from customer dissatisfaction, product failures, ethical breaches or negative publicity. Incidents such as social media backlash, corporate scandals or critical media coverage can quickly erode public trust and stakeholder confidence.

- **Cyber security risks** concern the protection of an organisation's digital assets, including the integrity, confidentiality and availability of data and IT systems. As cyber threats become increasingly sophisticated, risks such as data breaches, ransomware attacks, phishing and insider threats have grown in both frequency and impact, demanding robust cyber security measures.

- **Human risks** are linked to the behaviour and actions of individuals within or connected to the organisation. These can include fraud, misconduct, challenges with talent retention or workplace health and safety issues. Since human factors can be unpredictable, organisations must foster strong ethical cultures and implement safeguards to mitigate such risks.

- **Environmental risks** involve the impact of natural events or environmental changes on an organisation's operations or infrastructure. These include natural disasters such as earthquakes and floods, as well as long-term threats such as climate change or global pandemics. Environmental risks can disrupt supply chains, damage assets and require costly recovery efforts.

Steps in risk identification

Risk identification is a multi-step process that involves gathering input from various sources, evaluating the internal and external environment and documenting potential risks.

Define the risk identification scope
The first step is to clearly define the scope of the risk identification process. This involves determining:

- the departments, assets and processes to be considered (e.g. IT systems, supply chain, human resources);

- the timeframe for the identification process (e.g. short-term vs long-term risks);

- the geographical boundaries (e.g. risks affecting local operations vs global operations).

A well-defined scope ensures the risk identification process is thorough and relevant.

Gather input from stakeholders
Risk identification should be a collaborative effort, involving key stakeholders across the organisation. Engaging a diverse group of stakeholders helps to ensure that risks are not overlooked and that all relevant perspectives are considered.

This can include:

- **senior management** to identify strategic risks and evaluate the impact on organisational objectives;
- **operational teams** to understand risks associated with day-to-day operations, resource allocation and process efficiency;
- **IT and security professionals** to identify risks related to cyber security and data protection;
- **compliance officers** to address regulatory and compliance-related risks;
- **legal teams** to spot risks concerning contracts, liabilities or potential legal action.

Use structured techniques for risk identification

There are several structured techniques for identifying risks, which can be used individually or in combination:

- **Mind mapping** can be a group activity where participants generate as many risk scenarios as possible. Mind mapping can be done in person or virtually, and helps to bring out diverse ideas.
- **Interviews and surveys** with key stakeholders or sending out surveys to a broader group within the organisation can provide valuable insights into potential risks.
- **Strengths, weaknesses, opportunities and threats (SWOT) analysis** is used for identifying internal strengths and weaknesses, as well as external opportunities and threats. This analysis helps to highlight areas where risks may arise.
- **Risk checklists**, which could be predefined lists of common risks, are often based on industry standards, regulations or lessons learned from past incidents. These can serve as a starting point for identifying risks that might apply to the organisation.
- **Process mapping and flowcharts**, using visual tools that help to identify where risks may occur within processes or workflows, are especially helpful for operational risk identification.
- **Root cause analysis** is used to identify underlying causes of past incidents or problems, helping to uncover potential risks before they escalate.

Monitor the external and internal environments

Risk identification requires an awareness of both the internal and external environments:

- **Internal factors:** These include organisational structure, culture, processes and systems that may contribute to or mitigate risks.
- **External factors:** These involve changes in the market, industry, technology, regulation and broader economic, political or environmental conditions.

Regular monitoring and analysis of these factors are critical for identifying emerging risks and staying ahead of threats.

Document and categorise risks

A risk register is a structured document or tool used to identify, assess and manage risks within an organisation. In security, it helps in tracking threats to assets, systems or processes and outlines mitigation strategies. Key components typically include:

- **risk ID:** a unique identifier for each risk;
- **description:** a clear explanation of the risk and its potential impact;
- **likelihood:** the probability of the risk occurring (e.g. high, medium, low);
- **impact:** the potential consequences or severity of the risk;
- **risk rating:** a combined score based on likelihood and impact;
- **mitigation plan:** measures to reduce or eliminate the risk;
- **owner:** the individual or team responsible for managing the risk;
- **status:** the current state of the risk (e.g. open, mitigated, under review);
- **review date:** when the risk will next be evaluated.

Review and update regularly

As stated earlier, risk identification is not a one-time task. As internal and external conditions change, so too should the risk register. Regular reviews at least annually or after major organisational changes help to ensure the risks identified are still relevant and that emerging risks are accounted for. Any accepted risks that are not within risk tolerance should be reviewed on a regular basis, even monthly, to ensure there is no change to the level of risk or whether it can now be addressed properly.

Tips for effective risk identification

- **Foster a risk-aware culture:** Encourage employees at all levels to identify and report risks. A culture that prioritises risk awareness will ensure that risks are spotted early.

- **Use a holistic approach:** Consider both internal and external risks, including operational, financial, technological, environmental and reputational factors. The broader the approach, the more comprehensive the risk identification process will be.

- **Incorporate historical data:** Learn from past incidents, including near misses. Past experiences provide valuable insights into potential risks and help to prevent repeat incidents.

- **Use technology:** Use appropriate and suitable risk management software, monitoring tools and predictive analytics to identify risks more effectively, especially in complex and dynamic environments such as cyber security or financial markets.

- **Involve external experts:** Sometimes external consultants or industry experts can provide a fresh perspective on risks that internal teams may overlook.

- **Document everything:** Ensure that all identified risks are documented in a structured manner. A risk register should be easily accessible, regularly updated and reflect any changes in risk levels.

- **Be open to all ideas:** Encourage diverse perspectives during the identification process. Risks can arise from unexpected sources, and a broad view is necessary to identify hidden risks.

Disaster Incubation Theory

Professor Barry Turner was a British sociologist who worked on understanding how organisational and systemic factors contribute to disasters. His book, *Man-Made Disasters* (1978), introduced the concept of 'Disaster Incubation Theory', which outlines a sequence of stages through which disasters develop due to the accumulation of unnoticed events and organisational oversights.

Turner's research highlighted that major organisational disasters often stem from socio-technical and systemic patterns, suggesting that such events could be anticipated and prevented. He emphasised the importance of recognising 'failures of foresight', where organisations overlook or misinterpret warning signs due to cultural and informational factors.

His developmental sequence for understanding disasters begins with a 'notionally normal starting point' and progresses through stages of incubation, precipitating events, onset, rescue and salvage, culminating in a full cultural readjustment. This framework underscores how unnoticed events can accumulate, leading to significant organisational failures.

Turner's Disaster Incubation Theory can also be effectively applied to security by examining how security failures develop over time due to systemic weaknesses, unnoticed signals and cultural blind spots. Outlined below is Turner's theory and how it can be applied to organisational security within logging, monitoring and incident response.

Disaster incubation and cyber security incidents

- **Turner:** Disasters develop in an incubation period when early warning signs are overlooked.

- **Security parallel:** Major security breaches, such as SolarWinds or Colonial Pipeline, often have early indicators such as misconfigurations, failure to patch, failed security audits or minor policy violations that are ignored until a full-blown incident occurs.

- **Solution:** Adequate logging and monitoring as well as regularly reviewing risk registers, policy and procedures and performing a gap analysis will mitigate this.

Failures of foresight in security

- **Turner:** Organisations fail to foresee disasters due to cultural and informational barriers.

- **Security example:** Many breaches occur because companies fail to patch known vulnerabilities, despite having prior knowledge of the risk (e.g. the Equifax breach due to an unpatched Apache Struts vulnerability).
- **Solution:** Security teams should analyse near misses, aggregate threat intelligence and foster a culture of proactive risk management.

The notionally normal state and security baselines

- **Turner:** Disasters often originate from a 'normal' starting state where risks accumulate unnoticed.
- **Security parallel:** Attackers frequently exploit 'business as usual' activities, such as default credentials, excessive privileges or poor access control.
- **Solution:** Zero trust principles can help to challenge assumptions and enforce least privilege as well as enhanced monitoring of accounts, especially privileged accounts.

Structural and cultural contributors to security failures

- **Turner:** Organisational structures can reinforce ignorance of risk.
- **Security example:** Many security breaches occur due to siloed security teams or poor communication between security, IT and other business units.
- **Solution:** Foster cross-functional security awareness, encourage blameless post-mortems, accept criticism as learning and understand that people are the biggest asset and greatest risk to an organisation. Never assume the correct level of awareness or knowledge of employees either. Train them to succeed with the correct skill set.

Precipitating events and security triggers

- **Turner:** Small incidents can act as triggers that lead to full-scale disasters.
- **Security parallel:** A phishing email leading to credential theft could escalate into full domain compromise.
- **Solution:** Implement layered defences, assume breach mentality and monitor. Make use of IoCs and threat intelligence to enable a more proactive approach.

Lessons from post-event cultural readjustment

- **Turner:** After disasters, organisations reframe their understanding and (ideally) improve.
- **Security application:** Security teams should conduct rigorous post-incident reviews and make use of lessons learned, and ensure a root cause analysis is performed to identify how to prevent a reoccurrence.
- **Solution:** A root cause analysis should be undertaken after any disaster to find out why and how it happened to then improve the DR plan, policy and procedure.

RISK EVALUATION

Risk evaluation is a crucial component of the risk management process in any enterprise. It involves assessing the risks identified in the previous phase (risk identification) to determine their potential impact and likelihood, and subsequently prioritising them based on their significance to the organisation. The goal of risk evaluation is to provide decision-makers with the necessary information to determine how to respond to each risk, whether through mitigation, acceptance or further monitoring.

Risk evaluation helps an organisation to allocate resources efficiently, ensuring that the most significant risks are addressed first while balancing the cost and effort of mitigation strategies. Below is a detailed explanation of the risk evaluation process, including the steps involved, the importance of each step and practical tips for conducting it effectively within an enterprise.

Importance of risk evaluation

Risk evaluation is essential for several reasons:

- **Prioritisation:** Not all risks pose the same level of threat to an organisation. Risk evaluation enables organisations to prioritise which risks need immediate attention and which can be monitored over time.

- **Resource allocation:** Evaluation helps in the effective allocation of resources, ensuring that time, money and effort are spent on mitigating the most critical risks.

- **Informed decision-making:** By understanding the significance of each risk, organisations can make more informed decisions about how to respond, such as mitigate, accept, transfer or avoid risks.

- **Compliance and legal requirements:** In many industries, there is a legal or regulatory requirement to evaluate and address risks, particularly in areas such as data protection, safety and financial reporting.

- **Business continuity:** Evaluating risks ensures that the organisation can continue to operate effectively by addressing the risks that could lead to significant disruptions.

Risk evaluation process

The risk evaluation process involves assessing each identified risk in terms of its likelihood of occurrence and its potential impact on the organisation. This typically includes the following steps.

Establish risk criteria
Before evaluating individual risks, it is essential to establish risk criteria that will be used to assess each risk. Risk criteria include factors such as:

- **Impact:** What would happen if the risk materialises? The impact could be financial, operational, reputational or even legal.

- **Likelihood:** How likely is the risk to occur? This is usually based on historical data, expert judgement and quantitative or qualitative analysis.

- **Tolerance:** How much risk is the organisation willing to tolerate in various areas, such as operational, strategic, financial and compliance risks? This is often guided by risk appetite and risk tolerance levels set by senior management.

Risk criteria should be consistent and aligned with the organisation's risk management objectives. They provide a foundation for comparing and evaluating different risks.

Assess the likelihood and impact of each risk

After defining risk criteria, each identified risk needs to be assessed in terms of two main components:

- **Likelihood (probability):** The likelihood refers to how probable it is that the risk will materialise. This can be rated on a scale (e.g. low, medium, high) or numerically (e.g. 1–5, where 1 is highly unlikely and 5 is highly likely).

- **Impact (consequence):** The impact refers to the consequences the organisation would face if the risk occurred. Similar to likelihood, impact can be rated (e.g. low, medium, high) or on a scale that reflects potential financial loss, reputational damage or operational disruption.

The combination of likelihood and impact forms the basis for evaluating the risk's overall significance. For example, a risk with a high likelihood and high impact would be prioritised over a risk with low likelihood and low impact.

Use a risk matrix (risk assessment matrix)

A risk matrix is a tool used to evaluate risks by plotting them on a grid based on their likelihood and impact. It helps organisations to visualise the relative severity of risks and facilitates prioritisation. An organisation needs to define its own likelihood and impact based on past history, threat intelligence, threat modelling and internal or external knowledge.

The matrix typically has one axis for likelihood (e.g. from 'Rare' to 'Almost Certain') and another for impact (e.g. from 'Insignificant' to 'Catastrophic'). Each risk is assigned a position on the matrix based on its likelihood and impact ratings.

The matrix helps to categorise risks into four or five levels, such as:

- **high risk:** requires immediate attention and mitigation;
- **medium-high risk:** requires monitoring and possibly mitigation;
- **medium-low risk:** requires monitoring, with periodic reviews;
- **low risk:** can be accepted, with no immediate action needed.

This matrix is an effective visual tool for making risk evaluation more intuitive and guiding decision-making.

Consider existing controls and mitigating factors

When evaluating risks, it's important to consider the existing controls and mitigation measures already in place. These can reduce both the likelihood and the impact of risks. For example, the presence of strong cyber security measures might lower the likelihood of a data breach. Evaluating the effectiveness of existing controls helps to refine the overall risk assessment and determine if additional actions are needed.

- **Effectiveness of current controls:** Are the current mitigation strategies sufficient to manage the risk, or are additional controls required?
- **Residual risk:** This refers to the level of risk that remains after considering the existing controls. If residual risk is still unacceptable, further mitigation may be necessary.

Prioritise risks

After evaluating the risks, it's time to prioritise them. This step is essential to ensure that the organisation focuses its resources and efforts on the most critical risks first. Prioritisation is typically done by considering both:

- the severity of the risk, which includes the likelihood and impact;
- the strategic importance of the risk in terms of the organisation's objectives.

Prioritisation should be documented in a risk register, which includes a clear ranking or categorisation of risks and outlines appropriate actions or mitigation measures for each.

Tips for effective risk evaluation

Involve key stakeholders

Risk evaluation should not be an isolated process. Involve key stakeholders, such as senior leadership, risk management teams and department heads, to ensure that all perspectives are considered in the evaluation process.

Use quantitative and qualitative methods

Depending on the available data, risk evaluation can be based on quantitative (numerical data, statistical models) and qualitative (expert judgement, qualitative scales) methods. Combining both provides a more holistic view of the risk landscape.

Review risk context and strategic objectives

Always evaluate risks in the context of the organisation's strategic objectives. Risks should be assessed based on their potential to disrupt or enable the organisation's ability to achieve its goals.

Use historical data and benchmarking

Refer to historical data and industry benchmarks to inform your risk evaluation. This includes analysing past incidents, learning from industry trends and using best practices to assess similar risks.

Update regularly

The risk environment can change, so risk evaluation should be an ongoing process. Regularly update risk assessments to account for changes in the organisation's internal and external environments, including new business objectives, regulatory changes or emerging threats.

Ensure transparency and documentation

Properly document the risk evaluation process, including the criteria used, the rationale for assessments and the prioritisation of risks. This ensures transparency and allows for better communication with stakeholders.

RISK TREATMENT

Risk treatment is an important phase in the risk management process where an organisation decides how to deal with the identified and evaluated risks. It involves selecting and implementing appropriate measures to modify risk to an acceptable level. The aim is to reduce the potential for loss or potential opportunities, while ensuring the continuity and resilience of the organisation.

The risk treatment process entails making decisions on how to handle risks and then implementing actions to manage them. This process needs to be dynamic, regularly updated and aligned with the strategic goals and risk appetite of the enterprise. Let us have a comprehensive look at risk treatment, detailing the types of risk treatment options, steps involved in the process and some practical tips for effective implementation.

Deter, detect, delay and respond

From a security perspective, deter, detect, delay and respond can form the foundation of a layered security strategy designed to protect assets, mitigate risks and ensure resilience against attacks. Each stage plays a critical role in a defence-in-depth approach, integrating physical, technical and procedural security controls.

> A multi-layered security approach is fundamental to modern risk management, incorporating deterrence, detection, delay, and response to mitigate threats effectively (Schneier, 2019).

Deter or displace

Prevent attacks before they happen by reducing the likelihood of an attack through making the target less attractive or more difficult to compromise. This could be: psychological deterrence to make attackers believe the risk outweighs the reward; physical deterrence using barriers, guards or environmental design to discourage attempts; and technical deterrence by the deployment security measures that increase the effort required to breach defences.

Security measures include:

- visible security presence (closed-circuit television (CCTV) cameras, security guards, signage);
- hardened infrastructure (reinforced doors, security lighting, perimeter fencing);
- cyber deterrence techniques (firewalls, access control, MFA);
- deception technologies (honeypots, decoys, false data) to mislead adversaries.

Detect

Identify potential threats and anomalies before they can cause damage. Detection enables a swift response, reducing the impact of an attack. Early detection helps organisations to stop threats before escalation. Comprehensive monitoring ensures that even low-level suspicious activities are logged and analysed.

Security measures include:

- IDSs and IPSs;
- SIEM for centralised event analysis;
- user and entity behaviour analytics (UEBA) to detect anomalies;
- continuous network monitoring for suspicious activity;
- physical intrusion alarms and biometric access controls.

Delay

Slow down attacks to allow time for response. Even if deterrence and detection fail, delaying an attack can provide valuable time to respond effectively. Essentially, delaying an intruder's progress increases the chances of detection and intervention. Using layered security measures ensures that breaching a single control does not lead to full system compromise.

Security measures include:

- network segmentation (limits lateral movement of attackers);
- rate limiting and throttling (reduces automated attack effectiveness);
- time-based access controls (restricting access to sensitive systems outside working hours);
- multi-layer authentication and verification (prevents rapid escalation of privilege);
- physical delay measures (reinforced doors, vehicle barriers, turnstiles).

Respond

Mitigate the impact and restore normal operations. Once an attack is detected and delayed, organisations must contain, neutralise and recover from the threat. This can be a rapid response to minimise damage and prevent further compromise. This could be the use of automated responses to stop attacks before human intervention is required. Also implement incident response plans to ensure teams act decisively under pressure.

Security measures include:

- incident response plans with predefined workflows;
- automated threat containment (e.g. disabling compromised accounts);
- forensic analysis tools to understand attack vectors;

- DR and backup solutions to restore operations;
- public relations and legal response planning to manage reputational and regulatory impacts.

The deter, detect, delay and respond framework is important in both physical and cyber security. Each layer reinforces the next, ensuring that even if one measure fails, there are multiple backup defences in place. This approach aligns with defence-in-depth strategies to enhance an organisation's overall protection against threats.

Understanding risk treatment options

There are four main strategies for treating risk, each with different implications for the enterprise. They are avoid, mitigate, transfer and accept.

Risk avoidance
This strategy involves eliminating the risk entirely by avoiding the activity or condition that creates the risk. If the potential impact of a risk is too high and cannot be mitigated cost-effectively, the organisation may choose to avoid the risk by discontinuing the associated activity.

- **Example:** A company might decide not to enter a new market with unstable regulatory conditions to avoid the risk of regulatory fines or restrictions.
- **Considerations:** While risk avoidance can eliminate certain risks, it may also limit opportunities and the ability to achieve strategic objectives. It should be used cautiously.

Risk mitigation
This approach seeks to reduce the likelihood of the risk occurring or minimise its impact if it does occur. Risk reduction can be achieved through implementing controls, policies or processes that make the risk less severe.

- **Example:** Implement cyber security measures such as firewalls, IDSs and employee training to reduce the risk of a data breach.
- **Considerations:** Risk reduction often involves upfront and ongoing costs, so it is crucial to ensure that the cost of mitigation measures is justified by the reduction in risk exposure.

Risk transfer
Risk transfer involves shifting the impact of a risk to a third party by sharing; however, the organisation still owns the risk. This is commonly achieved through insurance policies, outsourcing or contractual agreements.

- **Example:** A company may purchase insurance to transfer the financial impact of a natural disaster or liability claims. Alternatively, a business might outsource non-core activities to a specialised third-party vendor, transferring associated risks.
- **Considerations:** Risk transfer does not eliminate the risk, but it does shift the financial burden. It is essential to carefully consider the terms and conditions of insurance policies or contracts to ensure effective coverage.

Risk acceptance

When the cost of mitigating or transferring a risk outweighs the potential impact, an organisation may decide to accept the risk. This strategy is appropriate for low-impact or low-likelihood risks that are within the organisation's risk appetite.

- **Example:** A company may accept the risk of minor supply chain delays if the impact on operations is negligible.

- **Considerations:** Risk acceptance requires monitoring to ensure the risk does not become more significant over time. It is also important to have a contingency plan if the risk materialises unexpectedly.

Steps involved in risk treatment

Risk treatment involves a structured approach to ensure risks are managed effectively and efficiently. The key steps in the process are set out below.

Identify and evaluate risk treatment options

- Review each risk identified and evaluated in the previous stages and consider the available treatment options. The choice of treatment should align with the organisation's risk appetite and strategic objectives.

- Conduct a cost–benefit analysis to compare the cost of implementing a risk treatment option against the potential benefit (e.g. reduced likelihood or impact of the risk).

Select the appropriate risk treatment

Choose the most suitable risk treatment option for each risk based on its impact, likelihood and alignment with organisational priorities. The decision should be informed by the enterprise's overall risk tolerance and financial considerations. Ensure that the selected treatment is practical, sustainable and does not introduce new, unintended risks.

Develop a risk treatment plan

A risk treatment plan outlines the actions required to manage each risk, the resources needed, timelines for implementation and the individuals or teams responsible for carrying out the treatment.

The plan should include clear objectives, measurable outcomes and deadlines to ensure accountability and effective execution. Components of a risk treatment plan are:

- description of the risk;
- chosen treatment strategy;
- specific actions to be taken;
- assigned responsibilities;
- timeline and milestones;
- monitoring and review procedures.

Implement risk treatment measures

- Execute the actions defined in the risk treatment plan. This may involve implementing new policies, setting up controls, or negotiating contracts with third parties.

- Ensure that the implementation is well-coordinated, with regular communication between teams and departments to maintain alignment with overall business objectives.

- Track progress against the plan and adjust as needed.

Monitor and review the effectiveness of risk treatments

Risk treatment should be an ongoing process, with regular monitoring and review to ensure that the chosen measures are effective. Evaluate whether the risk treatment actions are achieving the desired outcomes and if any adjustments are needed. This step involves collecting performance data, reviewing incident reports and conducting audits to assess the effectiveness of controls. Adjust the treatment strategy if the risk environment changes, or if new risks emerge that affect the treatment plan.

Document and report

- Maintain comprehensive records of the risk treatment process, including decisions made, actions taken and the rationale for each treatment option. This documentation is critical for transparency, accountability and compliance with regulatory requirements.

- Report the status of risk treatments to senior management and relevant stakeholders. This helps to ensure that risk management remains a strategic priority, and that decision-makers are informed of any emerging threats or issues.

Tips for effective risk treatment

Involve key stakeholders, such as department heads, risk owners and subject matter experts, in the risk treatment process. Their input is valuable for selecting practical and effective treatment options and supporting your strategy. Risk treatment should support the organisation's strategic goals and objectives. Ensure that the chosen measures do not hinder the business from achieving its desired outcomes. Focus on treating the risks that pose the greatest threat to the organisation first. Use a risk-based approach to allocate resources where they are most needed and can have the most impact. Risk treatment measures should be flexible enough to adapt to changing circumstances. As the risk landscape evolves, treatment plans may need to be scaled up or down accordingly.

Risks often have interdependencies, where treating one risk may affect another. Be aware of these relationships and assess the broader impact of risk treatment measures on the enterprise. Use risk management software where appropriate, and evaluated fully, to automate tracking, reporting and analysis. Technology can enhance the efficiency of monitoring risk treatments and ensure timely updates, but ensure the technology does not introduce new risk and has been fully tested, so that the organisation knows it is fit for purpose. Avoid over-mitigating risks, as this can be costly and may limit the organisation's flexibility. Balance the need to manage risk with the potential benefits of taking calculated risks to drive innovation and growth. Define how the success of each risk treatment will be measured. Use key performance indicators (KPIs) to monitor effectiveness and ensure that treatment measures are delivering the expected benefits.

Keep communication channels open across all levels of the organisation. Ensure that risk treatment updates are shared and that there is a clear understanding of roles and responsibilities. The risk landscape is dynamic, so regular reviews of risk treatment strategies are essential. Stay informed about emerging threats, regulatory changes and shifts in the business environment.

RISK MONITORING

Risk monitoring is a crucial part of the risk management process in an enterprise. It involves the continuous observation and assessment of identified risks and the effectiveness of implemented risk treatments. The primary goal of risk monitoring is to ensure that the risk environment is fully understood and that any changes in risk exposure are promptly detected and managed. This ongoing vigilance helps organisations adapt to evolving threats and opportunities, maintain compliance with regulations and make informed strategic decisions.

Importance of risk monitoring

Risk monitoring is vital for several reasons:

- **Proactive risk management:** By continually observing the risk environment, enterprises can identify new or emerging risks early, giving them a chance to take timely corrective action.

- **Effectiveness of controls:** Effective controls help in assessing whether risk mitigation measures are working as intended. If certain controls are found to be ineffective, they can be adjusted or replaced.

- **Adaptability:** As the business environment is constantly changing, risk monitoring ensures that an organisation's risk management strategies evolve in line with shifts in external and internal factors, such as regulatory changes, market dynamics or technological advancements.

- **Compliance:** As many industries have strict regulatory requirements that necessitate continuous monitoring and reporting of risks, compliance is important. Effective risk monitoring ensures that organisations remain compliant.

- **Resource optimisation:** By understanding risk trends and control effectiveness, organisations can better allocate resources to areas that need the most attention, reducing waste and enhancing efficiency.

Steps involved in risk monitoring

Establish a risk monitoring plan

- Develop a comprehensive plan outlining the approach to risk monitoring, including which risks will be monitored, how frequently and by whom.

- The plan should include details on data collection methods, performance indicators and reporting mechanisms.

Key components of a risk monitoring plan

- **Scope and objectives:** Define what will be monitored and why.

- **Roles and responsibilities:** Assign responsibilities to individuals or teams for monitoring specific risks.

- **Monitoring frequency:** Establish how often each risk will be reviewed, which may vary based on the risk's criticality.

- **Tools and technology:** Identify any tools or systems required for data collection and analysis.

Track identified risks

- Continuously observe the risks identified during the risk assessment phase. This involves monitoring any changes in the likelihood or impact of each risk and keeping an eye on the risk landscape for new developments.

- Update the risk register regularly to reflect any changes in the risk profile. This includes recording incidents, near misses or any factors that could alter the nature of a risk.

Example If an organisation has identified cyber security threats as a significant risk, risk monitoring might involve tracking the frequency and severity of cyber incidents and observing threat intelligence feeds.

Assess the effectiveness of risk treatments

- Evaluate whether the implemented risk mitigation measures are working as expected. This could involve conducting regular audits, control testing or performance evaluations.

- Use both qualitative and quantitative methods to assess control effectiveness. For example, quantitative measures might include statistical analysis of incident trends, while qualitative assessments could involve interviews with key personnel.

- If controls are not performing effectively, investigate why and make necessary adjustments. This could involve strengthening security measures, retraining staff or updating policies.

Monitor key risk indicators (KRIs)

- KRIs are metrics used to provide early warning signs of increasing risk exposure. KRIs are often tied to specific thresholds and, when these thresholds are breached, they trigger alerts or further investigation.
- Examples of KRIs include:
  - the number of failed login attempts (indicating potential cyber security threats);
  - market share fluctuations (indicating competitive risk);
  - changes in regulatory compliance metrics.
- Regularly review KRIs and ensure they remain relevant and aligned with the enterprise's risk appetite.

Identify new and emerging risks

In addition to monitoring known risks, enterprises should remain vigilant for new or emerging risks. This can be done by staying informed about industry trends, changes in legislation and technological advancements.

To identify emerging risks, organisations should make use of structured tools such as SWOT analysis or horizon scanning. These methods help to proactively uncover potential new threats and opportunities, allowing for early intervention. When new risks are identified, it is essential to update the risk register and corresponding risk treatment plans to ensure they remain accurate and relevant. Once risks have been identified, the next step is to collect and analyse data from various sources to assess trends, patterns and the overall effectiveness of existing risk management practices. Employing data visualisation tools such as dashboards can help to present complex risk data in a clear, concise and actionable manner, aiding informed decision-making across the organisation.

Regular risk reporting is critical for maintaining awareness and accountability. Reports should be shared with senior management and other key stakeholders, providing insights into current risk trends, the status of risk treatments, any incidents that have occurred and recommendations for future action. Tailoring these reports to suit the intended audience is important. Executives typically require high-level summaries, while operational teams benefit more from detailed, actionable intelligence. Organisations should also periodically review and update their risk management framework based on the insights gained through ongoing monitoring. This ensures that the framework remains aligned with strategic goals and continues to effectively address the evolving risk landscape. Regular risk reviews may include reassessing the organisation's risk appetite, updating relevant policies and refining risk treatment strategies.

Finally, fostering a culture of continuous improvement is vital. Lessons learned from monitoring activities should be actively used to enhance and mature the organisation's risk management practices over time. This not only strengthens resilience but also embeds risk awareness into day-to-day decision-making processes.

Tips for effective risk monitoring

Use automation and technology
Using technology can significantly enhance the efficiency and effectiveness of risk monitoring. Risk management software can automate data collection, monitor KRIs and generate real-time alerts when thresholds are breached. By automating routine tasks, risk management teams are freed up to focus on higher-level strategic analysis and decision-making. However, it's essential to ensure that any automation used is appropriate, reliable and does not introduce new risks or dependencies.

Maintain a comprehensive risk register
An up-to-date and comprehensive risk register is a cornerstone of effective risk management. It should include detailed information about each risk, such as its current status, changes in exposure and any incidents or mitigation actions. The register should be easily accessible to relevant stakeholders and regularly reviewed. Categorising risks by department or business unit can further enhance visibility and enable targeted risk monitoring and response.

Establish clear communication channels
Clear and open channels for communicating risk information are vital across the organisation. Employees should be encouraged to report incidents or concerns without fear of blame or reprisal, helping to foster a culture of transparency. Regular meetings, workshops and updates should be used to keep teams informed about current risks, incident trends and the effectiveness of mitigation strategies.

Conduct regular training and awareness
Ongoing training is essential to keep employees engaged and informed about risk management practices. This is especially important in high-risk areas such as cyber security, where staff act as the first line of defence. Training should cover how employees can identify and report risks, as well as giving updates to relevant policies or changes in the risk landscape. Building awareness helps to embed risk-conscious behaviour throughout the organisation.

Set meaningful KRIs and KPIs
KRIs and KPIs should be carefully selected to align with organisational objectives. These indicators need to be specific, measurable and actionable, providing clear insights into both risk exposure and performance. Regular reviews of KRIs and KPIs are necessary to ensure they remain relevant and useful, particularly as the business environment evolves.

Conduct scenario analysis and stress testing
Scenario analysis and stress testing provide valuable insight into how the organisation might respond to various risk events, including high-impact, low-likelihood scenarios. These exercises help to identify gaps in preparedness and inform improvements to risk treatment plans. By simulating adverse conditions, organisations can strengthen their resilience and readiness to respond effectively under pressure.

Engage with industry groups and forums
Participation in industry-specific risk management groups or professional forums is a valuable way to stay informed about emerging threats, regulatory changes and evolving

best practices. Engaging with peers allows organisations to gain new perspectives, identify potential risks that may not have been considered internally and benchmark their practices against industry standards. Sharing experiences and knowledge with others fosters continuous improvement and innovation in risk management.

Be risk aware

Have risk awareness embedded in daily operations. Encourage employees to think about risk in their decision-making and to escalate concerns when necessary. Ensure employees understand and are given appropriate awareness training. Never 'assume' employees know what a risk is – always assume they know nothing, and devise awareness training from that perspective. Recognise and reward proactive risk management behaviours, reinforcing the importance of continuous risk monitoring.

5   SYSTEM SECURITY

In this chapter we will look at the system security found within an organisation, looking at network security before moving onto network and software hardening, cryptography, cloud, containers, zero trust and PAM, AI and, finally, quantum computing.

This is a more technical chapter, but it is important for a security architect or cyber engineer to understand security technology and use cases. Technology should be an enabler adding demonstratable value to an organisation. At the same time, technology is not always the answer and is just one element of people, process and technology. Technology should be thoroughly evaluated and tested prior to deployment – this includes risk and impact – to ensure that it fully meets organisational needs and does not add unnecessary risk and cost.

NETWORK SECURITY

Intrusion detection is another security device designed to detect attacks. It can be software based and installed on devices such as a server – called host intrusion detection (HID) – and placed inline in a network – called network intrusion detection (NID). More sophisticated detection devices or software can also prevent the intrusion. These are called host intrusion prevention (HIP) and network intrusion prevention (NIP). There is also wireless intrusion prevention (WIP).

IDS is designed to monitor network or system activities for malicious activities or policy violations. It analyses traffic patterns to detect potential threats and alerts administrators to suspicious activity. IDS can be either network-based (NIDS) or host-based (HIDS), depending on where they are deployed.

IPS is a more advanced version of an IDS that not only detects but also prevents identified threats. It sits in line with network traffic and can take immediate action, such as blocking malicious traffic, dropping packets or resetting connections, to stop attacks in real-time.

A **proxy firewall** is an early type of firewall. A proxy firewall serves as the gateway from one network to another. Proxy firewalls can also provide additional functionality such as security by preventing direct connections from outside the network coming in or inside connections going out.

A **stateful inspection firewall** blocks or allows traffic based on its state, port and protocol. It monitors all activity from when the connection is opened until it is closed. It can make filtering decisions based on rules as well as context. It uses information from previous connections and packets that belonged to the same connection.

A **unified threat management** (UTM) firewall typically combines the functions of a stateful inspection firewall with intrusion prevention and anti-virus. It may also include additional services and cloud management.

A **next-generation firewall** (NGFW) is a very evolved firewall used to block modern threats such as advanced malware and application-layer attacks. While these capabilities are increasingly becoming the standard for most companies, NGFWs can do more.

Micro-segmentation is a security approach that divides a network into granular, isolated segments to control and restrict the flow of traffic within a network environment. It uses software-defined policies, rather than traditional physical network configurations, to provide granular security controls, ensuring that, even if one segment is compromised, the breach is contained and does not spread easily to other parts of the network.

Anti-virus traditional malware defence

Anti-virus software has long been the primary line of defence against malware infections on computers and other devices. Operating in the background, anti-virus programs continuously monitor files, processes and activities to identify and block malicious software. This functionality is often referred to as real-time protection, on-access scanning or resident scanning.

The traditional anti-virus approach relies heavily on virus signatures, which are unique sequences of bytes that identify specific malware strains. These signatures are stored in a database that the anti-virus software uses to match against files and programs. However, malware developers often employ obfuscation techniques – such as encryption, polymorphism or code injection – to disguise malicious code and evade signature-based detection. To counter these efforts, modern anti-virus solutions supplement signature-based detection with heuristic analysis, which examines a program's behaviour for signs of malicious activity. This proactive approach enables anti-virus software to identify new or previously unknown malware based on suspicious patterns or anomalous behaviours.

Although anti-virus remains an essential tool for individual users, its effectiveness is limited against advanced threats. In organisational settings, anti-virus now forms one part of a broader security strategy, integrated into EDR solutions for enhanced protection.

EDR beyond anti-virus

Endpoint detection and response tools represent an evolution of endpoint security, providing a more comprehensive approach to identifying and responding to threats. Gartner's Anton Chuvakin defines EDR as a system that 'records and stores endpoint-system-level behaviours, uses various data analytics techniques to detect suspicious system behaviour, provides contextual information, blocks malicious activity and provides remediation suggestions to restore affected systems' (Barros and Chuvakin 2016).

Unlike traditional anti-virus, which focuses on blocking known malware, EDR solutions are designed to detect advanced threats, investigate incidents and respond effectively to minimise damage. Key features of EDR include:

- **Advanced threat detection:** EDR uses behavioural analysis, machine learning and threat intelligence to identify complex attacks, including zero-day threats and fileless malware.

- **Incident investigation and triage:** Security teams can analyse detailed logs and activity records to pinpoint the root cause of an incident and assess its impact.

- **Threat hunting:** EDR tools enable proactive searching for potential threats that may not trigger automatic alerts.

- **Malicious activity containment:** Once a threat is identified, EDR can isolate compromised endpoints to prevent further spread while remediation takes place.

EDR's ability to provide endpoint visibility and actionable insights makes it indispensable for modern security operations. However, as attackers increasingly exploit multiple vectors beyond endpoints, organisations are turning to more integrated solutions such as XDR.

XDR, a holistic security approach

XDR builds on the capabilities of EDR, offering a more advanced and integrated security solution. While EDR focuses solely on endpoints, XDR collects and correlates data across multiple layers of an organisation's infrastructure, including endpoints, networks, servers, cloud environments and email systems. By unifying these data sources, XDR delivers a holistic view of security incidents, enabling faster and more accurate detection and response. The key advantages of XDR include:

- **Unified threat visibility:** XDR breaks down silos between security tools, allowing teams to see the full scope of an attack, including lateral movements across the network.

- **Efficient threat detection:** By correlating data from diverse sources, XDR identifies sophisticated threats that might go unnoticed by isolated tools. For example, it can detect phishing emails that lead to endpoint compromise or malicious activity originating from a cloud application.

- **Streamlined incident response:** XDR employs automation and advanced analytics to reduce response times. Automated workflows can isolate infected endpoints, block malicious IPs and update firewall rules without manual intervention.

- **Simplified security operations:** By integrating multiple security functions into a single platform, XDR reduces the complexity of managing separate tools, making it easier for security teams to operate efficiently.

The use of automation in XDR not only accelerates threat detection and response but also alleviates the burden on security teams, who are often overwhelmed by alert fatigue. By prioritising high-risk incidents and providing context-rich insights, XDR empowers teams to focus on critical tasks, improving the overall effectiveness of security operations.

Access control

Access control relies on various technologies to ensure secure authentication, authorisation and accountability. These technologies are implemented to control and monitor access to resources based on predefined security policies, safeguarding sensitive information and systems.

One of the foundational technologies is IAM systems. IAM frameworks provide a centralised way to manage user identities and enforce access policies across an organisation. These systems often include tools for authentication, single sign-on (SSO) and MFA. SSO simplifies user access by enabling a single set of credentials to access multiple systems, while MFA adds an additional layer of security by requiring a combination of factors such as passwords, biometrics or security tokens. IAM systems also streamline the implementation of access control models such as RBAC and ABAC.

Kerberos, used with Windows, is another technology used in access control, particularly in enterprise environments requiring a robust authentication mechanism (Figure 5.1). It operates on a ticket-based system, using symmetric key cryptography to allow secure authentication between users and services. Kerberos works by issuing time-limited tickets through a trusted key distribution centre (KDC) consisting of an authentication server (AS) and a ticket granting server (TGS). This system mitigates the risk of password transmission over the network and ensures secure access to resources within a domain, such as in active directory environments.

Figure 5.1 Kerberos authentication process

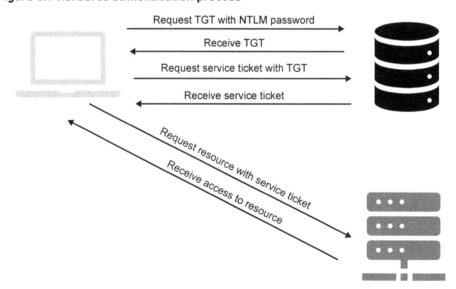

Key components

- **KDC:** a trusted authority that manages authentication;
- **AS:** verifies user identity;
- **TGS:** issues tickets for accessing services;
- **client:** the user or device requesting access;
- **service server:** the resource or service the client wants to access.

Authentication process

Initial authentication (getting a ticket granting ticket (TGT)):

- The client sends an authentication request to the AS containing the username.
- The AS checks the username and sends back an encrypted TGT along with a session key, encrypted using the user's password hash.
- The client decrypts the TGT using their password (typically handled securely via a local credential cache).

Service ticket request:

- The client presents the TGT to the TGS and requests access to a specific service.
- The TGS verifies the TGT and issues a service ticket encrypted using the service's secret key.

Accessing the service:

- The client sends the service ticket to the requested service.
- The service decrypts the ticket and validates the client.
- If valid, the client is granted access.

New Technology LAN Manager (NTLM)

Microsoft NTLM is a legacy authentication protocol used in Windows environments for securing network logins. It relies on a challenge–response mechanism and hash-based authentication instead of transmitting passwords directly over the network. While NTLM was widely used in earlier Windows versions, it has largely been replaced by Kerberos in modern environments due to security concerns.

The NTLM authentication process involves several steps. First, the client initiates authentication by sending a request to the server. The server then responds with a random challenge (a nonce). The client encrypts this challenge using the user's password hash (stored locally or in active directory) and sends it back to the server. Finally, the server verifies the response by checking it against its stored hash, granting access if the values match.

NTLM has significant security weaknesses. It is vulnerable to relay attacks, where an attacker can intercept and reuse authentication messages to gain unauthorised access.

Additionally, NTLM does not support mutual authentication, meaning the client has no way to verify the identity of the server. This makes NTLM susceptible to man-in-the-middle attacks.

Due to the weakness of NTLM, Microsoft recommends using Kerberos (they have deprecated NTLM), which provides stronger security features, including mutual authentication and ticket-based access control. NTLM is still present in some legacy systems and remains a fallback option in certain Windows environments.

NTLM vs Kerberos

NTLM and Kerberos are both authentication protocols used in Windows environments, but they differ significantly in terms of security, functionality and efficiency.

Authentication mechanism

NTLM uses a challenge–response mechanism, where the server sends a challenge and the client responds with an encrypted hash of the user's password. This process occurs for every authentication request, making it inefficient. In contrast, Kerberos uses a ticket-based system, where a user authenticates once and receives a TGT from the KDC. This allows for SSO and eliminates the need to repeatedly send hashed credentials.

Security

NTLM is vulnerable to pass-the-hash and relay attacks, as it does not support mutual authentication. Attackers can capture NTLM authentication traffic and reuse it to gain unauthorised access. Kerberos mitigates these risks by requiring both the client and the server to authenticate each other, reducing the chances of credential replay attacks. Also, Kerberos uses tickets that time out and encrypted communication, making it more resistant to attacks.

Performance and efficiency

Since NTLM requires authentication for each request, it leads to higher overhead in large networks. Kerberos, on the other hand, allows for SSO, meaning that once a user is authenticated, they can access multiple services without needing to re-enter credentials. This makes Kerberos significantly more efficient in enterprise environments, reducing issues with password resets and users being overwhelmed with passes so that they end up using bad passwords.

Mutual authentication

Kerberos provides mutual authentication, meaning that both the client and the service verify each other's identity before establishing a connection. NTLM lacks this feature, making it more susceptible to man-in-the-middle attacks.

Wireless Fidelity (Wi-Fi)

Wireless networks are used everywhere and it is the most common way we connect to our various home hubs or routers. Organisations have put in wireless networks to allow for agile working and hot desking. A wireless network refers to wireless local area networks (WLANs) based on IEEE 802.11 standard, which allows devices to access the network from anywhere within the range of an access point. There are several secure connection standards for devices to connect to a Wi-Fi network (Figure 5.2).

Figure 5.2 Wi-Fi handshake process

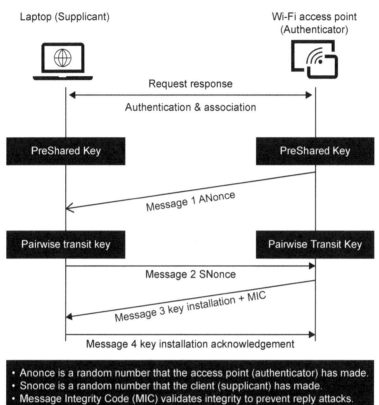

WPA2 was released in 2004, is still considered strong and is widely in use.

- WPA2-Personal uses a setup password (PreShared Key (PSK)) to protect unauthorised network accesses. In PSK mode, each wireless network device encrypts the password exchange using a 128-bit key, which is derived from a passphrase of 8 to 63 American Standard Code for Information Interchange (ASCII) characters.

- WPA2-Enterprise uses centralised client authentication, using multiple authentication methods such as token cards, Radius and Kerberos. Users are assigned login credentials by a centralised server, which they must use to access the network.

WPA3, released in 2019, is an advanced implementation of WPA2 providing improved protocols. Adoption is slow due to the extra cost and WPA2 still being considered secure.

- WPA3-Personal is a PSK-based authentication using the Simultaneous Authentication of Equals protocol, also known as Dragonfly Key Exchange, for secure key exchange. WPA3 is resistant to offline dictionary attacks and key recovery attacks.

- WPA3-Enterprise protects sensitive data using several cryptographic algorithms. Provides authenticated encryption.

Public Wi-Fi has always been a security risk due to the ability of anyone to connect to the network and be able to listen in (sniff) and see unencrypted traffic using a freely available tool called Wireshark. When using public Wi-Fi, it is always best practice to use a VPN and avoid sending or retrieving any sensitive data. The vast majority of organisations use VPNs such as CISCO Anytime, Fortinet or BIG IP to secure laptops for use at home or work. Some will not even allow the VPN to connect on public Wi-Fi. Consideration for Wi-Fi security is paramount to ensuring devices cannot connect to hostile Wi-Fi hotspots.

VPN

A VPN is used to establish a secure and encrypted connection over a less secure network, such as the internet. It enables users to send and receive data as if their devices were directly connected to a private network, maintaining privacy and security. By encrypting data traffic and masking the user's IP address, a VPN ensures activities remain confidential and protected from eavesdropping or unauthorised access, even when using public Wi-Fi networks.

VPNs operate by creating a virtual 'tunnel' between the user's device and a remote server managed by the VPN service provider. All data passing through this tunnel is encrypted, making it unreadable unless decrypted. VPNs can bypass geographic restrictions by routing traffic through servers in different countries, enabling access to region-specific content and services.

VPNs are now widely used in both personal and professional environments. Organisations often deploy VPNs to allow employees secure remote access to corporate resources, such as internal servers and databases. However, the effectiveness of a VPN depends on the provider's policies and technical implementation, particularly concerning data logging, encryption standards and jurisdiction.

Internet Protocol Security (IPSec)

IPSec is a group of protocols for creating a secure connection between devices. Its main use case is as a VPN and it works by encryption of IP packets and authentication of the source the packets are coming from. IP is the main protocol used on the internet for data flow using IP addresses. IPsec adds security either by encrypting the payload in the packet (transport mode) or both the packet and IP address (tunnel mode).

In networking, a protocol is a set of standard rules to format data so that any device on the network can understand the process and interpret the data.

The following protocols make up the IPSec suite:

- **Authentication header (AH):** The AH protocol is used to ensure data packets are from a trusted source and that the data has not been tampered with. The headers do not provide encryption and are a tamper-proof seal.

- **Encapsulating Security Protocol (ESP):** ESP encrypts the IP header and the payload of each packet unless transport mode is used. If transport mode is used, only the data payload is encrypted.
- **Security association (SA):** SA is used for negotiating encryption keys and algorithms. Internet Key Exchange (IKE) is the most commonly used SA protocol.

TLS

TLS is used for privacy and data security of internet communication. An example is the encryption of traffic between web applications and servers, such as web browsers loading a website. TLS can be used to encrypt other communications such as Voice-over Internet Protocol (VoIP), email and messaging. Hypertext Transfer Protocol Secure (HTTPS) is an implementation of TLS that added security to the insecure HTTP for data exchange used to fetch websites.

TLS replaced Secure Sockets Layer (SSL) in 1999. SSL was originally developed by Netscape in 1994. SSL is now deprecated and considered insecure, but is still used in books and industry to describe TLS. The change of name to TLS was due to SSL being the intellectual property of Netscape, and they no longer wanted to be involved. So, the Internet Engineering Task Force (IETF) took over and created TLS. Its latest iteration is TLS 1.3, which was released in 2018. It has a shortened handshake protocol that resists rollback and key compromise attacks. It can enforce a set cryptographic level and remove obsolete cypher suites to prevent downgrade attacks. TLS 1.0 and 1.1 are now deprecated and should not be used. There are ongoing efforts centred on adding quantum-resistant algorithms in a hybrid mode for key exchange and authentication within the existing TLS framework, such as Open Quantum Safe's fork of OpenSSL. The Open Quantum Safe project is a collaborative open-source initiative designed to facilitate the transition to quantum-resistant cryptography. It operates as part of the Linux Foundation's Post-Quantum Cryptography Alliance.

DLP

DLP has grown dramatically over the last few years. It is a set of strategies and tools used to ensure sensitive or critical information does not go outside the organisation's network. The primary goal of DLP is to prevent data breaches and unauthorised access to sensitive data.

The most critical factor is identifying and classifying data. DLP solutions can identify and categorise sensitive data, such as personally identifiable information (PII), financial data, intellectual property and other confidential information. Once data is identified, it is classified based on its sensitivity and criticality, which helps in applying appropriate policies and controls

DLP also focuses on data monitoring and protection. DLP tools continuously monitor data in use (endpoints), data in motion (network traffic) and data at rest (stored data) to detect any anomalies or unauthorised access attempts. They can enforce policies that prevent unauthorised sharing, copying or transferring of sensitive data, which can include encryption, access controls and other protective measures. Instead of waiting to check security after a new feature is developed, tested and released into production, it's more effective to perform security testing at every phase. This allows for immediate resolution of security issues as they arise.

Incident response and reporting are essential components of DLP. When a potential data breach or policy violation is detected, the DLP system generates alerts and detailed reports for administrators to review. DLP tools can trigger automated responses, such as blocking the transfer of data, quarantining affected files or notifying security teams for further investigation. DLP is often integrated with other security solutions for a more comprehensive security posture. This includes anti-virus, firewalls, intrusion IDS/IPS and SIEM solutions.

DLP helps compliance and risk management by ensuring that the organisation complies with regulatory requirements such as GDPR, HIPAA, PCI DSS and others through warranting that sensitive data is adequately protected. By preventing data breaches and ensuring data protection, it can reduce the overall risk to the organisation.

There are different types of DLP solutions:

- **Network DLP** monitors and protects data in motion across the network.
- **Endpoint DLP** monitors and protects data in use on endpoint devices such as laptops, desktops and mobile devices.
- **Storage DLP** protects data at rest stored in databases, file servers and other storage systems.
- **Cloud DLP** extends DLP capabilities to data stored in and transmitted to/from cloud services.

The benefits of DLP are significant. It protects intellectual property by preventing the theft or unauthorised sharing of trade secrets and proprietary information. It prevents data breaches by detecting and blocking unauthorised data transfers. It ensures compliance with data protection regulations, helping organisations to avoid hefty fines. It enhances data visibility by providing better visibility into data flows and usage within the organisation, and it improves the overall security posture by integrating with other security measures.

However, there are challenges and considerations when implementing DLP. It can be complex and resource-intensive to implement and manage. Balancing data protection with user privacy rights can be challenging. Ensuring accurate detection to minimise false positives and negatives is crucial for effective DLP. Additionally, DLP tools can sometimes affect system performance if not properly configured.

A false positive occurs when there is an incorrect indication of the presence of a condition or attribute that is not actually present. For example, an IDS might flag legitimate network traffic as malicious, resulting in an unnecessary alert.

A false negative occurs when there is an incorrect indication to a condition or attribute that is actually present. For example, IDS might fail to detect actual malicious activity, allowing an attack to proceed unnoticed.

Demilitarised zone (DMZ)

DMZ, or screened subnet, is a subnetwork in a network that contains public-facing resources such as web servers for company websites. The DMZ isolates these public-facing resources from the enterprise's private local area network (LAN). It can also be referred to as a perimeter network or screened subnet. The DMZ is an additional layer of network security. It is where any traffic from the internet or other locations outside the enterprise domain boundary should be terminated, inspected and authenticated if necessary (Figure 5.3).

Figure 5.3 DMZ network diagram

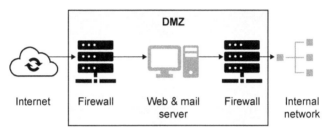

| Internet | Firewall | Web & mail server | Firewall | Internal network |

HARDENING

System and software hardening refers to the practice of securing a computer system or application by reducing its vulnerabilities and limiting its attack surface. It involves implementing various security measures and configurations to protect systems from malicious attacks, unauthorised access and data breaches. Hardening is a crucial aspect of information security, aimed at minimising the risk of exploitation by making the system or software as secure as possible.

The primary goal of hardening is to reduce the attack surface, which is the total set of ways an attacker can try to exploit a system. By minimising unnecessary features, services and settings, the opportunities for an attacker to gain unauthorised access are significantly reduced. For instance, disabling unused network ports and removing unused software applications are common ways to reduce the attack surface. Hardening makes systems more resilient by making it harder to find and exploit weaknesses.

Operating system hardening

OS hardening involves configuring the OS to enhance its security posture. Some key techniques used are:

- **Update and patch management**, by keeping the OS up to date with the latest security patches, is critical. Vulnerabilities are often discovered and disclosed, and software vendors release patches to fix them. Consistently applying these updates helps to prevent attackers from exploiting known weaknesses.

- **User account management**, by creating a strict user account policy, is vital. This includes disabling or removing default accounts, ensuring that all users have strong, unique passwords and using the principle of least privilege. The principle of least privilege means users and applications should only have the minimum access rights necessary to perform their tasks.

- **Disabling unnecessary services and features** using 'If you don't use it lose it', is vital. Many OSs come with default settings that enable various services that might not be needed. Disabling unnecessary services reduces the risk of exploitation, for example disabling Telnet or File Transfer Protocol (FTP) in favour of Secure Shell (SSH) or SSH File Transfer Protocol (SFTP) or turning off file-sharing features if they are not required.

- **Configuring security settings**, including setting up firewalls, enabling encryption and configuring system security policies, is vital. Enforcing password complexity requirements and setting account lockout policies are also important security measures.

- **Using Secure Boot and trusted platform modules** (TPMs) is vital. Secure Boot ensures that only trusted software can load during the system boot process. TPMs provide hardware-level security and are used for tasks such as securely storing cryptographic keys.

Application and software hardening

Software hardening focuses on making applications less vulnerable to attacks. This involves several best practices:

- **Input validation**, by ensuring that all user input is properly validated and sanitised, is essential to prevent common attacks such as Structured Query Language (SQL) injection and XSS. Input validation ensures that data entering the application meets expected formats and does not include malicious code.

- **Software must be securely configured** as it often comes with default settings that may be insecure. Hardening involves configuring the software securely, such as disabling debugging features in a production environment and turning off error messages that might reveal system details – having fail closed instead of failing open.

- **Applying security updates** by keeping application software up to date is vital. Vendors often release patches to fix vulnerabilities, and applying these updates promptly is crucial for security.

- **Use of secure coding practices** by developers is vital so that they follow secure coding guidelines to avoid introducing vulnerabilities into software. For example, using parameterised queries to interact with databases can prevent SQL injection attacks.

- **Implementing authentication and authorisation** is vital, as all applications should have robust authentication mechanisms to ensure that only authorised users can access specific features or data. MFA is a commonly recommended approach to enhance security.

- **Disabling unused features and modules** if they are not in use in an application is vital, as disabling them can help to reduce the attack surface. For instance, if an application has a built-in API but it is not required, it should be turned off to limit potential vulnerabilities.

Network hardening

Network hardening is another essential aspect of system and software security. This involves securing network infrastructure to prevent attacks and unauthorised access:

- **Firewall configuration:** Firewalls act as a barrier between trusted and untrusted networks and configuring them properly is a fundamental security measure. This includes setting rules to allow only necessary traffic and blocking everything else by default.

- **Network segmentation:** Separating the network into segments based on sensitivity and access needs can limit the damage caused by a breach. For example, isolating guest Wi-Fi networks from the main corporate network reduces the risk of unauthorised access to sensitive resources.

- **Using VPNs:** VPNs encrypt data in transit, protecting it from interception by attackers. They are particularly useful for securing communications over untrusted networks, such as public Wi-Fi.

- **IDPS:** These systems monitor network traffic for suspicious activities and take action to prevent potential threats. They can be configured to block malicious traffic or alert administrators of a possible attack.

- **Implementing strong encryption protocols:** Using strong encryption protocols, such as TLS, ensures that data transferred over the network is secure. Legacy protocols, such as SSL, should be avoided in favour of more secure alternatives.

Database hardening

Databases often store sensitive information, making them a prime target for attackers. Database hardening practices include:

- **Access control:** Limiting access to the database based on user roles and responsibilities ensures that only authorised users can view or modify data. Implementing strong authentication and authorisation mechanisms is crucial.

- **Data encryption:** Encrypting data at rest and in transit protects it from unauthorised access. Database encryption mechanisms should be used to safeguard sensitive information, such as using transparent data encryption (TDE).

- **Regular backups:** Taking regular backups of databases and ensuring they are stored securely is critical for DR and protection against data loss.

- **Monitoring and logging:** Setting up monitoring to track access and activities on the database helps to detect suspicious or unauthorised activities. Logs should be regularly reviewed to identify potential security incidents.

Hardening frameworks and best practices

Many organisations follow established frameworks and guidelines for hardening systems, and software vendors often produce hardening guidelines and best practices. Some wider examples are:

- **CIS benchmarks:** The CIS provides detailed configuration guidelines for securing OSs, software and network devices.

- **NIST security guidelines:** NIST offers a comprehensive set of guidelines and frameworks for information security and hardening.

- **OWASP Application Security Verification Standard (ASVS):** Created by the Open Web Application Security Project, the ASVS is a framework for assessing the security of web applications. It provides a set of requirements and best practices for building, maintaining and testing secure applications, especially against common web threats.

- **Cloud Security Alliance (CSA) security guidance:** This guidance provides a set of best practices and recommendations for securing cloud computing environments. The CSA's Cloud Control Matrix and Consensus Assessments Initiative Questionnaire are widely used for cloud hardening and assessing cloud provider security.

- **Microsoft security baselines:** Developed by Microsoft, these baselines provide a set of recommended security settings and configurations for Windows OSs, Office applications and other Microsoft products. These baselines help to ensure a secure starting point for deploying Microsoft products.

- **NCSC cloud security principles:** Developed by the National Cyber Security Centre, this framework outlines a set of principles to help organisations secure cloud services. The guidance covers areas such as data protection, asset management and supply chain security for cloud environments.

- **European Union Agency for Cybersecurity (ENISA) Critical Information Infrastructure Protection (CIIP):** Produced by ENISA, the CIIP guidelines focus on protecting critical information infrastructure. They offer security recommendations specific to sectors such as energy, finance and healthcare.

CRYPTOGRAPHY

Symmetric encryption

Symmetric encryption is where the same key is used for both the encryption and decryption processes (shared key). The problem with a shared key is that it must be exchanged with both parties and, if it is intercepted during exchange, any communication can be easily decrypted. Therefore, keeping the key secure during key exchange is critical, as the security of symmetric encryption relies on the strength of the key and the robustness of the encryption algorithm (Figure 5.4).

One of the most widely used symmetric encryption algorithms currently is the Advanced Encryption Standard (AES). AES was established as a standard by the US NIST in 2001,

Figure 5.4 Symmetric encryption

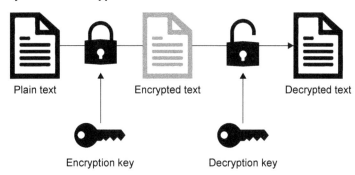

Plain text   Encrypted text   Decrypted text

Encryption key   Decryption key

replacing older, less secure algorithms. It operates on fixed block sizes of 128 bits and supports key sizes of 128, 192 or 256 bits. The longer the key, the stronger the encryption, but this also comes with an increase in computational complexity. AES is efficient, secure and suitable for a broad range of applications, from encrypting data at rest to securing communications over networks. AES instruction sets are now built into some modern computer processors too.

AES can function in several modes of operation to enhance security. These modes determine how plaintext blocks are encrypted to avoid patterns that can be exploited by attackers. One of the most commonly used modes is cipher block chaining, where each block of plaintext is regarded as 'exclusive OR' (XOR) with the previous ciphertext (unreadable, encrypted data) block before being encrypted, ensuring that identical plaintext blocks yield different ciphertexts. Galois/Counter Mode (GCM) is another important mode, often used in applications that require both confidentiality and data integrity. GCM combines counter mode encryption with Galois field multiplication to provide authenticated encryption, which is essential for protecting the integrity of the data.

The primary advantage of AES and symmetric encryption is speed and efficiency. Unlike asymmetric encryption, which uses complex mathematical operations, AES can quickly encrypt and decrypt large volumes of data with relatively low computational overhead. This makes it an ideal choice for securing data in environments such as real-time applications or when encrypting files on disk with a small computational overhead.

However, symmetric encryption does come with challenges, particularly regarding key distribution and management. Since both parties must have the same key, securely sharing and maintaining these keys can be difficult. In large systems with many users, the number of required unique keys increases significantly, making key management a complex task. Additionally, if a key is ever compromised, all data encrypted with it becomes vulnerable, necessitating proactive key rotation and robust management practices.

In modern applications, AES is used extensively for securing data, whether it is data at rest, such as files stored on a computer (BitLocker, New Technology File System (NTFS), TDE), or data in transit (IPSec, HTTPS), such as information exchanged over the internet using protocols such as TLS. AES at 256 bits is also currently considered, in theory, resistant to quantum computing attacks.

Symmetric encryption using AES works through a series of well-defined steps to securely transform plaintext into ciphertext and then back again when necessary.

The shared secret key

The fundamental aspect of symmetric encryption is the use of a single, shared secret key. Both the sender and the receiver need this key to perform encryption and decryption. The key must be kept secret because, if compromised, an attacker could decrypt the encrypted data.

Encryption process

When data needs to be protected, the following steps occur during encryption:

- **Input:** The plaintext data and the shared secret key are fed into an AES encryption algorithm.

- **Block division:** AES works by dividing the data into blocks of 128 bits (16 bytes). If the data isn't a perfect multiple of 128 bits, it is padded to reach the appropriate length.

- **Rounds of transformation:** Depending on the key size (128, 192 or 256 bits), AES performs multiple rounds of transformation to make the encryption secure:

  - **SubBytes:** Each byte of the block is substituted with another byte using a substitution table (S-box) to create confusion in the data.

  - **ShiftRows:** The rows of the data block are shifted to the left in a specific pattern to mix up the data further.

  - **MixColumns:** The columns of the data block are mixed to create more diffusion, spreading out the bits of the data.

  - **AddRoundKey:** The block is combined with a portion of the secret key using a bitwise XOR operation. This step is performed multiple times in each round.

- **Final round:** The final round is slightly different, omitting the MixColumns step. The resulting data is the ciphertext, which appears as a random and unreadable series of characters.

Decryption process

To decrypt the data and convert the ciphertext back into plaintext, the process is essentially reversed:

- **Input:** The ciphertext and the same shared secret key are fed into the AES decryption algorithm.

- **Reversing rounds:** The decryption algorithm goes through the rounds in reverse order, undoing each step performed during encryption:

- **AddRoundKey:** The original key is applied using XOR, reversing the encryption and transforming the ciphertext back into plaintext.

- **Inverse MixColumns:** The columns are mixed back to their original state.

- **Inverse ShiftRows:** The row shifts are reversed to restore the original order.

- **Inverse SubBytes:** The substitution is reversed.

After all the rounds, the original plaintext is recovered.

Example of how it works

Suppose Alice wants to send a confidential message, 'HELLO WORLD', to Bob using AES encryption with a 128-bit key:

1. Alice and Bob agree on a 256-bit shared secret key beforehand through a secure channel.

2. Alice's message, 'HELLO WORLD', is converted into binary data and padded to a 256-bit block if necessary.

3. Alice uses the AES encryption algorithm, applying the shared key and multiple transformation rounds to convert the plaintext into ciphertext.

4. She sends the ciphertext to Bob. Without the shared key, the message appears as random data to anyone intercepting it.

5. Bob uses the same shared secret key and the AES decryption algorithm to transform the ciphertext back into the original message, 'HELLO WORLD'.

Asymmetric encryption

Asymmetric encryption, also known as public key encryption, is a type of encryption where two different keys are used: a public key for encryption and a private key for decryption (Figure 5.5). This method addresses a major limitation of symmetric encryption, namely the challenge of securely sharing and managing a secret key between parties. In asymmetric encryption, the public key can be freely distributed, while the private key remains confidential, allowing secure communications even between parties that have not previously shared a secret.

One of the most well-known asymmetric encryption algorithms is Rivest–Shamir–Adleman (RSA). Developed in 1977, RSA relies on the mathematical complexity of prime factorisation. The algorithm generates a pair of keys: a public key, used for encrypting messages, and a private key, used for decrypting them. The security of RSA comes from the difficulty of factoring the product of two large prime numbers. To illustrate how RSA works, when a sender wants to send a secure message, they use the recipient's public key to encrypt the message. Only the recipient, who has the matching private key, can decrypt the message. RSA is commonly used in secure data transmission protocols such as HTTPS.

However, as quantum computing technology advances, RSA and other encryption schemes based on number theory face significant threats. Quantum computers could theoretically solve prime factorisation problems exponentially faster than classical

Figure 5.5 Asymmetric key encryption

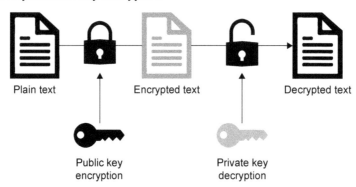

Plain text   Encrypted text   Decrypted text

Public key
encryption

Private key
decryption

computers, making RSA vulnerable to future quantum attacks. Hackers are likely to exploit quantum algorithms that optimise certain tasks. One was published in 1996 by Lov Gover of AT&T Bell Labs to help quantum computers search for permutations. A permutation is an arrangement of objects in a definite order and used in cryptography. An earlier algorithm published by Peter Shor in 1994, when working for Bell Labs, is used to find prime factors of integers incredibly fast. Public key infrastructure (PKI) such as RSA is vulnerable to the algorithm due to the mathematics relying partly on how difficult it is to reverse-engineer the result of multiplying exceptionally large prime numbers together. The theory is that a powerful quantum computer could crack a 1,024-bit implementation of RSA in less than a day running Shor's algorithm.

One such post-quantum encryption algorithm is Kyber, part of a family of algorithms known as lattice-based cryptography. Kyber was selected for standardisation by the NIST and is the standard for Federal Information Processing Standards (FIPS) 203 as part of the effort to secure communications against quantum attacks. Unlike RSA, which depends on prime factorisation, Kyber's security is based on the learning with errors (LWE) problem, a hard problem in lattice mathematics that even quantum computers are not expected to solve efficiently. The Kyber algorithm is efficient and secure, making it a promising solution for encryption in a post-quantum world.

Kyber works by generating a pair of keys, similar to RSA, but the underlying mathematics involve operations within a high-dimensional lattice structure. The public key is used to encrypt data and the private key, derived from the lattice structure, is used to decrypt it. The encryption and decryption processes are designed to be both computationally efficient and resilient against attacks, even from quantum computers. Kyber is particularly valued for its speed and efficiency, which make it suitable for a wide range of applications, including secure internet communications and protecting data in transit.

Despite their differences, both RSA and Kyber play crucial roles in the realm of asymmetric encryption. RSA is used in many existing systems due to its proven security and widespread adoption. It has laid the foundation for secure communications over the internet, providing the backbone for digital signatures, secure key exchange and encrypted data transmission. Kyber represents the future of encryption in a quantum-secure world. Its development ensures that our data remains secure as computing technology continues to evolve, safeguarding sensitive information from potential quantum threats.

How asymmetric encryption works

Asymmetric encryption (public key encryption) uses two separate but mathematically linked keys, a public key and a private key. This allows secure communication without needing to share a secret key in advance.

Key pair generation
The process starts with the creation of a key pair:

- **Public key:** This key is used for encrypting data and can be safely shared with anyone. It is called 'public' because it does not need to be kept secret.

- **Private key:** This key is used for decrypting data that has been encrypted with the corresponding public key. The private key must be kept confidential and secure, as anyone with access to it can decrypt the encrypted messages.

The keys are generated using complex mathematical operations that ensure a strong link between the two, making it computationally infeasible to derive the private key from the public key.

Encryption process
When someone wants to send a secure message:

- The sender encrypts the message using the recipient's public key. This ensures that only the intended recipient can decrypt the message.

- The encryption process transforms the plaintext (readable data) into ciphertext (unreadable, encrypted data) using the public key. The ciphertext cannot be decrypted using the same public key; only the matching private key can decrypt it.

For example, if Alice wants to send a secure message to Bob, she would use Bob's public key to encrypt the message. Even if an attacker intercepts the ciphertext, they would not be able to decrypt it without Bob's private key.

Decryption process
When the recipient receives the ciphertext:

- They use their private key to decrypt the message. The private key, being the only key capable of reversing the encryption process, converts the ciphertext back into plaintext.

- Since the private key is never shared, only the rightful owner of the private key (in this case, Bob) can decrypt and read the message.

This separation of keys ensures that communications remain secure, even if the public key is widely available.

How RSA works

To understand asymmetric encryption, let's look at how RSA functions:

- **Key generation:** RSA starts by generating two large prime numbers and multiplying them to produce a large composite number, which forms part of the public and private keys. The security of RSA comes from the difficulty of factoring this large composite number.

- **Encryption:** The sender uses the recipient's public key, which includes the composite number and an exponent, to perform mathematical operations on the plaintext. The result is ciphertext.

- **Decryption:** The recipient uses their private key, which includes information about the original prime numbers, to reverse the mathematical operations and recover the plaintext.

The private key operations are computationally infeasible to deduce from the public key, making RSA secure under classical computing assumptions.

How Kyber works

CRYSTALS Kyber is designed to be secure even against quantum computers. It uses lattice-based cryptography and works by:

- **Key generation:** Kyber creates a public and private key pair using complex operations on high-dimensional mathematical lattices. The public key is derived from a lattice structure and the private key contains information needed to work with that lattice.

- **Encryption:** The sender uses the recipient's public key to encrypt the message, creating ciphertext based on mathematical problems related to lattice structures. These problems, like the LWE problem, are extremely difficult to solve, even for quantum computers.

- **Decryption:** The recipient uses their private key to interact with the lattice structure, solving the decryption problem and converting the ciphertext back into plaintext.

Kyber's security relies on the mathematical difficulty of lattice problems, which are considered resistant to quantum attacks. This makes Kyber an essential part of the effort to secure future communications as quantum computing advances.

Uses of asymmetric encryption

- **Secure data transmission:** Asymmetric encryption is widely used to secure data transmitted over the internet, as in TLS protocols, which protect sensitive information such as credit card details during online transactions.

- **Digital signatures:** The private key can also be used to sign a message or piece of data, creating a digital signature. This signature can be verified using the public key, proving the authenticity and integrity of the message.

- **Key exchange:** Asymmetric encryption allows secure key exchange in protocols such as Diffie–Hellman, enabling two parties to establish a shared symmetric key for fast encryption.

Hashing

Hashing is a cryptographic process used to transform data into a fixed-length string of characters, which is typically a sequence of numbers and letters. Unlike encryption, hashing is a one-way function, meaning that the original input data cannot be retrieved from the hash output. Hashing is crucial for ensuring data integrity and securely storing sensitive information such as passwords.

Hash functions are designed to take input data of any size and produce a unique hash value of a fixed length. For example, no matter how long or short the input data is, the resulting hash from the secure hash algorithm (SHA) family will always be a fixed length, depending on the specific version used (256 bits for SHA-256). This predictable output length makes hashes useful for various security purposes, such as generating digital signatures, verifying file integrity and ensuring that stored passwords are securely obscured.

The SHA family is one of the most commonly used hashing families. Developed by the National Security Agency and NIST, SHA algorithms have evolved over time, starting with SHA-1 and progressing to the more secure versions SHA-2 and SHA-3. SHA-1, which produces a 160-bit hash value, is now considered insecure and deprecated due to vulnerabilities that allow for hash collisions, where different inputs produce the same hash value. SHA-2, which includes SHA-224, SHA-256, SHA-384 and SHA-512, is currently the standard for secure hashing.

SHA-256, part of the SHA-2 family, is one of the most widely used hashing algorithms. It produces a 256-bit (32-byte) hash value, usually represented as a 64-character hexadecimal number. The process involves taking the input data and applying multiple rounds of bitwise operations, modular additions and compression functions to scramble the data and produce a seemingly random hash output. Even a small change in the input data, such as changing one character, results in a completely different hash, a property known as the avalanche effect. This ensures that hashes are sensitive to input variations, making it virtually impossible to guess the original input based on the hash.

The SHA-2 family is highly secure and resistant to most types of cryptographic attacks, such as preimage attacks (where an attacker tries to reverse-engineer the input from the hash) and collision attacks (where an attacker tries to find two different inputs that produce the same hash). This security makes SHA-256 a preferred choice for applications such as securing digital certificates, validating software downloads and protecting blockchain data. However, as technology continues to advance, there is always the need to remain vigilant against potential vulnerabilities, especially in a future where quantum computing, as it evolves, could challenge current cryptographic standards.

To prepare for future threats, the cryptographic community developed SHA-3, a newer member of the SHA family, standardised in 2015. Unlike SHA-2, which uses a Merkle–Damgård construction, SHA-3 is based on the Keccak cryptographic sponge construction.

This design offers a different method of hashing, making SHA-3 an alternative resistant to specific attacks that could potentially affect SHA-2. SHA-3 algorithms, such as SHA3-256, provide the same level of hash output security as their SHA-2 counterparts, but their internal structure is fundamentally different, offering an extra layer of robustness.

Hashing is not used to secure data in transit or encrypt it for confidentiality, but rather to ensure data integrity and securely store information. For example, passwords stored in a database are hashed so that even if the database is compromised, attackers cannot easily recover the original passwords. When a user attempts to log in, the system hashes the provided password and compares it to the stored hash. If the hashes match, access is granted. Hashing also plays a critical role in digital signatures and certificates, where it helps to verify that data has not been tampered with.

Salting

Salting is the process of adding a random value mathematically (the salt) to a password before hashing it. This technique enhances security by preventing attacks such as rainbow table and precomputed hash attacks due to a longer length and the salt having to be cracked as well as the password.

When a user creates a password, a unique salt is generated and combined with the password before hashing. The resulting hash is then stored alongside the salt. During authentication, the system retrieves the salt, appends it to the entered password and hashes it again to verify the match.

By using salts, even if two users have the same password, their stored hashes will be different. This makes it significantly harder for attackers to crack passwords using precomputed hash databases. For added security, salts should be long, random and unique for each password.

FIPS

FIPS is a set of standards developed by NIST for use in computer systems by non-military US government agencies and contractors. These standards ensure a minimum level of security and interoperability for sensitive but unclassified information. FIPS 140 is a series of security standards specifically for cryptographic modules, covering their design, implementation and operation. The most well-known are FIPS 140-2 and FIPS 140-3, which define security requirements for cryptographic modules that handle sensitive data.

FIPS 140-2

FIPS 140-2 (released in 2001, superseded by FIPS 140-3 in 2019) specifies four security levels, each increasing in security and assurance.

FIPS 140-2 security levels

Level 1 – Basic security

- There are no physical security requirements beyond using an approved cryptographic algorithm.

- Software or hardware implementation is allowed.
- There is no mandatory role-based authentication.

Level 2 – Enhanced physical security

- This adds requirements for role-based authentication.
- Tamper-evident coatings or seals are required to detect physical access attempts.
- Software or hardware implementation is allowed.

Level 3 – High security

- This requires identity-based authentication.
- Tamper-resistant mechanisms are used to prevent access.
- Physical security is used to protect against key extraction.
- Cryptographic keys must be zeroized (erased) if the module is tampered with.

Level 4 – Highest security

- Physical security provides strong resistance against attacks, including environmental conditions.
- There is protection against tampering in extreme temperatures and voltages.
- Zeroization must occur upon any security compromise.

FIPS 140-3

FIPS 140-3, which replaced FIPS 140-2 in 2019, is based on ISO/IEC 19790:2012 (now replaced by ISO/IEC 19790:2025). It retains the four security levels but introduces stricter testing requirements, modernised security requirements and additional protection mechanisms. The levels in FIPS 140-3 are essentially the same as FIPS 140-2 but incorporate updates in cryptographic best practices, testing methodologies and vulnerability assessment frameworks.

FIPS 203, 205 and 205

FIPS 203, 204 and 205 focus on data in use, particularly in cloud computing and trusted execution environments. New cryptography standards for these were approved on 14 August 2024, specifying the latest digital signature schemes. FIPS 203 specifies Module-Lattice-Based Key Encapsulation Mechanism (ML-KEM). ML-KEM is derived from the CRYSTALS Kyber algorithm and is intended as the primary standard for general encryption. FIPS 204 specifies the Module-Lattice-Based Digital Signature Algorithm (ML-DSA), which is derived from the CRYSTALS-Dilithium submission. FIPS 205 specifies the Stateless Hash-Based Digital Signature Algorithm (SLH-DSA), which is derived from the SPHINCS+ submission.

ML-DSA   The ML-DSA is a cryptographic scheme designed to provide digital signatures with post-quantum security. It is based on the hardness of problems related to module lattices, a specialised structure within lattice-based cryptography. This makes ML-DSA resistant to attacks from both classical and quantum computers, ensuring its viability in a post-quantum era. The underlying security of ML-DSA comes from the difficulty of solving problems such as the shortest vector problem (SVP) or LWE within module lattices.

Module lattices are a more structured and efficient generalisation of standard lattices, allowing ML-DSA to achieve computational efficiency without compromising on security. The algorithm follows the general principles of digital signature schemes: it guarantees authenticity, integrity and non-repudiation. Specifically, a private key is sampled from the lattice and the corresponding public key is derived in a way that maintains efficiency and security. Signatures are generated using a lattice-based trapdoor mechanism, which allows the signer to create a valid signature for a message while ensuring that the process remains computationally secure. Verification is performed using the public key to confirm the signature's validity, without exposing the private key.

One of the primary advantages of ML-DSA is its quantum resistance, as it is built to withstand attacks from quantum computers. The use of module lattices also improves efficiency by reducing key sizes and computation time, compared to generic lattice-based approaches.

SLH-DSA   SLH-DSA is a cryptographic scheme designed for digital signatures in the security of cryptographic hash functions. As a member of the post-quantum cryptography family, SLH-DSA is highly resistant to quantum and classical attacks, making it an ideal choice for securing digital systems in the face of advancing quantum technologies. It differs from traditional hash-based signature schemes by eliminating the need for maintaining a state during signing, which simplifies implementation and reduces the risk of mismanagement.

SLH-DSA uses one-time or few-time signature mechanisms, such as Lamport or Winternitz signatures, which rely solely on the security of the underlying hash function. These signatures are constructed to be computationally efficient and easy to verify. To address scalability challenges and enable the signing of multiple messages without requiring state tracking, SLH-DSA uses a hierarchical structure of hash-based signatures. This structure allows the creation of a virtually unlimited number of signatures while maintaining the security of individual key pairs.

However, SLH-DSA is not without its limitations. A key challenge is the relatively large size of signatures and public keys compared to traditional algorithms. These larger sizes can pose storage and transmission challenges, particularly in resource-constrained environments. Additionally, the hierarchical structure introduces some computational overhead, though this is generally outweighed by the benefits of being stateless.

SLH-DSA is particularly well-suited for applications requiring long-term security and robustness against future quantum threats. Its use cases include secure software updates, blockchain technologies and systems requiring reliable authentication.

How hashing works

Hashing is a cryptographic process that transforms input data of any length into a fixed-length output called a hash or digest (Figure 5.6). The output hash is a seemingly random sequence of numbers and letters, and it serves as a unique representation of the original data. The key aspect of hashing is that it is a one-way function. Once data is hashed, it is computationally infeasible to reverse the process and retrieve the original input.

Figure 5.6 Producing a message digest or hash

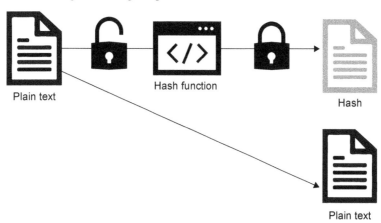

Input and hash function

The hashing process starts with an input, which can be a text, file or any other form of digital data. This input is then passed through a hash function, a mathematical algorithm designed to scramble the input data and generate a fixed-length hash value. Regardless of the size of the input, the output hash will always have the same length, which depends on the specific hash algorithm being used.

For example, the SHA-256 algorithm from the SHA-2 family always produces a 256-bit hash value (32 bytes), even if the input is a single character or a large file. This fixed-length output ensures uniformity and makes it easy to compare hashes.

Data transformation and scrambling

Hash functions apply a series of mathematical transformations to the input data. These transformations include bitwise operations (such as AND, OR and XOR), shifts and modular additions. The input data is often divided into blocks, and the hash function processes each block through multiple rounds of computation.

These operations are designed to achieve two key properties:

- **Diffusion:** This property ensures that every bit of the input affects many bits of the hash output. A small change in the input, such as modifying a single character, causes a completely different hash value. This behaviour, known as the avalanche effect, is crucial for making the hash unpredictable.

- **Confusion:** The relationship between the input and the hash output is deliberately obscured, making it hard for anyone to infer the original data from the hash.

Fixed-length hash output

After processing all the input data, the hash function generates a fixed-length output. For example, SHA-256 produces a 256-bit hash, represented as a 64-character hexadecimal string. The fixed length makes hash values easy to store, compare and use in digital systems.

Key properties of hashing

Hash functions have several essential properties that make them useful for security purposes:

- **Deterministic:** The same input always produces the same hash value. This consistency is critical for data integrity verification.

- **Irreversibility:** It is computationally infeasible to reverse-engineer the original input from the hash value. This one-way property ensures that even if an attacker has the hash, they cannot retrieve the original data.

- **Collision resistance:** A hash function should make it extremely difficult to find two different inputs that produce the same hash value (known as a collision). Strong collision resistance ensures the security and reliability of the hash function.

- **Avalanche effect:** A slight change in the input should result in a vastly different hash output. This ensures that even small alterations in the data are easily detectable.

How SHA hash functions work

To illustrate how hashing works, let's look at the SHA-256 algorithm in more detail:

- **Input pre-processing:** The input data is first padded to ensure its length is a multiple of 512 bits. Padding involves adding a 1-bit followed by enough zeros to reach the required length, and the total length of the original input is appended as well.

- **Block processing:** The padded data is divided into 512-bit blocks and SHA-256 processes each block through a series of rounds.

- **Initialisation and compression:** SHA-256 starts with a set of initial hash values, which are constants derived from the fractional parts of the square roots of the first eight prime numbers. Each block of data is then processed through 64 rounds of compression, where bitwise operations and modular arithmetic scramble the data.

- **Final hash value:** After processing all the blocks, the final hash value is produced by combining the results from the compression rounds. The output is a 256-bit hash that serves as the unique fingerprint of the input data.

Applications of hashing

- **Data integrity verification:** Hashes are used to ensure data has not been tampered with. For example, when downloading a file, the hash value provided by the file's source can be compared with the hash of the downloaded file to verify its integrity.

- **Password security:** In password management, passwords are hashed before being stored in databases. When a user logs in, the system hashes the provided password and compares it with the stored hash. If the hashes match, the user is authenticated.

- **Digital signatures and certificates:** Hashing is used in digital signatures to provide a unique fingerprint of the data being signed. This ensures the authenticity and integrity of the signed document.

- **Blockchain technology:** Hashing is fundamental in blockchain, where it is used to secure and link blocks of data. The hash of each block is included in the next block, creating a tamper-proof chain.

Homomorphic encryption

Homomorphic encryption is a form of encryption that allows computations to be performed on encrypted data without decrypting it, ensuring data remains confidential even while being processed. The result of computations on encrypted data, when decrypted, matches the result of operations performed as if it had been conducted in plaintext.

One of the main characteristics of homomorphic encryption is data privacy, as it ensures that sensitive data can be processed without exposure. This is particularly beneficial in areas of high confidentiality such as government, healthcare, finance and military. It also supports operations on encrypted data, which can include addition, multiplication or both, depending on the type of homomorphism. Partially homomorphic encryption (PHE) supports either addition or multiplication, somewhat homomorphic encryption (SHE) supports limited operations with constraints and fully homomorphic encryption (FHE) supports arbitrary computations, allowing both addition and multiplication to be performed an unlimited number of times.

The security of homomorphic encryption is complex mathematical problems that are difficult to solve, such as lattice-based cryptography, making it resistant to conventional cryptographic attacks.

Applications of homomorphic encryption include secure data analysis, enabling analysis of sensitive data without exposing the raw data, cloud computing, allowing encrypted data to be processed while maintaining privacy, and encrypted search, facilitating searching over encrypted data without revealing the content or search queries.

However, there are challenges associated with homomorphic encryption. It tends to be computationally intensive and slower compared to traditional encryption methods due to the complex mathematical operations required. Developing and implementing homomorphic encryption systems is complex and requires a deep understanding of cryptography and mathematics. While FHE provides the most flexibility, it is not yet practical for all applications due to its high computational overhead. Ongoing development aims to make it more efficient and practical for broader use, though.

CLOUD

Cloud refers to the use of remote servers hosted on the internet to store, manage and process data, rather than relying on local servers or personal computers. It allows for on-demand access to a shared pool of configurable resources, such as servers, storage, databases and applications.

NIST 800-145 definition of cloud computing

> Cloud computing is a model for enabling ubiquitous, convenient, on-demand network access to a shared pool of configurable computing resources (e.g., networks, servers, storage, applications and services) that can be rapidly provisioned and released with minimal management effort or service provider interaction. This cloud model is composed of five essential characteristics, three service models and four deployment models (Mell and Grance, 2011).

There are now numerous cloud-based services, such as hosted email, photo sharing, streaming of video and music and social media. Many organisations will have some form of cloud for storage, third-party service or replication of the entire network. Cloud is often chosen as it is an operational expenditure, which means it can be paid for monthly, as opposed to on-premises equipment, which is more commonly a capital expenditure to pay for new on-premises devices such as a server.

For smaller organisations, cloud solutions can provide access to powerful computing tools that would previously have been out of their financial reach. These include such offerings as Microsoft's Office 365®, in which, rather than buying multiple copies of the MS Office suite of programs, individual users, small organisations and large organisations can subscribe to the online service, which includes an element of cloud storage and information sharing between teams.

Some of the advantages of using the cloud are:

- on-demand self-service;
- distributed storage;
- rapid elasticity;
- automated management;
- broad network access;
- resource pooling;
- measured service;
- virtualisation technology.

The NIST cloud computing reference architecture defines five major actors:

- **Cloud consumer:** A person or organisation that uses cloud computing services.
- **Cloud provider:** A person or organisation providing services to interested parties.
- **Cloud carrier privacy:** An intermediary for providing connectivity and transport services between cloud consumers and providers.
- **Cloud auditor:** A party for making independent assessments of cloud service controls.
- **Cloud broker:** An entity that manages cloud services in terms of use, performance and delivery and maintains the relationship between cloud providers and consumers.

Cloud computing types of service

- **Infrastructure as a service (IaaS)** provides virtual machines (VMs) and other hardware including OS, which may be controlled through a service API. Examples are Amazon Elastic Compute Cloud (EC2) and Microsoft Azure.
- **Platform as a service (PaaS)** offers on-demand development tools, configuration management and deployment platforms that can be used by subscribers to develop custom applications. Examples are Google App Engine, Microsoft Azure, Oracle Cloud Platform, Amazon Web Services (AWS) Lambda and Salesforce.
- **Software as a service (SaaS)** offers on-demand software to subscribers over the internet, such as web-based office applications. Examples are Google Docs, Zoom, Adobe Creative Cloud and Shopify.

Cloud deployment models

- **Public cloud** services are supplied over a network that is open for public use.
- **Community cloud** is a shared infrastructure between several organisations collaborating on a common goal and with common concerns of security.
- **Private cloud** is where all hardware and software resources are used exclusively and are accessible only by a single customer.

Cloud security

Cloud security is made up of technology, policy, procedures and security controls that are used to address internal and external security. Cloud security is used to ensure the privacy of data and address security concerns of the organisation around cloud usage. Regarding control of cloud access for users, devices and software, when using the cloud it is not always clear where the data is being stored. Users may inadvertently move data to a less secure location, increasing the risk of unauthorised access. I have heard of incidents where a third party has accidentally left customer data in a test environment that was publicly accessible. An organisation that created applications accidentally pushed an application in development into production and it contained a cloud admin password. After 20 seconds the developer realised and pulled the application down.

However, within 15 seconds attackers had gained access to the organisation's cloud and started to set up a bitcoin mining operation.

OWASP Top 10 2022 cloud security

The OWASP Top 10 highlights the top 10 most critical cloud security risks. Each of the risks are in a ranked order based on frequency, severity and magnitude for impact.

R1. **Accountability and data ownership:** Using the public cloud for hosting organisational services can cause severe risk for the recoverability of data.

R2. **User identity federation:** Creating multiple user identities for different cloud providers makes it complex to manage multiple user IDs and credentials.

R3. **Regulatory compliance:** There is a lack of transparency and there are different regulatory laws in different countries.

R4. **Organisation continuity and resiliency:** There can be organisational risk or monetary loss if the cloud provider handles the organisation's continuity improperly.

R5. **User privacy and secondary usage of data:** The default share feature in social websites can jeopardise the privacy of users' personal data.

R6. **Service and data integration:** Unsecured data in transit is susceptible to eavesdropping and interception attacks.

R7. **Multi-tenancy and physical security:** Poor logical segregation may lead to tenants interfering with the security features of other tenants.

R8. **Incidence analysis and forensic support:** Due to the distributed storage of logs across the cloud, law enforcement agencies may face problems in forensics recovery.

R9. **Infrastructure security:** Misconfiguration of infrastructure may allow network scanning for vulnerable applications and services.

R10. **Non-production environment exposure:** Using non-production environments increases the risk of unauthorised access, information disclosure and information modification.

It is also worth noting that attackers have generally relied upon stolen credentials and access tokens that did not require MFA to gain initial access to cloud and hybrid environments. With the adoption of MFA and increased security awareness there has been a shift towards social engineering with targeted campaigns to lure users into providing credentials and some highly innovative methods to circumvent MFA or exploit weaknesses in its implementation.

CASE STUDY

Cloud security architecture in a healthcare organisation

Scenario
A large healthcare provider managing sensitive patient data decided to transition to a hybrid cloud environment to improve operational efficiency, enable remote access to medical records and support emerging technologies such as telemedicine and AI-based diagnostics. However, the migration required a security-first approach to ensure compliance with stringent healthcare regulations such as HIPAA and GDPR while maintaining the trust of patients and stakeholders. The project focused on establishing a robust cloud security architecture tailored to the healthcare sector.

Focus areas

Design of a secure cloud architecture
The hybrid cloud architecture integrated on-premises systems with public cloud platforms, ensuring scalability while retaining control over critical systems:

- **Hybrid environment integration:** Core systems, such as health records and imaging data, remained on-premises for better control and security, while non-critical workloads, including scheduling and patient communications, were migrated to the cloud.

- **Zero trust framework:** All access to cloud resources was governed by a zero trust model, requiring continuous verification of user identities and device compliance.

- **Multi-cloud security management:** Centralised management tools were deployed to enforce consistent security policies across multiple cloud providers.

Data encryption strategies
Data protection was a top priority, given the sensitivity of healthcare records:

- **End-to-end encryption:** Patient data was encrypted both in transit and at rest using AES-256.

- **Tokenisation:** Identifiable patient data was tokenised before being transferred to the cloud, ensuring additional protection against data breaches.

- **Key management:** Encryption keys were centrally managed through hardware security modules, allowing the organisation to maintain exclusive control over encryption keys.

Cloud-native security tools

Use of cloud-native capabilities enabled the healthcare provider to integrate security more seamlessly into its workflows:

- **IAM:** RBACs were implemented to restrict user access to only the data and systems necessary for their roles.
- **Cloud security posture management:** Automated tools continuously monitored for misconfigurations, such as improperly configured storage buckets, which could expose patient data.
- **Threat detection, managed detection and response:** Services provided real-time insights into potential threats and unusual activity patterns in the cloud environment.

Secure data sharing across the organisation to enable collaboration while safeguarding patient privacy:

- **Secure APIs:** Data sharing between cloud applications and on-premises systems was facilitated through encrypted APIs.
- **DLP:** Policies were enforced to prevent the unauthorised sharing of sensitive data, both internally and externally.
- **Auditing and monitoring:** All access and data-sharing activities were logged and regularly audited to ensure compliance with healthcare regulations.

Challenges

Balancing security and accessibility

Ensuring clinicians and researchers could quickly access critical data without compromising security was a significant challenge. Adaptive authentication mechanisms, such as context-aware access (e.g. location and device type), were implemented to maintain accessibility while protecting sensitive data.

Managing data residency concerns

Regulations such as GDPR required patient data to remain within specific geographical regions. The organisation worked with cloud providers offering region-specific data centres to ensure compliance and implemented controls to prevent data from being transferred across borders.

Integrating security controls across multiple cloud providers

The hybrid cloud environment included multiple providers, each with its own tools and configurations. A centralised SOC was established to standardise controls, monitor activities and streamline incident response across the diverse environment.

Outcomes

Enhanced patient data protection
The deployment of encryption, tokenisation and robust access controls ensured that sensitive patient data was protected against breaches. A third-party audit confirmed compliance with HIPAA and GDPR, bolstering the organisation's reputation for safeguarding patient privacy.

Successful implementation of access controls
The adoption of IAM and context-aware access controls improved user experiences by streamlining secure access for authorised personnel while effectively preventing unauthorised access attempts.

Improved incident response in a cloud context
Incident response workflows were adapted to the cloud environment, leveraging automation to rapidly identify and mitigate threats. For example, during a simulated phishing attack targeting cloud-based email systems, automated detection tools flagged and quarantined malicious emails, preventing unauthorised access to patient data.

Key learnings

- Early engagement with legal and compliance teams ensures that security solutions align with regional and sector-specific regulations.

- Making use of cloud-native tools provides cost-effective, scalable security while reducing the operational burden on internal teams.

- Hybrid cloud environments require strong governance frameworks to prevent misconfigurations and ensure data residency requirements are met.

- Continuous monitoring and regular incident simulations are critical for maintaining resilience in dynamic cloud environments.

- A phased migration strategy allows organisations to address security challenges incrementally while maintaining service continuity.

EDGE COMPUTING

Edge computing is a distributed and decentralised computing model that brings data processing, storage and analysis closer to the data source, or 'edge', of the network, rather than relying on a centralised data centre or the cloud. This approach aims to reduce latency, enhance response times and improve the efficiency of data-driven applications. By processing data locally at extremely high speed, edge computing enables more immediate and actionable insights, which is crucial for applications that require real-time or near-real-time performance.

How edge computing works

The traditional model of cloud computing involves sending data from devices to a centralised server or data centre for processing and analysis. However, this model can introduce significant latency, especially when dealing with large amounts of data or when the centralised servers are located far away from the data source. In contrast, edge computing places computation and storage capabilities near the location where data is generated, such as on edge devices (IoT sensors, routers or gateways) or local servers.

For example, consider an autonomous vehicle that needs to make split-second decisions while navigating traffic. If data from the car's sensors were sent to a distant cloud data centre for processing, the delay would be too long to ensure safe operation. Instead, edge computing enables data to be processed within the vehicle itself, allowing for ultra-fast decision-making and increased safety.

Benefits of edge computing

- **Reduced latency:** By processing data closer to where it is generated, edge computing minimises the delay associated with data transmission to distant servers. This is crucial for real-time applications such as industrial automation, augmented reality (AR) and autonomous systems.

- **Enhanced bandwidth efficiency:** Due to edge computing reducing the need to transmit all raw data over the network to a centralised location, it conserves bandwidth and reduces network congestion. Only essential or summarised data may need to be sent to the cloud for long-term storage or analysis.

- **Improved data privacy and security:** Edge computing can help to improve data privacy and security by keeping sensitive data on local devices rather than transmitting it to remote servers. This is particularly important in sectors like healthcare and finance, where data privacy regulations are stringent.

- **Increased reliability and resilience:** Due to processing data locally, edge systems can continue to function even when there is limited or no connectivity to central servers. This makes edge computing ideal for remote or critical operations, such as those in remote oil fields or disaster response scenarios.

- **Scalability:** Edge computing enables the efficient scaling of applications across a wide network of distributed devices, making it suitable for large-scale IoT deployments.

Applications of edge computing

Edge computing is now found in a variety of real-time and high-stakes applications such as:

- **Autonomous vehicles:** Autonomous cars and drones rely heavily on edge computing to process vast amounts of sensor data, including inputs from cameras, light detection and ranging (LiDAR) – which is a remote sensing technology that uses laser pulses to measure distances and generate precise 3D maps of objects and environments – and radar to make driving decisions in real time. The onboard edge computing systems perform tasks such as obstacle detection, path planning and speed control to ensure safety and efficiency. Since even a fraction of a second's delay could lead to catastrophic outcomes, edge computing is critical to the successful deployment of self-driving vehicles.

- **Industrial automation and control:** In Industry 4.0 environments, edge computing supports industrial IoT (IIoT) systems that manage and monitor machinery in factories. By using edge devices to process data from sensors and actuators locally, industrial systems can automate processes and detect potential failures almost instantly. This leads to more efficient production lines, reduced downtime and predictive maintenance capabilities. For example, if a temperature sensor detects that a piece of equipment is overheating, the local edge system can shut down the machine immediately to prevent damage.

- **Smart cities and infrastructure:** Edge computing plays a vital role in smart city initiatives, where a network of connected devices monitors and manages urban infrastructure. For instance, edge devices in smart traffic lights can analyse traffic patterns in real time to optimise traffic flow, reducing congestion and improving emergency response times. Similarly, in smart buildings, edge computing can manage lighting, heating and security systems for greater energy efficiency and safety.

- **Healthcare and medical devices:** In healthcare, real-time data processing is critical for applications such as remote patient monitoring, robotic surgery and emergency medical services. Edge computing allows medical devices to process and analyse data close to the patient, enabling timely interventions. For example, wearable health monitors can track vital signs and alert healthcare providers of abnormalities in real time, even in areas with poor network connectivity.

- **Kiosks and retail automation:** Retail environments use edge computing for automated checkouts, digital kiosks and inventory management. Smart kiosks process data locally to deliver personalised customer experiences, such as recommending products based on past purchases. Edge-enabled cameras and sensors can also monitor stock levels in real time and alert staff when shelves need restocking, streamlining operations and enhancing the shopping experience.

- **Military and defence:** Edge computing is critical for defence and military applications, where reliable and secure data processing is necessary in the field. In battlefield environments, drones and other surveillance systems need to analyse and react to data without relying on distant data centres. Edge computing enables real-time situational awareness, threat detection and decision support, even in remote or adversarial environments where network connectivity may be limited or compromised.

- **AR and virtual reality (VR):** Edge computing enhances AR and VR experiences by minimising latency and ensuring smooth interactions. In applications such as remote assistance, training or gaming, even slight delays can disrupt the experience. By processing data at the edge, these technologies can deliver immersive and responsive user experiences.

Challenges and considerations

While edge computing offers numerous benefits, it also comes with its own set of challenges:

- **Infrastructure and deployment complexity:** Setting up and managing a distributed network of edge devices can be complex, requiring careful planning and orchestration.

- **Security risks:** Although edge computing can improve data privacy by keeping data local, the distributed nature of edge devices introduces new attack vectors. Each device must be secured to prevent tampering and data breaches.

- **Data management:** Handling and managing data across a distributed network can be challenging, especially when determining which data to process locally and which to send to the cloud for long-term storage and analysis.

- **Resource constraints:** Edge devices often have limited processing power and storage compared to centralised data centres, which can limit the complexity of algorithms and analyses that can be performed locally.

FOG COMPUTING

Fog computing, often referred to as fog networking or fog architecture, is a distributed computing model that extends cloud computing closer to the 'edge' of the network. It creates an intermediary layer between edge devices and centralised cloud servers to improve the efficiency and speed of data processing, storage and analysis. In a fog computing environment, computing resources (such as processing power, storage and networking) are distributed across devices that are located between the data source (edge devices) and the cloud infrastructure.

Fog computing can be thought of as a 'fog layer' that sits between the edge (where data is generated) and the cloud (where large-scale processing and storage occur). It enables data processing at intermediate nodes, such as local routers, gateways or servers, rather than transmitting all data to central cloud data centres.

How fog computing works

Fog computing operates on a decentralised model that uses local processing nodes situated geographically closer to the data source. The edge devices (IoT devices, sensors and smart devices) collect and transmit data and, instead of sending all this data directly to the cloud for processing, the fog layer processes it locally, reducing the need for long-distance data transfer.

Key components of fog computing include:

- **Edge devices** (e.g. IoT sensors, cameras or smart machines) generate data. They can be equipped with limited computing capabilities and typically operate as the starting point for data collection.

- **Fog nodes** are intermediary nodes that process, store and analyse the data before sending relevant insights to the cloud. Fog nodes can be located on local routers, gateways or intermediate servers that are strategically placed between the edge devices and the cloud infrastructure.

- **Cloud servers** provide the centralised infrastructure where large-scale storage, advanced analytics and complex computations are performed. However, the data sent to the cloud typically undergoes filtering and processing in the fog layer before transmission.

In a typical fog computing system, data flows as follows:

- **Data generation:** Edge devices (e.g. sensors or cameras) collect data.

- **Initial processing:** Fog nodes (local gateways or servers) process data locally, filtering and aggregating it to reduce redundancy.

- **Cloud transmission:** Only essential or summarised data is sent to the cloud for further analysis, long-term storage or advanced computations.

By processing data closer to the source, fog computing addresses the limitations of cloud computing, such as high latency, bandwidth constraints and dependency on centralised data centres.

Benefits of fog computing

- **Reduced latency:** Fog computing minimises the delay associated with data transmission by processing it locally. This is crucial for real-time applications where quick responses are essential, such as in autonomous vehicles or smart manufacturing.

- **Bandwidth efficiency:** By processing data locally, fog computing reduces the amount of raw data that needs to be sent to the cloud, conserving bandwidth. This is particularly important in environments with limited connectivity or high data volume.

- **Enhanced security and privacy:** Fog computing can improve security and privacy by keeping sensitive data on local devices or servers, reducing the need for data to travel over networks to distant cloud data centres.

- **Optimised data flow:** The fog layer acts as an intermediary that filters, processes and aggregates data before it is transmitted to the cloud. This ensures that only relevant or summarised data is sent, improving data management and reducing congestion.

- **Resilience and reliability:** By decentralising computation, fog computing enables more reliable systems. If a cloud server experiences downtime or connectivity issues, the fog layer can continue to operate independently, ensuring that critical operations are not disrupted.

- **Scalability:** Fog computing enables efficient scaling of applications across a distributed network of devices, ensuring that infrastructure and services can grow dynamically in response to demand.

Fog vs edge computing

- Edge computing focuses on processing data directly at the device or sensor level (i.e. 'on the edge'). It aims to reduce latency by processing data as close as possible to the data source.

- Fog computing extends this concept by adding an intermediate layer (fog nodes) between the edge devices and the cloud. These fog nodes handle more complex processing and storage than edge devices and are geographically distributed to serve as a bridge between the cloud and edge devices.

- Edge computing typically processes and stores data at the device level or local node, while fog computing decentralises this process across a wider network of intermediate devices.

Fog vs cloud computing

- Cloud computing is a centralised model that performs large-scale data processing, storage and analytics in remote data centres. It is well-suited for heavy workloads and long-term storage.

- Fog computing complements cloud computing by processing data closer to where it is generated. It provides a layer of intelligence between edge devices and cloud servers to handle real-time applications, local data processing and resource management, reducing the dependency on the cloud for time-sensitive tasks.

- While cloud computing excels at handling large datasets, fog computing is ideal for latency-sensitive applications that require faster decision-making.

Applications of fog computing

Fog computing is particularly beneficial for use cases that require real-time processing, low latency and local decision-making. Below are some examples where fog computing is applied effectively.

Smart cities and urban infrastructure

In smart cities, fog computing enables the collection and processing of real-time data from various sensors (e.g. traffic lights, CCTV cameras, environmental monitoring systems). For example:

- **Traffic management:** Fog nodes analyse traffic flow data in real time, enabling traffic lights to adjust based on traffic conditions, thereby reducing congestion and improving traffic safety.

- **Smart lighting:** Streetlights can adjust brightness based on local conditions, such as time of day, weather or traffic flow, thereby improving energy efficiency and safety.

IIoT and manufacturing

Fog computing is used in industrial automation and smart factories to improve operational efficiency, predictive maintenance and automation. By processing data locally, fog nodes can monitor equipment, detect anomalies and trigger real-time actions to prevent failures.

- **Predictive maintenance:** Fog computing analyses data from machinery sensors to predict failures before they occur, allowing for proactive maintenance and reducing downtime.
- **Real-time monitoring:** Fog nodes process operational data locally, providing managers with real-time visibility into manufacturing processes and equipment performance.

Autonomous vehicles

In the context of autonomous vehicles, fog computing processes data from sensors (such as LiDAR, cameras and global positioning systems (GPS)) in real time, allowing vehicles to make split-second decisions without needing to rely on distant cloud servers. This ensures safe and reliable operation, particularly in scenarios with limited or unreliable connectivity.

Healthcare and remote monitoring

Fog computing enhances healthcare applications by providing local data processing and decision-making for real-time health monitoring. For instance:

- **Wearable devices:** Health-monitoring devices, such as smartwatches or biosensors, can process vital signs data locally and immediately alert healthcare providers if abnormal patterns are detected, without waiting for cloud processing.
- **Medical devices:** In critical care environments, fog computing enables medical equipment to process and analyse data from patients, making quick decisions that could save lives.

Smart grids and energy management

In smart grids, fog computing helps to optimise energy distribution by processing data locally at various nodes (e.g. substations, smart meters) and adjusting the flow of energy in response to real-time conditions:

- **Energy consumption optimisation:** Fog nodes analyse usage data from smart meters to optimise the distribution of electricity across the grid, improving efficiency and reducing waste.
- **Fault detection and recovery:** Fog computing can quickly detect faults in the grid and take corrective action, such as rerouting power or notifying maintenance crews.

Retail and customer experience

In retail, fog computing supports applications such as:

- **In-store kiosks:** Processing customer interaction data locally on kiosks or in-store devices allows for immediate responses to customer queries, such as personalised product recommendations.
- **Inventory management:** Fog computing can aggregate data from in-store sensors, tracking real-time inventory levels and enabling automatic stock replenishment.

Challenges and considerations

- **Complexity of deployment:** Setting up and managing a distributed fog network requires significant effort, including the configuration of local nodes, ensuring seamless integration and maintaining connectivity.

- **Security risks:** The decentralised nature of fog computing creates additional points of vulnerability. Proper security measures, including encryption, authentication and secure communication protocols, are essential to protect sensitive data.

- **Resource constraints:** Fog nodes may have limited computational power and storage compared to cloud data centres, which can restrict the types of processing and applications that can be supported locally.

- **Interoperability:** Ensuring that different fog nodes, edge devices and cloud systems can work together seamlessly requires standardisation and careful planning.

Future of fog computing

As IoT devices become increasingly widespread and the demand for real-time data processing grows, fog computing will continue to be a vital technology for many industries. Technologies such as 5G and AI will further enhance fog computing by providing the high-speed connectivity and advanced analytics necessary to support more complex, data-driven applications. Fog computing is expected to become more integrated with edge and cloud systems, providing organisations with a more flexible, efficient and scalable approach to data management and processing.

CONTAINERS

Containers are lightweight, self-contained packages that include an application and everything needed to run it, such as libraries, configuration files, binaries and other dependencies (Figure 5.7). This encapsulation ensures that the application is isolated from its underlying environment and other processes running on the same system. By abstracting the application from the OS, containers eliminate compatibility issues and ensure consistent performance across diverse deployment environments. Whether running in a private data centre, public cloud or on a developer's local machine, containers maintain the same functionality and behaviour. This consistency significantly simplifies the development lifecycle and reduces the 'it works on my machine' problem that often arises when moving applications between environments.

One of the most notable features of containers is their ability to run independently of the host system's configuration. They can utilise a shared OS kernel but keep the application and its dependencies isolated. This allows containers to be lightweight compared to VMs, which require a full OS for each instance. As a result, containers are more resource-efficient, enabling higher density on the same hardware. They can be quickly created and destroyed, supporting agile development practices and rapid scaling based on workload demands. This dynamic behaviour makes containers ideal for microservices architectures, where applications are broken into smaller, independently deployable services.

Figure 5.7 Container architecture

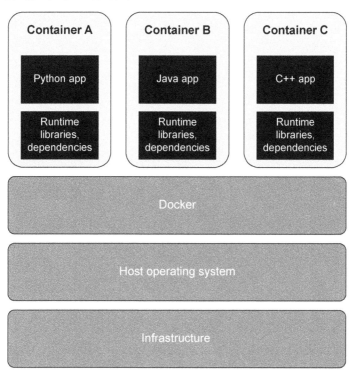

Portability is another cornerstone of container technology. Because containers include all necessary components and dependencies, they can seamlessly move across different environments, such as on-premises infrastructure, public cloud platforms (e.g. AWS, Azure and Google Cloud) or hybrid cloud setups. This portability ensures that developers can build and test applications in an environment that mirrors production, reducing integration issues and deployment failures. The ability to easily move containers across environments also supports modern DevOps workflows, enabling faster and more reliable software delivery.

Additionally, containers promote security by isolating applications. This isolation minimises the risk of interference or compromise between applications running on the same host. If one container is breached or malfunctions, the damage is limited to that specific container. Using automation such as Kubernetes, a new container can be quickly spun up to support availability. Combined with practices such as image scanning and runtime security policies, containers should be used to enhance the overall security of an organisation's infrastructure.

They provide a streamlined, consistent and secure way to build, deploy and run applications across a wide range of environments, together with their lightweight nature, resource efficiency, portability and ability to support modern software development like microservices and DevSecOps.

Container vulnerabilities

- **Impetuous image creation:** This is careless creation of images by not considering the security safeguards or control aspects, using unsafe or untested code.

- **Unreliable third-party resources:** Untrusted third-party resources make the resources vulnerable to malicious attacks.

- **Unauthorised access:** Gaining access to the user accounts leads to privilege escalation attacks.

- **Insecure container runtime configurations:** Improper handling of the configuration option and mounting sensitive directories on the host can cause faulty and insecure runtime configurations.

- **Data exposure in Docker files:** Docker images exposing sensitive information such as passwords and SSH encryption keys can be exploited to compromise the security of the container.

- **Embedded malware:** A container image may be embedded with malware after creation, or hard-coded functions may download malware after image deployment.

- **Non-updated images:** Outdated images may contain security loopholes and bugs that compromise the security of images.

- **Hijacked repository and infected resources:** Security misconfiguration and bugs may allow attackers to gain unauthorised access to the repository so that they can poison the resources by altering or deleting files.

- **Hijacked image registry:** Mismanaged configurations and vulnerabilities can be exploited to compromise the registry and image hubs.

- **Exposed services due to open ports:** Misconfiguration of an application may allow open ports that expose sensitive information upon port scanning.

- **Exploited applications:** Vulnerable applications can be exploited using various techniques such as SQLi, XSS and radio frequency interference (RFI).

- **Mixing of workload sensitivity levels:** Orchestrators place workloads having different sensitivity levels on the same host. One of the containers hosting a public webserver with vulnerabilities may pose a threat to the container processing sensitive information.

Cloud containerisation

Containers in the cloud are typically managed and orchestrated using container orchestration platforms such as Kubernetes, Docker Swarm or Amazon Elastic Container Service (ECS). These platforms provide tools and services for deploying, scaling and managing containerised applications in a cloud environment.

Kubernetes
Kubernetes is an open-source container orchestration platform that automates the deployment, scaling and management of containerised applications. Originally developed by Google and now maintained by the Cloud Native Computing Foundation, Kubernetes is designed to handle complex containerised applications at scale.

Core features

- **Automated deployment and rollouts:** Kubernetes manages the deployment of containers and can roll out updates seamlessly, ensuring zero downtime. It also supports rollbacks in case of deployment failures.

- **Scalability:** Kubernetes automatically scales applications based on resource utilisation or custom-defined metrics, ensuring optimal performance under varying workloads.

- **Self-healing:** If a container crashes, Kubernetes detects the issue and restarts or replaces it automatically, maintaining the desired state of the application.

- **Networking and service discovery:** Kubernetes provides built-in networking features, such as load balancing and service discovery, to enable seamless communication between services.

- **Deployment environments:** Kubernetes clusters are highly portable and can run on diverse infrastructures, including on-premises data centres, hybrid clouds and major public cloud providers such as Google Cloud (via Google Kubernetes Engine (GKE)), AWS (via Elastic Kubernetes Service (EKS)) and Azure (via Azure Kubernetes Service (AKS)).

Use case: Kubernetes is ideal for enterprises adopting microservices architectures or those requiring highly available, scalable and distributed systems. Its robust ecosystem includes tools such as Helm (for managing application packages) and Istio (for service mesh capabilities), further enhancing its capabilities.

Docker Swarm

Docker Swarm is a native clustering and orchestration tool for Docker containers. It simplifies managing and scaling containerised applications by treating a group of Docker hosts as a single virtual system. While not as feature rich as Kubernetes, Docker Swarm offers simplicity and ease of use, making it a great choice for smaller projects or teams already familiar with Docker.

Core features

- **Integrated with Docker:** Docker Swarm is built into the Docker engine, providing a seamless experience for developers using Docker containers. There's no need for additional installations or tools.

- **Declarative services:** Developers can define the desired state of their application, and Docker Swarm ensures that it is maintained.

- **Load balancing:** Docker Swarm automatically distributes incoming requests across the cluster, ensuring high availability.

- **Scalability:** With simple commands, developers can scale services up or down based on application requirements.

- **Deployment environments:** Docker Swarm is particularly suited for on-premises deployments or small-to-medium-scale applications that do not require the advanced features of Kubernetes.

Use case: It's best for teams already using Docker who need lightweight, easy-to-configure orchestration without the complexity of Kubernetes.

Amazon Elastic Container Service

Amazon ECS is a fully managed container orchestration service provided by AWS. It allows users to deploy, run and scale containerised applications seamlessly on AWS infrastructure. ECS is tightly integrated with other AWS services, such as IAM for security, CloudWatch for monitoring and Application Load Balancer for networking, offering a comprehensive ecosystem for container management.

Core features

- **AWS integration:** ECS integrates natively with AWS services, enabling features such as automatic scaling, secure identity management and seamless logging and monitoring.

- **Flexible deployment options:** Users can run ECS on AWS Fargate (a serverless compute engine) or EC2 instances for more control over the underlying infrastructure.

- **Task scheduling:** ECS supports scheduling tasks across the cluster based on resource requirements, availability or custom-defined parameters.

- **Cost optimisation:** With ECS on Fargate, users only pay for the resources consumed by containers, eliminating the need for managing and provisioning servers.

- **Deployment environments:** ECS is designed to run within AWS but supports hybrid architectures through AWS Outposts, enabling workloads to extend to on-premises environments.

Use case: ECS is ideal for organisations already invested in the AWS ecosystem, offering a tightly integrated, easy-to-use solution for container orchestration without the need to manage complex infrastructure.

Microservices

Microservices is an architectural style that structures an application as a collection of small, autonomous services, each designed to perform a single function or a set of related functions (Figure 5.8). Microservices and containers are closely related and often used together to enhance the benefits of a microservices architecture. Containers encapsulate a microservice along with its dependencies, ensuring that it runs consistently across different environments. This isolation helps to maintain the independence of each microservice, preventing conflicts and making deployments more predictable. Containers can be easily scaled up or down, facilitating the horizontal scaling of microservices. Each microservice can be scaled independently based on its load, optimising resource utilisation. Containers provide a lightweight, portable environment that can run on any system. This portability aligns with the microservices principle of being able to deploy services independently across different environments.

Figure 5.8 Microservices

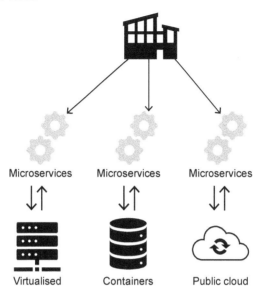

Microservices	Microservices	Microservices
Virtualised	Containers	Public cloud

Docker

Docker is an open-source platform designed to simplify the creation, deployment, management and operation of containers. It enables developers to package applications with all necessary dependencies, including libraries, configuration files and binaries, into lightweight, portable containers that run consistently across different environments. This portability and consistency make Docker a key enabler of modern development practices, such as microservices and cloud-native architectures.

Comparison with VMs
While Docker is conceptually similar to VMs in that both isolate applications for better performance and security, Docker operates at the process level rather than at the OS level. VMs require a full OS installation, along with virtualised hardware resources, which can result in significant overhead. This makes VMs more resource-intensive, as each instance consumes central processing unit (CPU), memory and storage even when idle.

Docker containers, on the other hand, share the host OS kernel, eliminating the need for a separate OS per application. This drastically reduces resource consumption, enabling higher density on the same hardware. Containers are also faster to start and stop compared to VMs, as there is no need to boot a full OS. This agility not only improves operational efficiency but also reduces infrastructure costs, particularly in cloud environments where costs are tied to resource utilisation.

Resource efficiency and cost benefits
Docker's lightweight nature makes it particularly well-suited for cloud environments, where scaling resources on-demand is critical. Containers can be spun up or down within seconds, consuming resources only when active. This leads to optimised utilisation of

145

compute resources, which directly translates into cost savings. In cloud platforms such as AWS, Azure or Google Cloud, where pay-as-you-go pricing models dominate, Docker ensures organisations only pay for what they use. Moreover, its ability to reduce waste by consolidating workloads helps to further minimise expenses.

Integration with DevSecOps

The integration of Docker into DevSecOps pipelines is vital for maintaining security, efficiency and consistency across the software development lifecycle. Containers can be created, tested and deployed rapidly, enabling CI/CD. However, it's essential to embed security throughout this process:

- **Container image scanning:** Third-party and custom container images should undergo rigorous vulnerability scanning to ensure they do not introduce security risks. Tools such as Aqua Security, Trivy and Docker's built-in scanning features can help to detect issues in base images and application layers.

- **Role of immutable infrastructure:** Containers align well with the DevSecOps principle of immutable infrastructure, where containers are rebuilt from source and redeployed rather than patched in place, ensuring clean, consistent and secure deployments.

- **Automated security policies:** Security tools can be integrated into CI/CD pipelines to enforce policies, such as preventing the use of outdated or vulnerable base images.

Development and testing advantages

Docker also revolutionises development and testing processes. By using containers, developers can replicate production environments locally, ensuring that applications behave consistently across different stages of deployment. This eliminates the common 'works on my machine' problem and accelerates troubleshooting. Testing teams benefit from disposable and reproducible environments, where new test cases can be executed in isolated, clean containers without the risk of conflicts.

Ecosystem and community

Docker has a robust ecosystem supported by Docker Hub, a vast public repository of pre-built container images for a variety of applications and services. These images can be customised or used as-is to accelerate development. The active community around Docker ensures a continuous flow of innovations, updates and best practices.

In summary, Docker is a transformative tool for modern application development and deployment. By offering a lightweight, efficient alternative to VMs, it enables organisations to build scalable, cost-effective and secure solutions. Its alignment with DevSecOps principles ensures seamless integration into modern workflows, empowering developers to innovate quickly without compromising security or reliability.

ZERO TRUST

Zero trust is a security strategy. A misconception sometimes is that it is a product or service, when it is actually an approach for designing and implementing a set of security principles. Zero trust sees the network as hostile, and you treat it as if it has been compromised. Any device connected to the network should not have access to everything. Each and every request to access data has to be authenticated and authorised in line with the access policy. If the connection does not meet the access policy requirements, the connection is terminated.

A zero trust approach applies to the entire digital estate and should be part of the security and end-to-end strategy (Figure 5.9).

Figure 5.9 Zero trust security

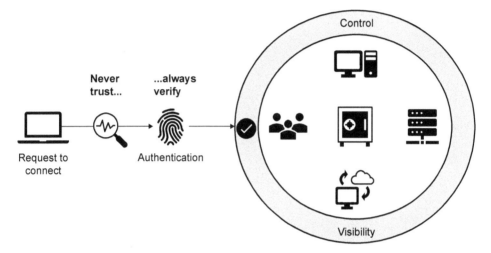

Steps to implement zero trust

- **Define the attack surface:** The attack surface of the network needs to be considered. Having full visibility of all assets is essential in ensuring necessary protection is put in place. Then break up the network to focus on areas where the most protection is required, such as the most valuable assets. This can be done by implementing policies and tools that meet security requirements of the security strategy.

- **Implement controls around network traffic:** Traffic flows throughout the network, and the dependencies will be a driver for how controls are implemented. An example is a central database that holds data required by several systems across the organisation.

- **Architecture:** A zero trust network is designed around the needs of the organisation in support of security. All networks are different, but some common aspects are likely NGFW, which helps to segment the network. MFA is another critical aspect to access control.

- **Create a zero trust policy:** With architecture in place, zero trust policies need to be developed. You can use the 'Kipling Method', which involves asking who, what, when, where, why and how for every user, device and network that requires access.

- **Monitor your network:** Network monitoring alerts you to IoCs or issues, as well as helping to optimise network performance.

Microsoft now has the Rapid Modernisation Plan (RaMP) to support rapid adoption of zero trust (Figure 5.10). It is essentially a technical zero trust deployment guide for organisations to follow.

Figure 5.10 Microsoft RaMP architecture for zero trust

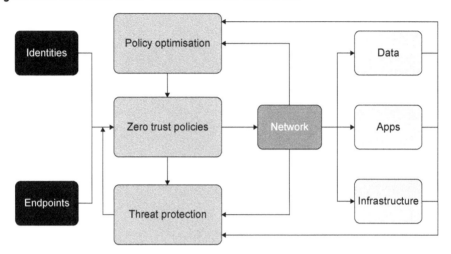

Google BeyondCorp

Google's BeyondCorp initiative is one of the most influential implementations of the zero trust security. The initiative was born out of necessity following a sophisticated cyberattack known as Operation Aurora in 2009.

Operation Aurora was a highly sophisticated and targeted cyberattack campaign that began in mid-2009 and was publicly disclosed in early 2010. The attack targeted several high-profile companies, including Google, Adobe Systems, Yahoo, Juniper Networks, Symantec, Northrop Grumman and Dow Chemical. It was linked to cyber-espionage operations believed to have originated from China, allegedly backed by Chinese state-sponsored groups. The campaign was classified as an advanced persistent threat (APT), meaning the attackers remained undetected within the networks for an extended period, gathering intelligence and exfiltrating data without alerting the victims.

The attackers used a zero-day vulnerability in Microsoft Internet Explorer (CVE-2010-0249) to gain remote access to compromised systems. This exploit provided a foothold for the attackers, allowing them to escalate privileges and move laterally within the targeted networks. The primary objectives of the campaign were intellectual property theft and espionage. Attackers sought to steal proprietary information and sensitive data, such as Google's source code and information from defence contractors and technology firms, indicating a strong espionage motivation.

Operation Aurora relied on spear phishing and social engineering techniques to deliver the initial payload. By targeting employees with specially crafted emails, attackers were able to compromise systems and deploy malware, establishing a backdoor for persistent access. This allowed the attackers to control infected machines remotely and exfiltrate valuable data. They also employed lateral movement and privilege escalation tactics, exploiting vulnerabilities and misconfigurations to reach high-value targets deeper within the network.

Google's role in disclosing the attack was significant. In January 2010, the company announced that it had detected a 'highly sophisticated and targeted attack' on its corporate infrastructure, which originated from China. Google revealed that some of its intellectual property had been stolen and stated that the incident was a major factor in reconsidering its business operations in China, particularly around issues of censorship.

The impact of Operation Aurora was far-reaching. It exposed significant security gaps, prompting organisations to strengthen their cyber security practices, such as adopting HTTPS encryption and improving incident response strategies. The attack also highlighted the growing threat of state-sponsored cyber actors, leading to a greater focus on defending against APTs. Additionally, the exploitation of a zero-day vulnerability in Internet Explorer brought increased scrutiny to the dangers of unpatched software, with Microsoft releasing security patches in response. Ultimately, Operation Aurora marked a pivotal moment in the global understanding of cyber espionage, shaping the cyber security landscape and prompting greater awareness of nation-state threats.

This incident drove Google to rethink its approach to securing access to corporate resources, moving away from the traditional perimeter-based model that had proven vulnerable.

Key components of Google's BeyondCorp architecture
IAM

- Every access request is validated through a strong identity verification process. This includes MFA, the use of security keys and constant checks to ensure that users are who they claim to be.
- RBAC ensures that users only have access to resources necessary for their role and that policies are dynamically enforced based on the user's context and behaviour.

Device security posture
Google maintains a comprehensive inventory of all devices used to access its resources, continuously monitoring their security posture. Devices must meet strict security criteria, such as having the latest software updates and security patches before they are allowed to access sensitive data.

Endpoint verification tools are used to assess the health and status of each device in real time. If a device's security posture changes (e.g. it becomes outdated or compromised), its access can be restricted or revoked.

Context-aware access

- BeyondCorp implements context-aware access controls that consider various factors such as the user's identity, device security status, geographic location and the type of resource being requested.

- Access decisions are made dynamically and continuously, not just at the point of initial connection. For example, a user's session can be terminated if there are signs of anomalous behaviour or if the device becomes untrusted during an active session.

Comprehensive logging and monitoring

- Google has implemented extensive monitoring systems that log every access request and action. This enables real-time threat detection and a quick response to potential incidents.

- Anomalies such as failed login attempts, unusual geographic locations or accessing resources outside normal working hours are flagged and investigated.

Lessons learned from Google's implementation

- **Identity as the new perimeter:** The transition to zero trust highlights that identity, rather than the physical network boundary, should be the primary security perimeter. Google's success emphasised the importance of robust identity verification and the role of MFA in reducing the risk of account compromise.

- **Continuous verification is crucial:** One of the most significant lessons is the importance of continuous validation rather than one-time authentication. Google's model shows that access needs to be continually reassessed based on context, rather than assuming a user remains trustworthy after an initial login.

- **Complexity and cultural shifts:** Implementing a zero trust model is not just a technical challenge but also a cultural and organisational one. Google had to change the way employees and teams viewed network security, placing a strong emphasis on user training and engagement to ease the transition.

- **Incremental implementation:** Google's adoption of zero trust was not an overnight transformation but rather a gradual, multi-year process. This phased approach helped to minimise disruption while ensuring that each component was thoroughly tested and optimised.

PAM

PAM is a security solution for monitoring, detecting and preventing unauthorised privileged access to critical areas or such as admin or service accounts. Like a lot of organisation technology, it relies on people, process and technology. It gives visibility on who has access and is accessing privileged accounts and what they are doing with those accounts. It also limits those that have access to admin accounts with additional layers to prevent attackers getting into those accounts.

In an enterprise environment, 'privileged access' is a term used to designate special access or abilities above and beyond that of a standard user. Privileged access allows organisations to secure their infrastructure and applications, run business efficiently and maintain the confidentiality of sensitive data and critical infrastructure. Privileged access can be associated with human users as well as non-human users such as applications and machine identities (CyberArk, n.d.).

PAM enforces security procedures and controls to limit and monitor privileged account access (Figure 5.11). It is made up of secure authentication, authorisation and auditing. This is to ensure only those that have the correct authorisation can access privileged accounts that contain sensitive data. PAM should also support session monitoring to quickly flag any strange behaviour or use of these accounts (Figure 5.12).

Figure 5.11 PAM benefits

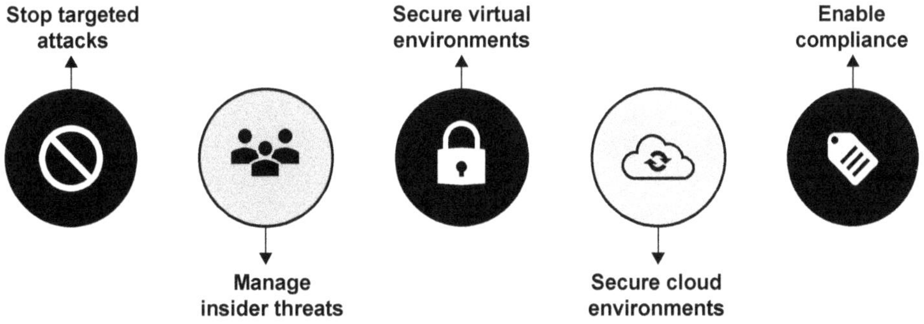

Stop targeted
attacks

Secure virtual
environments

Enable
compliance

Manage
insider threats

Secure cloud
environments

Figure 5.12 PAM solution

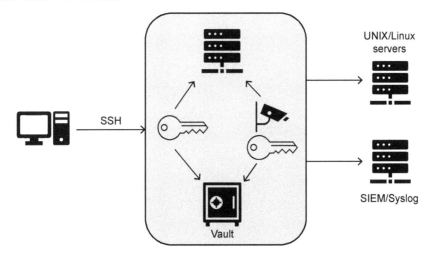

UNIX/Linux
servers

SSH

SIEM/Syslog

Vault

Some of the benefits of PAM are:

- providing JIT access to critical resources;
- allowing secure remote access with the use of password vaulting, with removal of password use;
- monitoring privileged access;
- detecting any unusual, privileged activity;
- ensuring all privileged accounts' events are logged for compliance audits;
- reporting on privileged user access and activity.

Conduct a thorough assessment

- **Identify privileged accounts:** Start by discovering all privileged accounts, including local admin accounts, domain admin accounts, service accounts and application accounts.
- **Assess risks:** Evaluate the risks associated with each privileged account and the potential impact of a breach.

Define a clear PAM strategy

- **Set objectives:** Define clear objectives and goals for your PAM implementation. Understand what you aim to protect and the compliance requirements you need to meet.
- **Create policies:** Develop comprehensive PAM policies that outline how privileged access will be managed and monitored.

Implement least privilege principle

- **Minimise access:** Ensure users only have the minimum level of access necessary to perform their jobs. Regularly review and adjust access levels as needed.
- **Time-based access:** Grant privileged access only for the time needed to complete a task (JIT access).

Use MFA

- **Add layers of security:** Implement MFA for all privileged accounts to add an extra layer of security beyond just passwords.

Deploy a PAM solution

- **Choose the right tool:** Select a PAM solution that fits organisational needs. Key features should include session recording, credential management and automated workflows.
- **Integrate with existing systems:** Ensure the PAM solution integrates well with existing IT infrastructure and security tools.

Automate and secure password management

- **Use password vaulting:** Store privileged credentials in a secure vault and automate password changes to ensure they are regularly updated and strong.
- **Eliminate hard-coded passwords:** Replace hard-coded passwords in scripts and applications with dynamic, vault-managed credentials.

Monitor and audit privileged access

- **Continuous monitoring:** Implement continuous monitoring of privileged accounts to detect and respond to suspicious activities.
- **Audit trails:** Maintain comprehensive audit trails of all privileged access activities to support forensic investigations and compliance reporting.

Implement session management

- **Session recording:** Record all privileged sessions to provide a detailed account of user actions for auditing purposes.
- **Real-time monitoring:** Monitor privileged sessions in real-time to detect and respond to unauthorised activities promptly.

Regularly review and update policies

- **Periodic reviews:** Conduct regular reviews of PAM policies, user access levels and privileged accounts to ensure they remain effective and aligned with current security threats.
- **Update policies:** Update PAM policies as needed to address emerging threats and changes in the IT environment.

Provide training and awareness

- **Educate users:** Train all users, especially those with privileged access, on the importance of PAM and secure practices.
- **Foster a security culture:** Promote a culture of security awareness throughout the organisation to ensure everyone understands their role in protecting sensitive information.

Implement incident response plans

- **Prepare for breaches:** Develop and test incident response plans specifically for privileged account breaches.
- **Quick remediation:** Ensure you have the tools and processes in place to quickly revoke privileged access and mitigate damage in case of a breach.

ARTIFICIAL INTELLIGENCE

AI has already found itself in a plethora of applications, and a quick search of the internet sees numerous websites that you can ask questions of, write CVs and cover letters or draft an entire book. Whilst it has been around for a number of years, it is only in the last few years it has become more mainstream. AI is still a growing and improving technology, and has steadily become more impressive, such as with picture creation, which is a concern when it comes to deep fakes. I have been told by the owner of a marketing and design organisation that copywriters are no longer required.

From a security architecture perspective, it must be considered as a tool that can help but at the same time brings in its own set of risks, which must be assessed and considered. Its use case and where the data it ingests will go is another consideration. Some of these will be pertinent questions to ask a vender offering a tool incorporating AI.

The term AI has become almost overused, encompassing a wide range of technologies that power many services and devices we use daily, from mobile phones and cars to chatbot applications for customer support. There is, however, some debate about whether all these technologies genuinely qualify as AI.

The concept of 'true artificial intelligence' is still subjective and heavily debated, depending on how you define intelligence. Current AI systems are not considered 'true AI' in the sense of possessing human-like understanding, consciousness or autonomy. Instead, they fall under the category of artificial narrow intelligence (ANI). ANI is designed to perform specific tasks efficiently, such as language processing, image recognition or strategic game-playing. While these systems can simulate intelligent behaviour, they operate purely based on learned patterns and lack any understanding or awareness of their actions.

True artificial intelligence would correspond to artificial general intelligence (AGI) or even artificial superintelligence (ASI). AGI would have the ability to understand, learn and apply knowledge across a broad range of tasks, comparable to human cognition. Unlike current AI, which is task-specific, AGI would demonstrate reasoning, problem-solving, creativity and adaptability, allowing it to switch seamlessly between tasks without retraining. Beyond AGI lies ASI, a form of intelligence that surpasses human capabilities in every respect, including creativity, wisdom and emotional intelligence. ASI would likely be capable of self-improvement, leading to exponential growth in capability. However, achieving AGI or ASI faces significant challenges, including our still not yet complete understanding of human intelligence and consciousness, ethical concerns and technical limitations. Quantum computing will certainly lend a hand in moving towards true artificial intelligence as the limit of classical systems is reached.

From a philosophical perspective, there is an ongoing debate about whether AI can ever be considered 'truly intelligent'. Some argue that, without consciousness or subjective experience, AI cannot be genuinely intelligent, regardless of its problem-solving ability. Others counter that intelligence does not necessarily require consciousness; if AI can learn and adapt autonomously, it could qualify as intelligent in a functional sense. Critics also point out that current AI systems only give the illusion of intelligence. For example, models such as ChatGPT appear thoughtful because they generate responses based on complex probabilistic patterns, not because they reason or understand like humans do. Some define ChatGPT as a more advanced 'Google' with the ability to write answers to questions and search for information and collate it.

Some examples of AI in use are:

- ChatGPT, DeepSeek and Google Bard, which use large language models (LLMs) to generate text in response to questions or comments inputted.
- Netflix uses machine learning algorithms to create personalised recommendations for users based on their previous viewing history.
- Tesla makes use of AI for its computer vision to power self-driving features on their cars.
- Face ID is used to unlock an iPhone, and virtual filters on Snapchat use AI.

LLMs are used to categorise foundation models trained using immense amounts of data, which helps the AI be capable of understanding and generating natural language and a wide range of content and tasks.

AI learns by machine learning, which is a subset of AI that enables computers to learn and improve independently by analysing and adapting to data fed into them (Figure 5.13). Several machine learning techniques exist. The three main techniques are supervised, unsupervised and reinforcement learning.

Figure 5.13 AI vs machine vs deep learning

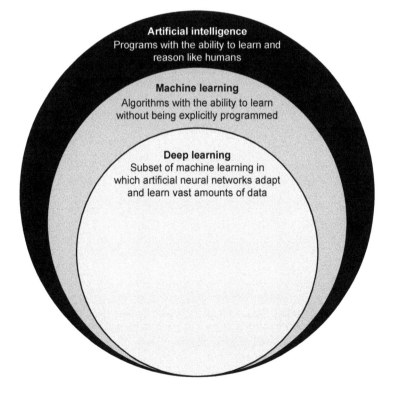

AI training

Training AI involves several key steps, each critical to developing an effective and accurate model. First, there is data collection. AI models, especially machine learning models, require vast amounts of data. This data can come from various sources, such as databases, online repositories or generated synthetically. The quality and relevance of the data are crucial for the performance of the AI.

Next is data pre-processing. Raw data often contains noise, missing values and inconsistencies. Data pre-processing involves cleaning the data by removing or imputing missing values and correcting errors, followed by normalisation or standardisation to ensure that different features contribute equally. For tasks such as image recognition, data augmentation is used to increase dataset diversity by applying transformations such as rotations and flips.

Choosing a model comes next. Depending on the task, such as classification, regression or clustering, different algorithms and models are chosen.

- **Supervised learning:** In supervised learning, a model is trained using labelled data, which consists of inputs and their corresponding desired outputs. The algorithm learns from these labelled data points and can then make predictions on new, unseen data. Examples of supervised learning include tasks such as image classification, spam detection and speech recognition.

- **Unsupervised learning:** Unsupervised learning involves discovering patterns in unlabelled data, where the dataset only contains inputs without any corresponding outputs. The algorithm searches for patterns and relationships within the data and utilises these patterns to make predictions on new, unseen data. Some examples of unsupervised learning are anomaly detection and dimensionality reduction.

- **Reinforcement learning:** Reinforcement learning entails training a model through trial and error by providing rewards or punishments for specific actions. The algorithm learns by interacting with an environment and receives rewards for correct actions and punishments for incorrect ones. Reinforcement learning is commonly applied in areas such as robotics, gaming and recommendation systems.

- **Other types of machine learning:** Apart from supervised, unsupervised and reinforcement learning, there are other commonly used machine learning techniques. These include semi-supervised learning. This is where the model learns from both labelled and unlabelled data and deep learning. This utilises neural networks to learn from vast amounts of data. Another popular technique is transferring learning, which involves using a pre-trained model as a starting point for a new task.

The data is typically split into three sets: training set to train the model, validation set to tune the model's hyperparameters and avoid overfitting (analysis that corresponds too closely or exactly to a particular set of data) and the test set to evaluate the model's performance on unseen data. It is also worth making sure that any data being used in models has been legally collated to ensure the organisation does not find itself in legal trouble.

The core training process involves feeding the training data into the model and adjusting the model's parameters to minimise the error called loss function. Hyperparameter tuning is also essential. Hyperparameters are settings that are not learned from the data but set prior to the training process, such as learning rate, batch size and the number of layers in a neural network. Techniques for tuning hyperparameters include grid search, random search and Bayesian optimisation.

The trained model is then evaluated using the test set to determine its performance. Common metrics include accuracy, precision, recall, F1 score and others, depending on the task. A good F1 score means that you have low false positives and low false negatives.

Once the model is trained and evaluated, it can be deployed into a production environment where it can make predictions on new data. After deployment, the model's performance should be continuously monitored. This involves checking for model drift, where the model's performance degrades over time due to changes in the underlying data distribution. Retraining and updating the model periodically is essential to maintain its accuracy.

In terms of techniques and tools, deep learning is often used for complex tasks such as image and speech recognition. Transfer learning can be utilised with pre-trained models on similar tasks to reduce training time and improve performance. Popular frameworks and libraries include TensorFlow, PyTorch, scikit-learn and Keras.

AI poisoning

An AI poisoning attack, also known as data poisoning, involves deliberately feeding incorrect or malicious data into an AI system's training process. The goal is to manipulate the AI model's behaviour, leading to incorrect predictions or decisions. These attacks can degrade the performance of the model, cause it to make specific errors or create vulnerabilities that can be exploited later. Such attacks pose significant risks, particularly in applications where AI systems are used for critical decision-making, such as in healthcare, finance or security.

AI security

As AI performance and ability increases, its use in attacks will rise. AI is being used to generate convincing spear phishing emails, blending in well with how an organisation formats and writes its communications, which can fool even the most vigilant employees. AI can create deepfakes such as pictures, videos and voices, meaning that the leadership team could be impersonated as an example. These can be used to deceive employees into authorising unauthorised fund transfers, which bring a new level of believability to social engineering. What about an AI generated email or WhatsApp communication that causes reputational damage and causes share prices to drop? The attackers could then buy shares at a cheaper price to profit later on.

AI could be used by an attacker to tamper with data on a system, such as the creation of a realistic looking stock portfolio that has been fabricated by AI. If the fraud goes undetected, the attackers can then profit from this false information.

Microsoft has created best practices for AI security risk management with an AI security risk assessment framework. This has been created to support auditing and tracking and improve the security of the AI systems. It looks at the risks and controls that need to be considered.

In 2023 OWASP created a Machine Learning Security Top 10 to highlight the top 10 security issues of machine learning systems:

1. **Input manipulation attack:** This is a type of attack in which an attacker deliberately alters input data to mislead the model.

2. **Data poisoning attack:** This occurs when an attacker manipulates the training data to cause the model to behave in an undesirable way.

3. **Model inversion attack:** Attacks occur when an attacker reverse-engineers the model to extract information from it.

4. **Membership inference attack:** This occurs when an attacker manipulates the model's training data in order to cause it to behave in a way that exposes sensitive information.

5. **Model theft attack:** This occurs when an attacker gains access to the model's parameters.

6. **AI supply chain attack:** This occurs when an attacker modifies or replaces a machine learning library or model that is used by a system. This can also include the data associated with the machine learning models.

7. **Transfer learning attack:** Learning attacks occur when an attacker trains a model on one task and then fine-tunes it on another task to cause it to behave in an undesirable way.

8. **Model skewing attack:** This occurs when an attacker manipulates the distribution of the training data to cause the model to behave in an undesirable way.

9. **Output integrity attack:** In an attack scenario, an attacker aims to modify or manipulate the output of a machine learning model in order to change its behaviour or cause harm to the system it is used in.

10. **Model poisoning attack:** This occurs when an attacker manipulates the model's parameters to cause it to behave in an undesirable way.

QUANTUM COMPUTING

Quantum computing makes use of specialised computer hardware and algorithms that take advantage of quantum mechanics. Quantum mechanics can be best described as a fundamental theory in physics to describe the behaviour of nature at and below the scale of atoms. The theory was developed in the 1900s, when experiments showed strange and counterintuitive results. In normal mechanics, objects exist in a specific place at a specific time. In quantum mechanics, objects exist in a world of probability. They have a probability of being at one point and another chance of being at a second point, and so on. An example is that if a tennis ball was thrown at a wall in the real world, it would bounce back each and every time from the same wall. However, in the quantum world this same tennis ball has a probability that it could also bounce back from the opposite side of the wall, from the side of the wall or the front of the wall.

The era we are currently in is called NISQ, which stands for noisy intermediate scale quantum. Noise is the single biggest issue to overcome, as noise currently prevents building larger sized quantum computers.

What is a qubit?

A qubit (short for quantum bit) is the fundamental unit of information in quantum computing, analogous to the classical bit in traditional computing. A quantum system using two quantum states, and superpositions of them, is called a qubit. A bit of information in a classical computer is either 0 or 1, but a qubit of information is much more crowded. It can be viewed as a sphere. However, unlike a classical bit, which can only represent one of two states 0 or 1, a qubit can exist in a superposition of both states simultaneously. This property allows quantum computers to process information in ways that classical computers cannot.

> Whenever we represent a number in a computer we will specify it to a particular precision – 32 bits is a pretty conventional approach. So, to represent the state of a qubit we need about 64 bits. This may sound pretty standard, but the trick comes when we add more qubits. Instead of just needing another 64 bits for each qubit (which would be called linear scaling), the memory requirement grows exponentially! Two qubits still requires 128 bits. But three requires 256; four is 512; five is 1024; six is 2048, and so on. By the time we have increased it to 30 qubits, the working memory of most desktop computers would be exhausted. At only 75 qubits, the number of bits required to match the information would be more than all the data created in the world (300 zettabytes) (Q-CRTL, 2024).

A qubit is typically realised using physical systems that exhibit quantum behaviour, such as electrons, photons or atomic nuclei. These systems have two distinct states that represent the binary values 0 and 1. For example, the spin of an electron or the polarisation of a photon can be used to encode a qubit. When in superposition, a qubit's state is described by a combination of 0 and 1.

Bloch sphere

The Bloch sphere is a geometric representation of a qubit, the fundamental unit of quantum information, in a two-level quantum system. It is widely used in both quantum computing and quantum mechanics to visualise the state of a qubit.

The Bloch sphere is a unit sphere in a three-dimensional space. The north pole represents the state 0 and the south pole represents the state 1. Any point on the surface of the sphere represents a valid qubit state, which is a superposition of 0 and 1. Pure states lie on the surface of the Bloch sphere. Mixed states (probabilistic mixtures rather than coherent superpositions) are inside the sphere. Quantum operations (like gates) correspond to rotations of the Bloch sphere.

A Bloch sphere provides a way to understand qubit states and quantum gates. With quantum computation, single qubit operations (like the Hadamard, Pauli and phase gates) can be visualised as rotations on the sphere (Figure 5.14). Finally, entanglement and measurement collapses the state to either |0⟩ or |1⟩, represented as a projection onto the z axis.

Figure 5.14 Bloch sphere (https://en.wikipedia.org/wiki/File:Bloch_sphere.svg)

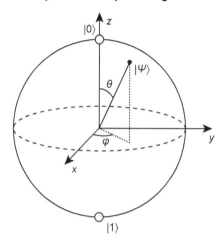

Figure 5.15 One qubit quantum computer

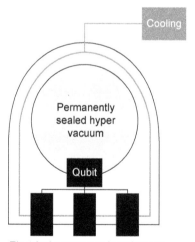

One thing that quantum computers cannot do is to provide computational solutions to problems that classical computers cannot solve – irrespective of the resources required – such as the famous halting problem formulated by Alan Turing in the 1930s. Quantum computers can be simulated by classical computers, so any computational problem that can be solved by a quantum computer can also be solved by a classical computer, though it might take the classical computer much, much longer to find a solution (IBM Quantum Learning, 2025).

A standard computer uses what is now referred to as classical bits and a quantum computer uses quantum bits, or qubits, which work in a unique way (Figure 5.15). A normal bit can store either a zero or a one, whereas a qubit can store a zero, a one, both a zero and a one, or an infinite number of values in between. Essentially it can be in multiple states at the same time. Because a quantum computer can store multiple numbers at once, it can also process them simultaneously too. Numbers are stored in qubits through a concept called superposition. Superposition is where two waves add to make a third one, which now contains both of the first two waves (Figure 5.16). It is a bit like the sound from an instrument where there is the fundamental frequency and overtones, known as harmonics, which are all stored simultaneously.

For a classical computer, both the input and output are binary and throughout computation, bits are either in zero or one state. Similarly, a quantum computer also takes binary input and produces binary output. However, during computation, qubits can exist in a superposition of both 0 and 1 (Figures 5.16 and 5.17). Unlike classical bits, qubits are manipulated through quantum operations, which allow them to exist in multiple states simultaneously. This superposition cannot be directly observed, though. When a qubit is measured, its state collapses to either 0 or 1. The probability of collapsing into one state or the other depends on the operations that were applied to the qubit. If the arrow shown in Figure 5.16 is up, then the probability of getting back a zero is higher. Conversely, if the arrow is down, the probability of getting back a one is higher. If the arrow is horizontal, then there is a 50/50 chance of getting back a one or a zero.

Another property, called entanglement, means entangled qubits can talk to one another even if they are some distance apart. Entanglement amplifies the power of superposition, which allows a quantum computer to do far more things far more quickly, as it no longer has to process anything in a one-at-a-time, sequential process. As quantum computers work in parallel, they can undertake an enormous amount of processing at a single point in time, making them millions of times faster than a conventional computer.

Kets

A ket, denoted as $|\psi\rangle$, is a vector in an abstract complex vector space used to describe quantum states. It encapsulates all the information about a quantum system, including probabilities and phase relationships in superpositions. The ket notation, introduced in Dirac's bra-ket formalism (Steane, 2023), provides a compact and convenient way to express quantum states and their transformations.

Figure 5.16 Superposition

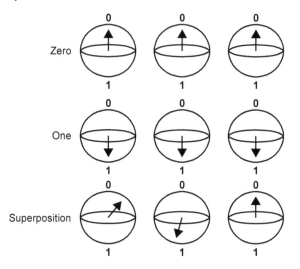

Figure 5.17 Output classical and qubit

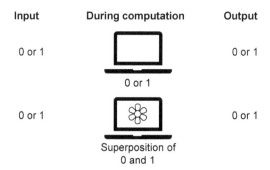

The technical definition is that $|\psi\rangle$ is a vector in an abstract complex vector space.

- **Complex:** This means superpositions can contain complex numbers, not just real numbers. These complex numbers represent phases (Phase is what turns the Bloch circle into the Bloch sphere).

- **Vector space:** This is a collection of objects that can be combined (added) in superposition and follow certain mathematical rules. It's abstract because many different sets of objects (such as numbers) can satisfy these rules.

- **Vector:** This is a single element in this set. The notation $|\psi\rangle$ is called a ket. This notation is useful because it represents everything about a quantum state.

Quantum circuit

In computer science, circuits serve as computational models where information flows through a network of gates via interconnected wires, with each gate performing operations on the transmitted data. Quantum circuits are a specialised form of this general concept, adapted for quantum computation (Figure 5.18). Despite the term 'circuit' suggesting a circular structure, computational circuit models typically exclude circular paths, meaning they are acyclic by design. Quantum circuits represent a finite sequence of operations without feedback loops.

Figure 5.18 Quantum circuit example

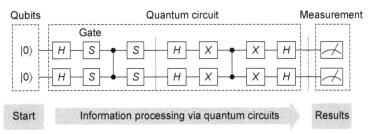

A quantum circuit is a model for quantum computation, analogous to classical logic circuits but designed to operate using qubits instead of classical bits. It consists of quantum gates that manipulate the quantum state of qubits through unitary transformations. The simplest possible quantum circuit does nothing at all, it is just a single quantum wire.

Mathematically, the circuit is trivial. But physically it's far from trivial. In many physical systems, the quantum wire is actually one of the hardest quantum computations to implement!

The reason is that quantum states are often incredibly fragile. If your qubit is being stored in some tiny system – perhaps a single photon or a single atom – then it's very, very easy to disturb that state. It really doesn't take much to upset an atom or a photon. And so while quantum wires are mathematically trivial, they can be one of the hardest elements to build in real systems (Matuschak and Nielsen, 2019).

Quantum noise

Controlling noise in quantum computing is one of the biggest challenges in making quantum computers practical. It is the single biggest technical challenge to still be fully overcome. As quantum systems are extremely sensitive to their environment, any unwanted interactions introduce quantum noise, which leads to decoherence and errors in computations. Creating quantum noise in an offensive manner could be used as a method of DoS attack, and mitigation around this potential attack vector may have to be considered from a security perspective.

Since qubits are extremely sensitive to their environment, even the slightest disturbances from electromagnetic fields, temperature fluctuations or quantum interactions can introduce errors. Qubits exist in superpositions, making them susceptible to decoherence (loss of quantum information) and gate errors. To counteract these effects, researchers use precise control methods, such as dynamical decoupling, pulse shaping and optimal control theory, to improve qubit fidelity and extend coherence times.

Cooling

Quantum computers, especially those using superconducting qubits, operate at temperatures close to absolute zero. Cooling the system is undertaken to isolate the quantum components, protecting them from external disturbances such as reducing thermal noise that occurs at higher temperatures. Particles within the quantum computer's components undergo increased thermal vibrations, which can disrupt the delicate quantum states of qubits. By cooling the system, these vibrations are minimised, reducing thermal noise and enhancing qubit stability.

Using cooling for preserving quantum coherence is important, as quantum states such as superposition and entanglement are highly sensitive to external conditions. Lower temperatures also help to extend the coherence time of qubits, allowing them to retain their quantum properties for longer periods, which is vital for complex computations, and minimising environmental interactions, as elevated temperatures increase interactions between quantum systems and their environment, leading to decoherence and information loss.

The cooling process involves multiple stages, starting from room temperature and progressively reducing through liquid nitrogen (77K) and liquid helium (4K). The final cooling stage is achieved using a helium-3 to helium-4 dilution process, which brings the system down to millikelvin temperatures. This multi-stage approach ensures that the qubits remain in a stable and controlled quantum state. This cooling method consumes around 10–20 kWh.

Quantum teleportation

Quantum teleportation enables secure quantum communication over long distances without violating the no-cloning theorem, which states that an arbitrary quantum state cannot be copied perfectly. Since cloning is impossible, teleportation does not transfer physical qubits, but rather reconstructs the state at a distant location using entanglement and classical communication (Figure 5.19). As quantum states cannot be perfectly copied, a sniffer or eavesdropper cannot be used to intercept and duplicate quantum keys without detection. Think of it like sending classical encrypted traffic (HTTPS, TLS, IPSec) across a network or the internet.

Quantum teleportation is one of the most important protocols in quantum information. By exploiting the physical resource of entanglement, quantum teleportation serves as a key primitive in a variety of quantum information tasks and represents an important building block for quantum technologies, with a pivotal role in the continuing progress of quantum communication, quantum computing and quantum networks. Here we review the basic theoretical ideas behind quantum teleportation and its variant protocols (Pirandola et al., 2015).

Figure 5.19 Quantum entanglement diagram

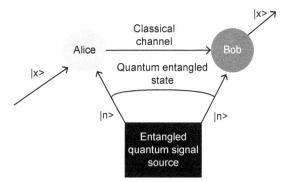

In February 2025, scientists at University of Oxford managed to link two separate quantum processors into a single, fully connected quantum computer, which is a real first step towards scalable quantum systems. The experiment paper has been published in *Nature* and demonstrates the feasibility of distributed quantum computing, a strategy that could eventually enable scalable and powerful quantum machines without the need for massive single-device architectures (Main et al., 2025). The quantum modules were separated by about two metres, with each containing dedicated network and circuit qubits.

- **Entanglement:** Two particles are entangled, meaning their quantum states are linked in such a way that the state of one particle instantly affects the state of the other, regardless of the distance between them.

- **Measurement:** The sender **Alice** has a quantum state **|n>** that she wants to teleport to a distant location **Bob**. She performs a measurement on her particle and the particle she wants to teleport, which destroys the original quantum state but also generates classical information (bits) in the process.

- **Transmission and reconstruction:** The classical information obtained from Alice's measurement is sent to Bob through a classical communication channel. Using this information and his entangled particle **|n>**, Bob can perform operations that allow him to recreate the original quantum state.

6   SECURITY LOGGING AND MONITORING

Security logging and monitoring are fundamental components of an organisation's cyber security strategy, providing visibility across systems, networks and applications. Effective logging allows security teams to detect, investigate and respond to security threats in real time, while monitoring ensures that deviations from normal activity are identified before they escalate into major incidents.

In this chapter we will explore the importance of security logging and monitoring, focusing on best practices for implementation. We will examine SIEM systems, their role in correlating security events and how they enhance situational awareness. Finally, we will discuss incident response, which is heavily reliant on accurate and timely logs to identify, contain and mitigate security incidents.

SECURITY LOGGING AND MONITORING

Security logging and monitoring refers to the practice of collecting, storing and analysing log data from various systems and devices within an organisation's IT environment. The goal is to detect, investigate and respond to security incidents effectively. This process provides crucial visibility into potential threats or malicious activities, helping to reduce harm by early detection and to ensure the safety and integrity of an organisation's information assets. Remember, though, that whilst confidentiality may keep data secure it won't prevent it from being stolen. Integrity may support accuracy but won't prevent tampering or loss, merely flag it up. Availability may keep systems running but won't prevent a breach or disruption. This lines up with the anti-CIA triad **Disclosure**, **Alteration** and **Disruption**, which is conceptually the opposite of the CIA triad. To be able to prevent a breach or prevent data from being stolen, we need to know an attempt is being made to enter our network or steal data. If a system is not functioning, we need to be alerted to it either not running properly or at all. This is why logging and monitoring is essential – it gives the organisation visibility as to what is happening, and having the correct coverage, monitoring wise, is just as important too.

A well-defined logging and monitoring strategy enables organisations to detect a wide range of security events, from unauthorised access attempts and malware infections to system failures and insider threats. Logs provide a historical record that aids forensic investigations, compliance reporting and risk management. However, not all events are equally important. Capturing too much data can lead to alert fatigue, increased storage costs and missed critical security nuances or IoCs.

To be effective, logging and monitoring should be strategically scoped to focus on the events most relevant to the organisation's threat landscape and risk posture. This requires defining:

- **What should be logged?** (e.g. authentication attempts, privileged access, configuration changes.)
- **How should logs be stored and protected?** (e.g. retention policies, encryption, integrity checks.)
- **How should monitoring be conducted?** (e.g. real-time alerting, anomaly detection, correlation of events.)

Security logging

Security logging involves recording events and activities generated by systems, networks, applications and security tools. These logs serve as a detailed record of everything that happens within the environment and are critical for detecting and diagnosing security incidents. There are different types of logs, such as system logs that track OS events like user logins and configuration changes, application logs that monitor software-specific activities and network logs that capture information about network traffic, including connection attempts and firewall events. Additionally, security device logs and audit logs provide further insights, tracking events from security tools and user activities on critical systems.

The primary purpose of security logging is to aid in incident detection, providing clues about unusual or suspicious activities such as repeated failed login attempts or strange data transfers. Logs also play a key role in forensic analysis, helping to reconstruct the timeline of events after a security incident. Furthermore, they are essential for compliance and assurance, as many regulations require certain activities to be logged to demonstrate adherence to security standards.

Security monitoring

Security monitoring is the continuous process of reviewing and analysing log data to identify threats, anomalies or security incidents in real time or near-real time. This proactive approach involves using a combination of tools and techniques to detect and respond to malicious activities before significant damage occurs. Key components of security monitoring include SIEM, which aggregates and analyses log data from across the network, and IDPSs, which monitor for signs of intrusion or attack.

Other critical tools include EDR solutions that provide monitoring and response capabilities for endpoints, and user behaviour analytics (UBA), which detect insider threats by analysing normal behaviour and flagging unusual patterns. Monitoring techniques range from rule-based monitoring, where predefined rules trigger alerts, to more advanced methods such as anomaly detection using machine learning and threat intelligence integration to prioritise threats based on known malicious actor behaviour.

Importance of security logging and monitoring

The importance of security logging and monitoring cannot be overstated. One of the most significant benefits is early threat detection, as continuous analysis of logs helps organisations to identify and respond to threats before they escalate. Additionally, logs are vital for incident response, providing crucial data to help security teams mitigate the impact of an incident.

Operational visibility is another key advantage, as logging and monitoring provide a clear view of the IT environment, allowing security teams to optimise defences and reduce risk.

Challenges in security logging and monitoring

Despite its benefits, security logging and monitoring comes with challenges. One of the biggest is the vast amount of log data produced by modern IT environments, making it difficult to collect, store and analyse effectively. False positives and negatives are also a concern; monitoring tools can generate numerous false alerts that overwhelm security teams or miss genuine threats, meaning that they have to be tuned properly, which can take skilled resources and time. Additionally, integrating logs from different sources and maintaining consistency in monitoring can be complex, especially in diverse or cloud-based environments. Tools have to be able to ingest various file types and it is essential to check that the chosen solution can ingest all file types in use.

Resource constraints can further complicate matters, as effective monitoring requires skilled personnel and robust infrastructure, which is costly. Sometimes logs have to be converted or ways looked at with the vendor on how they could be ingested and analysed. Part of developing a solution should include logging and monitoring and whether the solution works with the current SIEM or monitoring infrastructure.

Best practices

To implement an effective security logging and monitoring programme, organisations should follow several best practices. Centralised logging is essential, using systems such as SIEMs to collect and analyse data from all relevant sources. Establishing clear log retention policies is also important to ensure that important data is kept as long as necessary, especially for compliance or forensic purposes. Continuous monitoring strategies should be in place, incorporating real-time alerting and regular log reviews to identify and respond to threats quickly. Regular audits of logging and monitoring systems are also necessary to ensure they remain effective and up to date with the latest security threats.

SIEM

A SIEM solution plays a critical role in an organisation's security strategy by providing real-time analysis of security alerts generated across the IT infrastructure (Figure 6.1). The sooner an alert is raised and can be responded to, the quicker the response time to an IoC, a false positive or an actual attack. Essentially, a SIEM centralises and analyses data from various sources, such as firewalls, IDPSs, servers, applications and endpoint security tools. This centralisation enables the detection, monitoring, recording and analysis of security events in both real time and a historical context, empowering security teams to identify, investigate and respond to threats effectively.

Figure 6.1 SIEM architecture

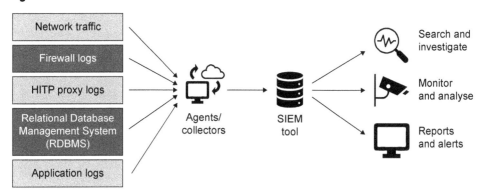

Security information and event management, or SIEM, is a security solution that helps organisations recognize and address potential security threats and vulnerabilities before they have a chance to disrupt business operations. SIEM systems help enterprise security teams detect user behaviour anomalies and use artificial intelligence (AI) to automate many of the manual processes associated with threat detection and incident response (IBM, 2023).

At the heart of a SIEM's functionality is the collection and aggregation of data. It captures logs from diverse sources and normalises them into a consistent format, which allows for efficient and effective analysis. The normalisation process ensures that events from different systems can be analysed in a structured manner. Once the data is ready, the SIEM applies correlation rules to link seemingly unrelated data points, detecting suspicious patterns that may indicate a potential security threat. For example, a SIEM could flag multiple failed login attempts followed by a successful one as a sign of a brute force attack. These rules help to prioritise alerts based on the severity of the threat, ensuring that security teams focus on the most critical issues.

When an event or series of events matches a known threat pattern, the SIEM generates an alert, notifying security analysts of possible security incidents. The SIEM platform usually provides intuitive dashboards and visualisations, giving analysts a comprehensive view of the security landscape. It also includes capabilities for incident management, with features like case tracking and documentation, making it easier for teams to manage and respond to alerts. Moreover, SIEM tools store logs for an extended period, ensuring compliance with regulatory requirements and aiding in forensic investigations, where historical data can provide crucial insights into the timeline and impact of an attack.

A significant advantage of SIEMs is their ability to enhance threat detection and response. By using real-time visibility, SIEMs help to identify and address threats swiftly, while integrating with external threat intelligence feeds to recognise and mitigate known attack techniques. The centralised approach also simplifies the compliance process for organisations in heavily regulated industries. Automated reports and dashboards can demonstrate adherence to data protection standards such as GDPR, PCI DSS or HIPAA. Additionally, SIEMs improve operational efficiency by automating tasks such as alerting and incident workflows, which helps to optimise the workload of security teams.

Despite their benefits, SIEM solutions come with challenges. They can be complex and expensive to deploy, requiring skilled personnel for configuration, monitoring and maintenance. Organisations may face issues with false positives, especially if correlation rules are not fine-tuned, leading to wasted time investigating non-issues. Scalability is another concern: as the organisation grows and generates more data, the SIEM must scale accordingly without sacrificing performance. Furthermore, seamless integration with other security and IT management tools can be difficult, particularly in environments with diverse and evolving technologies

AI and ML

The integration of ML and AI into a SIEM enhances their ability to detect, analyse and respond to threats.

One major application is anomaly detection, where ML models learn normal behaviours within networks, users and devices by analysing historical data. Once trained, these models detect deviations from the baseline, which could indicate insider threats, APTs or zero-day exploits. Coupled with this is behavioural analytics, where AI analyses user and entity behaviours through techniques such as UEBA. This helps to identify abnormal patterns, such as unusual file access or login attempts from unexpected locations.

SIEMs that use AI are adept at threat intelligence integration, ingesting vast quantities of real-time threat data. They match indicators such as malicious IPs or domains against logs and predict attack vectors based on the evolving threat landscape. Additionally, AI and ML help to manage the overwhelming volume of alerts generated by SIEM systems through incident prioritisation by correlating related events, suppressing noise and assigning risk scores.

AI and ML can also be used to power automated threat detection by recognising attack patterns and identifying subtle adversarial tactics using frameworks such as MITRE ATT&CK. Once an incident is detected, AI aids in root cause analysis, tracing the sequence of events leading to a breach and mapping the probable attack path. Many SIEM systems integrate with SOAR capabilities, where AI not only suggests responses but can also trigger automated actions, such as isolating compromised devices.

Beyond detection and response, AI can help a SIEM to perform predictive analysis. By utilising historical and real-time data, they forecast potential incidents and allow organisations to bolster their defences pre-emptively. Similarly, ML models excel at fraud detection, identifying subtle misuse patterns that traditional rule-based systems might overlook, such as irregular payment behaviours or phishing campaigns.

AI and ML continuously improve through learning techniques. Supervised learning refines detection using labelled data, unsupervised learning uncovers new patterns without predefined labels, and reinforcement learning optimises response strategies based on outcomes of past actions.

However, deploying AI and ML in SIEM systems is not without challenges. Poor-quality data, model drift and the need for regular updates can affect accuracy. Moreover, integrating and fine-tuning AI/ML within SIEM requires expertise, and overly sensitive models may generate false positives if improperly tuned. I was once involved with commissioning of CrowdStrike and, when turned on, it generated 10,000 false positives. These false positives were connected to engineers using Citrix to connect to remote servers using PowerShell commands. CrowdStrike saw the PowerShell commands as an attack. It had to both learn the environment and be tuned to understand the environment it was operating in.

Several SIEM platforms incorporate AI and ML capabilities. Splunk employs ML for predictive analytics and anomaly detection, IBM QRadar integrates AI (via Watson) for threat hunting and Microsoft Sentinel uses AI for alert correlation, behaviour analytics and automated response. AI will continue to further move SIEMs from reactive log aggregators into proactive systems capable of tackling and predicting threats.

Examples of SIEM solutions

Splunk
Splunk is a widely recognised SIEM tool for its robust data analytics, log management and real-time monitoring capabilities.

Core strengths: It excels in ingesting vast amounts of data from diverse sources, enabling powerful search, visualisation and reporting features. Splunk's Search Processing Language (SPL) allows users to extract actionable insights with high precision.

Key features:

- advanced data correlation and alerting;
- machine learning-based anomaly detection;
- pre-built dashboards and analytics for various use cases such as IT operations, compliance and security.

Use case: It is ideal for organisations needing a scalable solution with extensive customisation options and integrations for complex IT and security environments.

IBM QRadar
IBM QRadar is a leading SIEM platform that offers advanced threat intelligence, behaviour analysis and ML for efficient threat detection and response.

Core strengths: It integrates seamlessly with a wide range of IBM and third-party tools to provide comprehensive security visibility. Its automatic prioritisation of alerts reduces noise and improves incident triaging.

Key features:

- AI-driven threat detection using IBM Watson;
- out-of-the-box compliance reporting for regulations such as GDPR and HIPAA;
- network behaviour analytics for identifying suspicious activities.

Use case: It is ideal for large enterprises with complex security needs that are seeking a platform with deep integrations and automated threat intelligence.

ArcSight

ArcSight, by OpenText (formerly Micro Focus), is an enterprise-grade SIEM platform known for its powerful event correlation and scalability.

Core strengths: Its correlation engine can handle high-volume data from extensive IT infrastructures, making it suitable for organisations requiring deep insights across distributed environments.

Key features:

- real-time event correlation for identifying sophisticated threats;
- advanced UEBA;
- flexible deployment options (on-premises, hybrid or cloud).

Use case: It is best suited for enterprises with high compliance requirements and complex multi-network infrastructures, especially in industries such as finance and government.

LogRhythm

LogRhythm focuses on advanced security analytics, threat detection and rapid response. It is particularly well-suited for medium to large organisations looking for an intuitive, end-to-end solution.

Core strengths: Its integrated platform combines SIEM, log management and SOAR capabilities.

Key features:

- threat lifecycle management with automated workflows;
- AI-driven anomaly detection and behaviour analysis;
- built-in compliance modules and audit-ready reporting.

Use case: It is designed for security teams looking to streamline threat-hunting and incident response while meeting compliance needs efficiently.

Microsoft Sentinel

Microsoft Sentinel is a modern, cloud-native SIEM and SOAR solution that integrates with Microsoft Azure and Microsoft 365 environments.

Core strengths: As a cloud-native platform, Sentinel offers scalability, flexibility and tight integration with Microsoft's ecosystem, enabling rapid deployment and reduced operational overhead. Ingestion of Microsoft 365 logs is free but is costly for ingestion of external logs.

Key features:

- AI and machine learning for threat detection and incident prioritisation;
- built-in workbooks and connectors for seamless integration with Azure, AWS and third-party solutions;
- automated incident response workflows with Azure Logic apps.

Use case: Ideal for organisations heavily invested in the Microsoft ecosystem, especially those seeking a cost-effective and scalable cloud solution for monitoring hybrid or multi-cloud environments. Ideal for small to medium enterprises wanting greater emphasis and control on operational expenditure.

SOAR

SOAR is a category of security solutions designed to enhance the efficiency and effectiveness of security operations by integrating and coordinating various security tools and systems (orchestration), automating routine and repetitive tasks to reduce manual intervention (automation) and providing a structured framework for responding to security incidents (response) (Table 6.1).

Table 6.1 SIEM vs SOAR

Feature	SOAR	SIEM
Primary purpose	Automate, orchestrate and respond to security incidents	Collect, aggregate and·analyse security logs and events
Key functionality	Incident response automation, playbook execution, case management	Log management, event correlation, threat detection, compliance reporting
Data handling	Uses data from SIEM and other tools to automate response actions	Collects and normalises logs from multiple sources
Detection and response	Responds to threats via automation and workflow orchestration	Detects threats through correlation rules, ML and analytics
Automation level	High automation (e.g. automated triage, remediation, enrichment)	Limited automation (e.g. alerting, correlation rules)

(Continued)

Table 6.1 (Continued)

Feature	SOAR	SIEM
Human involvement	Reduces manual work through playbooks and automated actions	Requires analysts to investigate and respond to alerts
Integration	Integrates with SIEMs, firewalls, endpoint security, threat intelligence and ticketing systems	Integrates with various log sources, threat intelligence feeds and analytics tools
Alert management	Automates alert triage and response, reducing alert fatigue	Generates and prioritises alerts based on correlation rules
Use cases	Incident response automation, case management, threat hunting	Security monitoring, forensic analysis, compliance
Response time	Faster response due to automated workflows and playbooks	Dependent on SOC analysts' investigation and action
Complexity	Requires playbook creation and integration with multiple tools	Can be complex to configure and fine-tune rules
Example tools	Palo Alto Cortex XSOAR, IBM Resilient, Splunk SOAR, Microsoft Sentinel SOA	Splunk, IBM QRadar, ArcSight, Microsoft Sentinel

LOGGING AND MONITORING BEST PRACTICES

Define clear objectives and requirements

- **Set goals:** Before implementing a logging and monitoring strategy, outline the objectives clearly. Understand what you want to achieve, whether it's regulatory compliance, threat detection or performance monitoring.

- **Identify critical assets:** Identify which systems, applications and data are most critical to your organisation's operations and security. This prioritisation will guide where you focus your logging efforts.

- **Understand compliance needs:** Different industries have various regulations, such as GDPR, PCI DSS or HIPAA, which dictate specific logging and data retention requirements. Make sure you tailor your strategy to meet these obligations.

Centralise logging

- **Use a centralised log management system:** Collect and store logs from all devices and systems in a central repository. This approach simplifies analysis and ensures all relevant data is easily accessible. Solutions such as SIEM tools are commonly used for this purpose.

- **Standardise log formats:** Ensure logs are in a standardised format to make data aggregation and analysis more efficient. Normalising logs helps in faster correlation and reduces the complexity of monitoring.

Log the correct data

- **Prioritise key events:** Focus on logging events that are most critical for security and operational visibility. These include:

  - **authentication events:** successful and failed login attempts, account lockouts and privilege escalations;

  - **access events:** file and folder access, especially for sensitive data;

  - **network activity:** unusual outbound connections, firewall rule changes and VPN connections;

  - **configuration changes:** changes to critical system settings, software installations and user privilege modifications;

  - **application events:** errors, crashes and suspicious activities in business-critical applications.

- **Avoid over-logging:** Logging too much data can make analysis difficult and increase storage costs. Strike a balance to ensure essential events are logged without overwhelming the system.

Implement robust monitoring and alerting

- **Set up real-time monitoring:** Implement real-time monitoring to detect anomalies and security incidents promptly. Automated alerting mechanisms should notify the relevant teams when suspicious activities occur.

- **Define alert thresholds:** Configure alert thresholds based on the organisation's risk tolerance. Alerts should be prioritised to avoid alert fatigue and ensure critical threats are addressed immediately.

- **Tune alerts regularly:** Periodically review and adjust alerting rules to minimise false positives and improve detection accuracy. This process should be ongoing, as threats and the IT environment evolve.

Use correlation and contextual analysis

- **Correlation rules:** Create rules that connect related events to identify complex attack patterns. For example, correlate a successful login followed by a data transfer event to a high-risk location.

- **Contextual awareness:** Enhance logging data with contextual information such as the user's role, device health status and the sensitivity level of accessed data. This contextual data helps analysts to make better decisions during investigations.

Protect log integrity and security

- **Log tamper protection:** Implement measures to protect logs from tampering, such as write-once-read-many (WORM) storage or cryptographic hashing of logs. This ensures the integrity of logs for forensic analysis and compliance audits.

- **Access controls:** Restrict access to logs based on the principle of least privilege. Only authorised personnel should have access to sensitive log data.

- **Secure data transmission:** Use encryption protocols, such as TLS, to secure logs in transit and at rest, preventing unauthorised access during data transfer.

Implement log retention policies

- **Define retention periods:** Establish retention policies that comply with legal, regulatory and business requirements. Retaining logs for too long can increase costs and risk, but insufficient retention may hinder forensic investigations.

- **Automate archiving:** Automate log archiving processes and ensure that older logs are securely stored, but still accessible when needed for incident response or audits.

Regularly review and analyse logs

- **Proactive analysis:** Don't just rely on alerts. Conduct regular, proactive log reviews to spot trends and anomalies that automated systems may miss. This can include performing root cause analysis on recurring issues or looking for early signs of attack campaigns.

- **Utilise threat intelligence:** Integrate external threat intelligence feeds to identify emerging threats and adjust logging and monitoring practices accordingly. This helps to enhance the detection of sophisticated attacks.

Integrate with incident response

- **Automate responses where possible:** Automate common incident response actions, such as blocking an IP address or isolating a compromised device. Integration with incident response tools ensures a swift reaction to detected threats.

- **Document response procedures:** Have clear, documented procedures for responding to alerts. This ensures a coordinated and efficient response when a security incident occurs.

Audit and improve your logging and monitoring strategy

- **Conduct regular audits:** Periodically audit your logging and monitoring setup to ensure it remains effective and compliant. This includes reviewing logging configurations, storage systems and alerting mechanisms.

- **Stay updated on best practices:** Security threats are always evolving, so it's crucial to stay informed about the latest best practices and technologies. Regularly train your security team and keep your monitoring tools up to date.

- **Gather feedback from analysts:** Obtain feedback from security analysts to understand the effectiveness of current logging and monitoring processes. Analysts can provide insights into alert relevance, the volume of false positives and areas for improvement.

INCIDENT RESPONSE

Incident response is used to describe the process that an organisation uses in response to an incident. It is a structured approach to handling and managing the aftermath of an incident to reduce damage, recovery time and costs. The incident can be anything from a power outage, severe weather and fire to a data breach or cyberattack. Each incident needs to be managed effectively to reduce the impact and harm to the organisation. With the greater reliance on information processes and systems, if these are disrupted the financial and reputational damage can be huge.

I have been involved in several incidents, both local and global, such as the SolarWinds incident in December 2020. This incident impacted five of the seven African local markets I was supporting cyber security-wise for a global company. They were not attacked directly, but had software that required patching quickly due to a vulnerability, as well as undertaking a check for any IoCs. My role was to ensure systems were patched and a check for IoCs was performed, working with stakeholders at a local and senior level. What was also interesting was that, as soon as the vulnerability was known about, there was a huge increase in external scans looking for it.

The SolarWinds attack was a sophisticated supply chain cyber operation conducted by APT29, also known as Cozy Bear, and attributed to Russia's Foreign Intelligence Service. The compromise was discovered in December 2020. Cozy Bear had created customised malware and injected it into the SolarWinds Orion software build process. This was then distributed by a software update process unbeknown that it contained malware. As well as the malware, they used token theft, password spraying, spear phishing and API abuse along with other supply chain attacks to compromise user accounts to gain access. The US government assessed that, of the approximately 18,000 affected public and private sector customers of Solar Winds' Orion, only a small number were compromised with activity from Cozy Bear on their systems.

> **NIST 800-61** definition of an incident is: 'A security incident is the act of violating an explicit or implied security policy' (Nelson et al., 2025).

The security policy will be defined by the organisation and may differ from organisation to organisation. As an example, a personally enabled device being taken into a retail organisation would most likely not be an incident, but that same device taken into a government building that handles top secret information would be a serious incident.

An organisation should have an incident response (IR) plan in place that clearly defines what an incident is, with a guided process to follow in order to ascertain the severity of the incident and therefore the required response (Figure 6.2).

Figure 6.2 NIST 800-61 four stage incident response

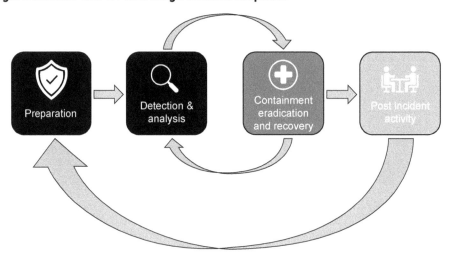

The need for an effective IR plan and management is often driven by change. Some of the trends and increased occurrences that can lead to changes are:

- a rise in information security incidents and losses such as ransomware;
- vulnerabilities in hardware and software;
- control failure;
- legal and regulatory changes;
- lack of security, with poorly managed IT;
- threat actor capability growing.

The IR plan must be supported by adequate policy and procedure and aligned to the overarching security strategy. The first step in creating an IR plan should be revisiting other information security policies to make sure that they are in place and that they are up to date and still fit for purpose, so that the IR plan is built on solid foundations.

A typical IR plan may include the following:

- mission;
- strategies and goals;
- organisation response to IR;
- triage and trigger for different IR levels;

- key decision-making employee and responsibilities;
- communication with the rest of the organisation and third parties or customers;
- an ability to measure the IR;
- capability and its effectiveness;
- lessons learned for ongoing IR improvement;
- senior management approval.

Preparation

The preparation phase is perhaps the most important phase. Here, the development of an IR plan and what is often called a computer emergency response team (CERT) is put together and trained. The goal is to ensure the organisation has the people, tools, polices and plans to respond to an incident. The plan cannot be considered implemented unless it has been tested.

- **Policies and procedures:** Establish and maintain IR policies, procedures and communication plans.
- **Tools and resources:** Ensure the availability of necessary tools, technologies and resources for effective incident management.
- **Training:** Provide regular training and awareness programmes for staff to recognise and respond to security incidents. This should be to test the incident plan too.

Detection and analysis

The next phase is the detection of an incident; it could just be IoC, intrusion or a full-blown cyberattack. The sooner you can detect, the sooner you can respond. A particularly important part is to check that it is an incident and not a false positive from a system failure or incorrect alerts. It is here where having monitors, vulnerability scanning, IDSs and log and network traffic analysis in place will help to get quick visibility and therefore response. With detection you also need to be able to undertake further analysis to determine the required response.

- **Detection:** Monitor systems to identify potential security incidents.
- **Analysis:** Assess the nature and scope of the incident to determine its impact and severity.

Containment, eradication and recovery

This third phase occurs after you have completed an analysis and know what you are dealing with. Even though it may not be full knowledge, you can look to contain the incident to prevent it spreading or affecting other critical systems or services. At this point you will also decide if you want to undertake collection for digital forensics' use or as required to keep for law enforcement, as eradication means removal of artefacts that may have been involved in the incident. Finally, recovery means ensuring the systems are running exactly as they were prior to the incident.

- **Short term:** Take immediate actions to contain the incident and prevent further damage, such as isolating affected systems.

- **Long term:** Take steps to maintain containment while preparing for full recovery, such as removing malware or closing vulnerabilities.

- **Restoration:** Bring affected systems back to normal operations, ensuring that data and systems are now clean and fully secure.

- **Monitoring:** Undertake ongoing monitoring to detect any signs of residual issues or new attacks.

Post-incident activity

This is the final phase and occurs after the incident has been resolved. Here, a root cause analysis should be completed if not completed during other phases. An organisation needs to know how and why it happened and what they can do to prevent it occurring again. The team can also look at their response and whether there is anything they could have done better, or any tools, policy or procedure that needs improvement – this can include the IR plan.

- **Post-incident analysis:** Conduct a thorough review of the incident to understand what happened, why it happened and how it was handled through a root cause analysis.

- **Improvement:** Update policies, procedures and security measures based on the findings to prevent future incidents.

Apply Disaster Incubation Theory

We can also use elements of Turner's Disaster Incubation Theory that we discussed in Chapter 4 within an organisational context:

- **Rigidities in perception and beliefs in organisational settings:** These can prevent accurate perception of the possibility of a disaster.

- **The decoy problem:** When some risk is perceived, the action taken to deal with the problem could distract attention from the problem that eventually causes a disaster.

- **Organisational exclusivity:** This is the organisational tendency to deny remote dangers, with management dismissing those who disagree with the organisation's policy as 'cranks'.

- **Information difficulties:** These divide among four classes:

  1. Completely unknown prior information.

  2. Prior information that is noted but not fully appreciated.

  3. Prior information that is noted by someone but not combined with other information at an appropriate time to build a holistic view.

  4. Prior information that is available but ignored because there was no place for it within prevailing modes of understanding.

CASE STUDY

Incident response and security architecture in a telecommunications firm

Scenario

A leading telecommunications company experienced a sophisticated cyberattack targeting its core infrastructure, resulting in service disruptions for customers and exposing vulnerabilities in its existing security architecture. The incident highlighted the need for a comprehensive review and overhaul of its security practices to better defend against future attacks. The company embarked on a mission to implement a more resilient security architecture and enhance its incident response capabilities while maintaining service availability for millions of customers across multiple regions.

Focus areas

Minimising the impact of future incidents

The security overhaul focused on building resilience into the architecture to contain and recover from attacks more effectively:

- **Resilient core infrastructure:** Critical systems such as domain name system (DNS), billing platforms and customer-facing services were hardened with advanced redundancy mechanisms.

- **Enhanced incident playbooks:** Detailed incident response playbooks tailored to telecommunications-specific threats, such as DoS attacks and Signalling System 7 (SS7) vulnerabilities, were developed.

- **Automation:** Tools for automated incident detection, containment and recovery were implemented, reducing response times significantly.

Network segmentation

The firm's flat network design was a key factor in the attack's ability to spread rapidly. The redesign introduced strict segmentation to limit lateral movement:

- **Customer data isolation:** Systems storing sensitive customer data were isolated from operational systems, with access strictly controlled via zero trust principles.

- **Segregation of administrative functions:** Privileged accounts and systems were placed in separate zones with enhanced monitoring and controls.

- **Regional segmentation:** Regional operations were segmented to ensure that breaches in one area did not impact global operations.

- **Robust SOC:** The SOC was restructured to provide real-time visibility across IT and telecommunications networks.

- **Threat intelligence integration:** Live feeds from telecom-specific threat intelligence sources were integrated to proactively identify risks such as signalling attacks or vulnerabilities in 5G and IoT devices.

- **SOC staffing and skills:** The SOC was staffed with experts in telecom protocols such as SS7, Diameter and session initiation protocol (SIP), enabling rapid response to sector-specific threats.

- **Advanced monitoring tools:** A combination of SIEM and UEBA tools was deployed to detect anomalous activities, such as unauthorised access to core switches or unexpected traffic patterns.

Challenges

Identifying critical assets to prioritise
Telecommunications infrastructures include a complex mix of legacy systems, new technologies and third-party integrations. A full asset inventory was undertaken, requiring collaboration between IT, engineering and network operations teams to map dependencies and identify critical assets for protection.

Ensuring minimal service disruption during redesign
The architectural overhaul had to be conducted in a live environment without disrupting essential services such as mobile, broadband and emergency communication channels. This was achieved by using phased rollouts, extensive testing in sandbox environments and fallback mechanisms to ensure service continuity.

Implementing effective logging and monitoring
Logging and monitoring needed to cover the expansive telecom environment, including base stations, data centres and interconnect networks. Challenges included standardising log formats across heterogeneous systems and ensuring logs were centrally aggregated for efficient analysis without introducing latency.

Outcomes

Enhanced incident response capabilities
The revamped incident response processes enabled faster detection and containment of threats. For example, during a simulated SS7 attack, SOC analysts identified and blocked malicious signalling traffic within 15 minutes, compared to several hours previously.

Faster threat containment
Network segmentation and automated containment tools limited the spread of attacks. In a follow-up penetration test, testers who gained initial access to a regional system were unable to escalate privileges or access core systems, demonstrating the effectiveness of segmentation.

Collaboration between security and engineering teams
Security and engineering teams worked more closely following the overhaul. Joint war games and incident simulations were conducted, fostering cross-functional collaboration and enabling teams to better understand each other's workflows and challenges.

Key learnings

- Proactive investment in segmentation and redundancy can significantly reduce the impact of breaches in critical infrastructures.

- Sector-specific threat intelligence and expertise are vital for effective monitoring and incident response in telecommunications.

- Collaborative incident simulations not only improve response times but also enhance trust and alignment across technical teams.

- Automation of detection and response processes allows faster and more efficient containment, crucial for large-scale and distributed infrastructures.

- Continuous refinement of security architectures ensures adaptability to emerging technologies such as 5G, IoT and edge computing.

7   SECURITY TESTING AND VERIFICATION

Security testing should be implemented in a way that integrates seamlessly into the SDLC, with automated tools providing continuous feedback and human experts conducting in-depth analysis. By embedding security from the earliest stages of development and maintaining a cycle of regular testing and monitoring, organisations can build more resilient and secure systems, reducing the risk of costly data breaches and enhancing overall software quality. In this chapter we will look at DevSecOps, security testing and SBD.

DEVSECOPS

DevSecOps is the integration of security practices in the software delivery model of DevOps (Figure 7.1). In DevSecOps everyone is responsible for security. The goal is to incorporate security in all the phases of the software development lifecycle by integrating security through tools, encouraging cross skills and establishing security as part of the software development culture.

Conventionally, security checks were performed at the end of the software development lifecycle after the product had been developed. This could lead to software that had to be reworked or extensively modified, adding to both the cost and the development time. Instead of waiting to check security after a new feature is developed, tested and released into production, it's more effective to perform security testing at every phase. This allows for immediate resolution of security issues as they arise.

DevSecOps requires developers, operations and security professionals to work together throughout the development lifecycle. The security team should advise the development and operations teams and support them in understanding and managing security. The security team should be involved in creating security policies, and choosing automation tools to identify security issues.

The benefits of DevSecOps are:

- It reduces security vulnerabilities in applications.
- Compliance can be incorporated at the initial stages.
- Developers can respond to code changes quickly.
- Early identification of vulnerabilities can be made.

Figure 7.1 DevOps vs DevSecOps

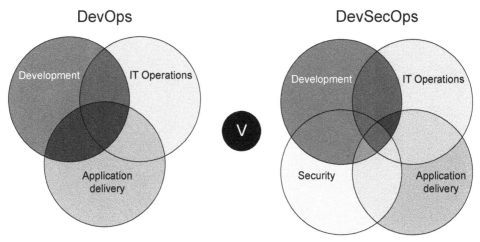

- Security teams can work faster.
- Every change can be tracked and monitored.
- It reduces cost and helps in the faster delivery of software.
- It offers transparency from the early stages of development.
- It is SBD with increased observability and traceability.
- It provides security, monitors resources and sends notifications earlier.
- Recovery from a security incident is faster.
- It improves overall security with immutable infrastructure.

Software is developed in a pipeline for DevSecOps, with security checks at every stage, and should follow these steps (Figure 7.2):

- **Plan:** Execute security analysis and develop a plan to determine the scenarios for when, how and where the security testing should be performed. Include threat modelling and risk assessment.
- **Code:** Protect API keys and passwords and ensure the use of secure code repositories. Use secure coding practices and conduct peer code reviews.
- **Build:** After building the code, use static application security testing (SAST) tools to identify security issues in the code before deploying to production. Use secure coding practices with code review.
- **Test:** To test the application during runtime, use dynamic application security testing (DAST) tools to identify errors such as those related to authentication, authorisation and injection. DAST tools should be complemented with other testing techniques, such as interactive application security testing (IAST), for more comprehensive coverage.

- **Release:** Use security analysis tools to perform penetration testing and vulnerability scanning before releasing the application, perform a final review of security policies and ensure compliance with relevant standards.

- **Deploy:** Once all the tests are completed at runtime, the secure build or infrastructure can be sent to production for deployment, monitoring and logging of security events post-deployment as part of an ongoing security requirement.

- **Operate:** Reliable and secure running of applications and infrastructure in production is vital. This involves deploying code in a controlled manner, enforcing runtime security policies, ensuring infrastructure is configured securely (e.g. using infrastructure as code with validated templates) and maintaining compliance with regulatory and organisational standards.

- **Monitor:** Ensure continuous visibility of the system's performance, security posture and user behaviour. Collect logs, metrics and telemetry data to detect anomalies, vulnerabilities or breaches in real time, ensuring that any threat or degradation in service is swiftly addressed to maintain system integrity and availability.

Figure 7.2 DevSecOps diagram

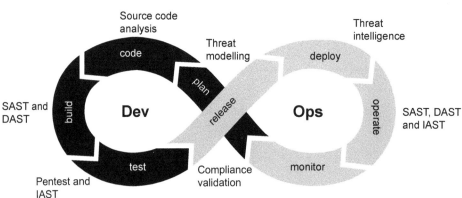

Proper testing of software including patches can be best highlighted by the CrowdStrike incident on 19 July 2024, when a flawed software update to CrowdStrike's Falcon Sensor caused severe disruptions, leading to blue screens of death on millions of Windows computers. This resulted in significant downtime globally, affecting commercial flights, broadcasters, banking, healthcare and emergency call centres. The incident had a substantial impact, causing CrowdStrike's share price to drop more than 11 per cent. The widespread system failures highlighted vulnerabilities in critical infrastructure and disrupted daily operations for numerous organisations and services, emphasising the critical importance of robust cyber security measures and quality control in software updates.

SECURITY TESTING

Security testing and verification are fundamental processes for identifying and mitigating vulnerabilities in software, systems or networks and they are integrated into the DevSecOps approach to ensure a robust security posture throughout the SDLC. DevSecOps represents a shift-left philosophy, where security practices are embedded into every stage of development from initial design to production deployment. Each time I have worked with a third party or on a project where security has not been consulted at the start, it has led to either delays or workarounds being required due to the lack of initial engagement or assumptions being made on security requirements.

Security testing focuses on detecting and addressing potential weaknesses within systems, and includes a variety of methods. Vulnerability scanning employs automated tools, such as Nessus or Qualys, to detect issues such as missing patches or misconfigurations; penetration testing (pentesting) involves simulating real-world attacks to find and exploit vulnerabilities, a task that often complements automated scans by assessing systems from an adversarial perspective. In a DevSecOps model, these tests can be incorporated into CI/CD pipelines, allowing for continuous validation of security controls.

Security code reviews are another critical aspect, where source code is analysed for insecure practices, either manually or using automated solutions such as Checkmarx. This step is vital in DevSecOps, as it ensures that developers can receive security feedback early and in real time. Threat modelling is also significant, helping teams to proactively identify and mitigate threats by evaluating application architecture. Using frameworks such as the STRIDE model, security threats are systematically analysed and mitigations are built into the development process. This proactive approach aligns with DevSecOps by embedding security considerations into design and implementation.

Techniques such as SAST and DAST are widely adopted in DevSecOps. SAST tools analyse code for vulnerabilities before execution, making them useful for early development phases, while DAST tools test running applications for weaknesses. Both are essential for providing comprehensive security coverage and integrating these into automated CI/CD pipelines to allow for consistent and continuous security checks. IAST combines elements of both SAST and DAST, offering a deeper level of security insight by analysing applications from within, fitting seamlessly into the DevSecOps framework.

Other key security testing methods include configuration testing, which assesses the security settings of components to ensure no exploitable misconfigurations remain, and fuzz testing (fuzzing), where applications are subjected to random inputs to uncover unknown vulnerabilities. These techniques are integral in a DevSecOps setup, where automated testing and fast feedback loops are essential.

Security verification is the process of validating that security controls are effective and compliant with security policies and standards. This involves activities such as manual code reviews, where security experts ensure that security measures are robust, and automated testing tools, such as OWASP ZAP or Burp Suite (API and web testing), which are critical for continuous security validation in DevSecOps. Compliance verification ensures adherence to standards such as ISO 27001, GDPR or PCI DSS, an important aspect that can also be automated to streamline security governance. In high-assurance environments, formal methods and model checking can provide guarantees of software security, often reserved for systems where failures would have severe consequences in terms of business impact should they not be available.

Security requirement testing ensures that all security specifications are correctly implemented. In DevSecOps, security requirements are defined early and continuously verified, ensuring they are upheld throughout the development lifecycle. This alignment with DevSecOps practices facilitates ongoing assurance that critical security measures are enforced.

The goals of security testing and verification include identifying vulnerabilities early, reducing remediation costs, ensuring compliance and enhancing overall system trustworthiness. In a DevSecOps context, these practices not only mitigate risk but also foster a culture of collaboration among development, security and operations teams, where security becomes a shared responsibility. This proactive approach prevents data breaches, safeguards sensitive information and promotes the delivery of reliable software.

Integrating security testing and verification within the SDLC involves several key steps, including defining security requirements during initial phases and conducting secure design reviews such as threat modelling to ensure that potential security issues are addressed before coding begins. Automated security testing integrated into CI/CD pipelines is a hallmark of DevSecOps, providing ongoing security assessments and ensuring any vulnerabilities are promptly fixed. Even post-deployment, systems are continuously monitored and tested to stay ahead of emerging threats. By embedding security throughout the SDLC, DevSecOps transforms the traditional security model into one that is agile, automated and integrated, enabling faster and safer software delivery.

Clean code

Clean code refers to well-structured, readable and maintainable code that follows best practices, making it easy to understand and modify. Key principles include:

- **readability:** clear naming conventions and well-organised structure;
- **simplicity:** avoids unnecessary complexity – follows the keep it simple, stupid principle;
- **modularity:** uses small, single-responsibility functions and classes;
- **consistency:** follows a uniform coding style and design patterns;
- **minimal comments:** code is self-explanatory – comments are used only when necessary;
- **efficient error handling:** uses proper exception handling and validation;
- **testability:** easily testable with unit tests.

Clean Code is code that's easy to read, maintain, understand for developers and other teams while improving the quality of their software through structure and consistency with performance demands. It lets you get the most value and purpose out of your software (Sonar, n.d.).

Security testing implementation

Implementing security testing effectively requires a comprehensive and structured approach, where security measures are woven throughout the SDLC. This process begins with establishing a strong foundation of security requirements during the planning and design phases. By clearly defining what needs to be protected and understanding the potential threats, development teams can create applications with built-in security measures rather than attempting to bolt them on later. This shift-left approach is fundamental to DevSecOps and encourages collaboration between developers, security experts and operations teams from the outset to ensure security issues are picked up and mitigated early on. Reworking or changing vendor or objectives due to a security failure at a later stage can be both time-consuming and expensive. An organisation must realise that security is as important as any other element in system development. It could be the reason not to proceed with a project due to cost or unacceptable risk.

Threat modelling, covered in Chapter 3, is a proactive step that should be implemented early on, where teams analyse the application architecture to identify possible attack vectors and vulnerabilities. This process will help to map out potential threats, such as data breaches or unauthorised access, and allows for prioritising the mitigation strategies. In this phase, using established frameworks such as STRIDE, TRIKE, VAST or PASTA can aid in thoroughly assessing risks and making informed security decisions.

SAST should be integrated into the development process to analyse the source code for vulnerabilities before the code is executed. This approach ensures that security checks occur early, catching issues such as hard-coded secrets or improper input validation at a stage where they are cheaper and easier to fix. Automated SAST tools, such as SonarQube or Checkmarx, can be set up to run within CI/CD pipelines, providing continuous feedback to developers and allowing them to address issues immediately. This integration is crucial in maintaining a fast development pace while ensuring security remains a top priority.

DAST complements SAST by testing the running application for security vulnerabilities in real time. This testing should occur in a staging environment that closely mirrors the production setting to ensure an accurate assessment of how the application would perform under attack. DAST can help to identify issues such as SQL injection or XSS that may not be evident from a static code analysis. Incorporating DAST into automated build processes ensures that security is continuously verified and any regressions are detected before they reach production.

Penetration testing is another essential component of testing, where ethical hackers simulate real-world attacks to expose vulnerabilities that automated tools may not detect. These tests should be scheduled regularly and after major changes to the system. They provide a deeper understanding of how an attacker might exploit a system, offering valuable insights into how security measures including controls perform. Penetration testing can be performed internally, with a focus on insider threats, or externally, to simulate the perspective of an external adversary. The results of these tests should be documented and fed back into the development cycle for remediation.

Fuzz testing adds another layer of robustness by subjecting the application to unexpected or random inputs to uncover flaws such as crashes or memory leaks. This type of testing is particularly effective in identifying vulnerabilities that might not be immediately obvious but could still be exploited by a determined attacker. Fuzz testing can be automated to run periodically, ensuring that the application remains resilient even as new features are developed.

Configuration testing is also important to ensuring that systems are not left with default or misconfigured settings that attackers could exploit. Misconfigurations is one of the top causes of breach or successful attack. It involves auditing the security settings of servers, databases and other components to ensure they are correctly configured and comply with security policies. Tools such as Center for Internet Security Configuration Assessment Tool can automate this process, making it easier to identify and rectify misconfigurations.

Security verification involves validating that all security requirements have been met and that the implemented controls are effective. This stage includes manual code reviews by security experts who ensure that critical parts of the application have been properly secured. It also involves automated testing using tools such as OWASP ZAP or Burp Suite, which can scan applications for vulnerabilities continuously. Security verification should also consider compliance with regulatory standards, such as GDPR, PCI DSS or ISO 27001, to ensure that the application meets industry requirements.

Post-deployment security testing and ongoing monitoring are crucial to maintaining a secure application. Even after the application goes live, it should be regularly assessed to protect against new and evolving threats. This can include running periodic vulnerability scans, IDSs and keeping an eye on threat intelligence feeds. Automation is key to efficiently managing these tasks in a DevSecOps environment, where continuous monitoring and incident response capabilities are essential to defend against sophisticated attackers.

SECURE BY DESIGN

The idea of SBD transforms security from being a reactive effort into a proactive one. By integrating security from the very beginning, organisations can build more resilient systems that are harder to exploit and easier to defend. This approach not only protects sensitive information and system functionality, but also instils a culture of security awareness throughout the development process, making it a crucial aspect of modern software and system engineering.

SBD emphasises embedding security measures into the architecture and design of a system right from the initial stages, rather than adding them as an afterthought. This concept ensures that security is a fundamental component of the system, significantly reducing the likelihood of vulnerabilities. The SBD philosophy prioritises proactive measures, ensuring that systems are built to withstand attacks and continue to function securely under adverse conditions.

The core idea behind SBD is to identify and mitigate security risks during the design phase of a project. This involves conducting thorough threat modelling and risk assessments to understand the attack surface and potential security challenges. Threat modelling is an analytical process that helps design teams to think like adversaries, mapping out possible attack vectors and weak points in the system architecture. By understanding these threats early, developers can design effective countermeasures and ensure that the system is resilient to known and emerging threats.

A critical aspect of SBD is defence in depth, which involves implementing multiple layers of security controls so that if one defence fails, others remain in place to protect the system. For example, a web application might use input validation and sanitisation to protect against injection attacks, while also employing authentication, authorisation and encryption to secure data. This layered approach ensures that even if an attacker bypasses one security measure, there are additional safeguards to prevent further exploitation.

Principle of least privilege is a foundational concept in SBD. It dictates that users and systems should have only the minimal level of access necessary to perform their functions. By limiting permissions, the potential damage from compromised accounts or insider threats is significantly reduced. This principle extends to system components, where microservices or modules should have restricted communication with each other, limiting the spread of attacks within the system. Implementing least privilege in the design phase helps to reduce the risk of lateral movement within an environment.

Secure defaults are another principle in SBD, meaning systems should be configured to be secure out of the box, without requiring extensive modifications. For instance, default settings should enforce strong password policies, disable unnecessary services and enable encryption for data at rest and in transit. This approach ensures that even if system administrators are not security experts, the system will still operate securely by default, reducing the risk of human error. Secure defaults are particularly important for reducing the attack surface, as they close off common entry points that attackers might exploit.

Data protection is a fundamental consideration in the SBD approach. Sensitive information should be protected both at rest and in transit using strong encryption algorithms. The design should include mechanisms for secure key management, ensuring that encryption keys are stored and used securely. Additionally, privacy principles, such as data minimisation and purpose limitation, should be applied to reduce the amount of sensitive information collected and processed. Implementing secure data handling practices ensures compliance with regulations such as GDPR and reduces the impact of data breaches.

Secure coding practices, which developers must follow to minimise vulnerabilities, include validating and sanitising all user inputs, using parameterised queries to prevent SQL injection and avoiding hard-coded secrets in the source code. Secure coding standards, such as those recommended by OWASP, provide guidelines that help developers to write secure software. Incorporating secure coding practices from the beginning of the development process helps to prevent common security issues and ensures that the application is resilient against various attack vectors.

Security reviews carried out on a regular basis along with design assessments are necessary to ensure the system remains secure as it evolves. These reviews should be integrated into the development lifecycle and involve security experts who can evaluate the design and architecture for weaknesses. As the system is developed, periodic assessments help to ensure that new features or changes do not introduce security flaws. Automated security tools can be employed to support these reviews, but manual oversight is also crucial for evaluating complex design elements that require human judgement.

Security testing is also critical in a SBD approach. Testing methods such as static analysis, dynamic analysis and penetration testing should be used to evaluate the security of the system throughout its development. The earlier that vulnerabilities are identified, the easier and cheaper they are to fix. By embedding security testing into the continuous integration and continuous deployment pipeline, teams can ensure that every code change is automatically checked for security flaws before deployment.

Resilience and incident response planning are essential components of a SBD strategy. Even with robust security measures, breaches may still occur, so it is important to design systems to be resilient and capable of quick recovery. This involves creating incident response plans, logging and monitoring for anomalies and designing systems that can continue to function in a degraded mode if necessary. Building resilience into the system ensures that, in the event of an attack, the impact is minimised and recovery is swift.

UK Government SBD principles

The UK Government's SBD principles are aimed to ensure security is embedded into the development of systems, software and services from the outset. These principles are outlined in various guidance documents from the NCSC and Department for Culture, Media and Sport (DCMS).

The core principles for the foundations required for embedding cyber security practices in digital delivery and building resilient digital services include:

- **Security as a foundation:** Security should be a fundamental part of design, not an afterthought.
- **Understanding the threats:** Systems should be built with a clear understanding of potential threats and risks via threat modelling.
- **Minimising the attack surface:** Unnecessary complexity and exposure to vulnerabilities must be reduced.
- **Secure defaults:** Systems should be secure by default, without requiring additional configuration.
- **Least privilege:** Users and processes should only have the minimum access needed to function.

- **Defence in depth:** Multiple layers of security must be implemented to protect against different types of threats.

- **Secure supply chain:** Ensuring that third-party components and services meet security standards is vital.

- **Secure deployment and maintenance:** Security should be maintained throughout the system's lifecycle, including updates and patching.

- **Security transparency and assurance:** Providing evidence that security measures are effective and verifiable is vital.

- **Resilience and recovery:** Systems should be designed to detect, respond to and recover from an event or incident.

APPENDIX

LEADERSHIP SKILLS

Leadership skills are critical in any role involving team collaboration, decision-making or achievement of goals. Leadership skills are not limited to management positions either, and are valuable for anyone aiming to make an impact or drive progress. Developing these skills often requires a combination of self-reflection, experience and continuous learning.

Leadership is all about influencing and taking a team on a journey. The team is a leader's greatest asset, and a leader should support and nurture the team by building skills, offering development opportunities, mentoring and listening to what the team has to say. Having empathy and understanding is important too. Leadership requires the ability to break down complex problems, identify their root causes and come up with fresh solutions. A leader may need to manage ambiguity, dealing with competing priorities that feel equally important.

Strategic vision and planning

This is the ability to align cyber security strategies with organisational goals and future-proof the security posture.

Application:

- developing long-term plans to counter emerging threats, such as zero-day vulnerabilities or quantum computing risks;
- balancing risk appetite and investment in security technologies.

Risk management and decision-making

This is the ability to assess risks, prioritise mitigation strategies and make informed decisions under pressure.

Application:

- leading risk assessments to identify potential threats to critical systems;
- deciding on trade-offs between security measures and business continuity during an incident.

Communication and stakeholder engagement

This is the ability to translate complex cyber security concepts into clear, actionable messages for diverse audiences.

Application:

- explaining the impact of a threat (e.g. ransomware) to non-technical stakeholders such as board members;
- leading awareness programmes to foster a security-conscious culture within the organisation.

Crisis management and incident response

This is the ability to stay calm, decisive and resourceful during cyber security incidents.

Application:

- leading the response to a critical event such as a data breach, ensuring swift containment, recovery and reporting;
- coordinating with legal, PR and IT teams to manage reputational and operational risks.

Technical knowledge and adaptability

This is the ability to understand cyber security frameworks, technologies and threat landscapes to make informed decisions.

Application:

- guiding the implementation of frameworks such as NIST, ISO 27001 or zero trust models;
- staying updated on emerging trends, such as quantum-resistant cryptography or AI-powered security tools.

Team building and mentoring

This is the ability to cultivate a skilled, motivated and cohesive cyber security team.

Application:

- recruiting and retaining top talent in specialised areas such as penetration testing or threat intelligence;
- providing career development opportunities and mentoring junior team members to grow their technical and leadership capabilities.

Collaboration and cross-functional leadership

This is the ability to foster collaboration across IT, legal, compliance and business teams.

Application:

- coordinating with DevOps teams to integrate security into software development (DevSecOps);
- engaging with compliance teams to address regulations such as GDPR or PCI DSS.

Ethical judgement and integrity

This is the ability to uphold ethical principles while handling sensitive information and making critical decisions.

Application:

- ensuring transparency during incidents, such as disclosing breaches to regulators and customers;
- avoiding shortcuts that could lead to regulatory or ethical violations.

Change management and innovation

This is the ability to lead organisational change to adopt new security technologies and processes.

Application:

- implementing advanced threat detection systems or migrating to cloud-based security architectures;
- driving the adoption of innovative solutions, such as AI for real-time threat analysis.

Influencing and advocacy

This is the ability to build a strong case for cyber security investments and influence key decision-makers.

Application:

- advocating for increased budgets for security tools and training;
- influencing board-level decisions to prioritise cyber security as a business enabler.

Cultural awareness and emotional intelligence

This is the ability to lead diverse teams and adapt leadership styles to cultural and situational nuances.

Application:

- managing a global incident response team with diverse cultural norms and communication styles;
- recognising and addressing burnout within the cyber security workforce.

Analytical thinking and problem-solving

This is the ability to break down complex problems and develop actionable solutions.

Application:

- analysing threat reports to anticipate and counter adversarial tactics;
- designing layered defences to mitigate vulnerabilities effectively.

CONCLUSION

Strong leadership in cyber security requires a unique balance of technical acumen, emotional intelligence and business insight. A successful cyber security leader not only defends the organisation against threats but also acts as a strategic partner, driving innovation and resilience.

BIBLIOGRAPHY

BOOKS

Department of the Army [US] (2021) *Field Manual 3–12: Cyberspace and Electronic Warfare Operations*. Washington, DC: Headquarters, Department of the Army. Available at: https://irp.fas.org/doddir/army/fm3-12.pdf.

Diston, R. (2024) *Real Security Management™*. London: The Real Security Doctor Ltd.

Green, J. (2024) *Information Management Security Principles*, 4th edition. Swindon: BCS.

ISACA (2022) *CISM Review Manual*, 16th edition. Schaumburg, Illinois: ISACA.

Katz, J. and Lindell, Y. (2015) *Introduction to Modern Cryptography*, 2nd edition. Abingdon: Chapman & Hall.

Moyle, E. and Kelley, D. (2020) *Practical Cybersecurity Architecture: A Guide to Creating and Implementing Robust Designs for Cybersecurity Architects*. Birmingham: Packt Publishing Ltd.

Nielsen, M.A. and Chuang, I.L. (2010) *Quantum Computation and Quantum Information*, 10th anniversary edition. Cambridge: Cambridge University Press.

Schneier, B. (2019) *Click Here to Kill Everybody: Security and Survival in a Hyper-connected World*. New York: W.W. Norton & Co.

Turner, B.A. (1978) *Man-Made Disasters: The Failure of Foresight*. London: Wykeham Publications.

CONFERENCE PAPERS

Grant, T. (2023) 'Detect, deny, degrade, disrupt, destroy, deceive: which is the greatest in OCO?'. *Proceedings of the 22nd European Conference on Cyber Warfare and Security*. Available at: https://papers.academic-conferences.org/index.php/eccws/article/download/1089/1166/4390.

Shor, P.W. (1994) 'Algorithms for quantum computation: discrete logarithms and factoring'. *Proceedings of the 35th Annual Symposium on Foundations of Computer Science*, pp. 124–134. Available at: https://doi.org/10.1109/SFCS.1994.365700.

REPORTS AND STANDARDS

Barker, E., Chen, L., Roginsky, A. and Vassilev, A. (2019) 'Special publication 800-56B rev. 2: recommendation for pair-wise key establishment using integer factorization cryptography'. *NIST*. Available at: https://nvlpubs.nist.gov/nistpubs/SpecialPublications/NIST.SP.800-56Br2.pdf.

Beasley, M. and Branson, B.C. (2024) '2024 state of risk oversight report: 15th edition'. *AICPA & CIMA*. Available at: www.aicpa-cima.com/resources/download/2024-state-of-risk-oversight-report-15th-edition.

Center for Internet Security (n.d.) 'The 18 CIS Critical Security Controls' [CIS controls v8.1]. *CIS. Center for Internet Security*. Available at: www.cisecurity.org/controls/cis-controls-list.

Center for Internet Security (n.d.) 'CIS Critical Security Controls navigator'. *CIS. Center for Internet Security*. Available at: www.cisecurity.org/controls/cis-controls-navigator.

Chen, L., Jordan, S., Liu, Y.-K., Moody, D., Peralta, R., Perlner, R. and Smith-Tone, D. (2016) 'NISTIR 8105: report on post-quantum cryptography'. *NIST*. Available at: https://nvlpubs.nist.gov/nistpubs/ir/2016/NIST.IR.8105.pdf.

ENISA (2010) 'Good practice guide for incident management'. *European Union Agency for Cybersecurity*. Available at: www.enisa.europa.eu/publications/good-practice-guide-for-incident-management.

ISACA (n.d.) 'COBIT, an ISACA framework. Effective IT governance at your fingertips: build your expertise in the globally accepted framework for optimizing enterprise IT governance'. *ISACA*. Available at: www.isaca.org/resources/cobit.

ISO (n.d.) 'ISO/IEC 19790:2012 – information technology – security techniques – security requirements for cryptographic modules' [withdrawn]. *ISO*. Available at: www.iso.org/standard/52906.html.

ISO (n.d.) 'ISO/IEC 19790:2025 – information security, cybersecurity and privacy protection – security requirements for cryptographic modules'. *ISO*. Available at: www.iso.org/standard/82423.html.

ISO (n.d.) 'ISO/IEC 27001:2022 – information security, cybersecurity and privacy protection – information security management systems – requirements'. *ISO*. Available at: www.iso.org/standard/27001.

ISO (n.d.) 'ISO 31000:2018 – risk management – guidelines'. *ISO*. Available at: www.iso.org/standard/65694.html.

McKay, K.A. and Cooper, D.A. (2019) 'SP 800-52 rev. 2: guidelines for the selection, configuration and use of transport layer security (TLS) implementations'. *NIST*. Available at: https://csrc.nist.gov/pubs/sp/800/52/r2/final.

Mell, P. and Grance, T. (2011) 'Special publication 800-145. The NIST definition of cloud computing: recommendations of the National Institute of Standards and Technology'. *NIST*. Available at: https://nvlpubs.nist.gov/nistpubs/Legacy/SP/nistspecialpublication800-145.pdf.

NCSC (2023) 'Cyber essentials: requirements for infrastructure v3.1'. *NCSC*. Available at: www.ncsc.gov.uk/files/Cyber-Essentials-Requirements-for-Infrastructure-v3-1-April-2023.pdf.

NCSC (2023) 'Cyber essentials plus: illustrative test specification v3.1'. *NCSC*. Available at: www.ncsc.gov.uk/files/Cyber-Essentials-Plus-Illustrative-Technical-Specification-v3-1-January-2023.pdf

NCSC (n.d.) 'Secure design principles'. *NCSC*. Available at: www.ncsc.gov.uk/collection/cyber-security-design-principles.

NCSC (n.d.) 'Security architecture anti-patterns: six design patterns to avoid when designing computer systems'. *NCSC*. Available at: www.ncsc.gov.uk/whitepaper/security-architecture-anti-patterns?source=techstories.org.

NCSC (n.d.) 'Zero trust architecture design principles: eight principles to help you to implement your own zero trust network architecture in an enterprise environment'. *NCSC*. Available at: www.ncsc.gov.uk/collection/zero-trust-architecture/introduction-to-zero-trust.

Nelson, A., Rekhi, S., Souppaya, M. and Scarfone, K. (2025) 'SP 800-61 rev. 3. Incident response recommendations and considerations for cybersecurity risk management: a CSF 2.0 community profile'. *NIST*. Available at: https://doi.org/10.6028/NIST.SP.800-61r3.

NIST (2018) 'SP 800-37 rev 2. Risk management framework for information systems and organizations: a system life cycle approach for security and privacy'. *NIST*. Available at: https://csrc.nist.gov/pubs/sp/800/37/r2/final.

NIST (2024) 'Announcing issuance of Federal Information Processing Standards (FIPS) FIPS 203, Module-Lattice-Based Key-Encapsulation Mechanism Standard, FIPS 204, Module-Lattice-Based Digital Signature Standard, and FIPS 205, Stateless Hash-Based Digital Signature Standard'. *Federal Register*. Available at: www.federalregister.gov/documents/2024/08/14/2024-17956/announcing-issuance-of-federal-information-processing-standards-fips-fips-203-module-lattice-based.

NIST (n.d.) 'Cybersecurity framework'. *NIST*. Available at: www.nist.gov/cyberframework.

NIST Joint Task Force (2020) 'Special publication 800-53 rev. 5: security and privacy controls for information systems and organizations'. *NIST*. Available at: https://nvlpubs.nist.gov/nistpubs/SpecialPublications/NIST.SP.800-53r5.pdf.

OWASP (n.d.) 'OWASP AI security and privacy guide'. *OWASP*. Available at: https://owasp.org/www-project-ai-security-and-privacy-guide/.

The Open Group (n.d.) 'The TOGAF® Standard, 10th edition'. *The Open Group*. Available at: www.opengroup.org/togaf.

ONLINE RESOURCES

Barros, A. and Chuvakin, A. (2016) 'Detection and response technologies and solutions'. *Gartner*. Available at: www.gartner.com/en/documents/3343417.

Braverman-Blumenstyk, M. (2023) 'Starting your journey to become quantum-safe'. *Microsoft*. Available at: www.microsoft.com/en-us/security/blog/2023/11/01/starting-your-journey-to-become-quantum-safe/?msockid=08b11b1ad9aa616b1fcb08ccd83a6022.

Cloudflare (n.d.) 'What is IPsec? How IPsec VPNs work'. *Cloudflare*. Available at: www.cloudflare.com/en-gb/learning/network-layer/what-is-ipsec/.

CRYSTALS (n.d.) 'Kyber'. *CRYSTALS*. Available at: https://pq-crystals.org/kyber/.

CyberArk Software Ltd (n.d.) 'What is privileged access management (PAM)?'. *CYBERARK, The Identity Security Company*. Available at: www.cyberark.com/what-is/privileged-access-management/.

Docker (2025) 'Get started with Docker: build applications faster and more securely with Docker for developers'. *docker*. Available at: www.docker.com/get-started/.

Evrin, V. (2021) 'Risk assessment and analysis methods: qualitative and quantitative'. *ISACA Journal*, 2. Available at: www.isaca.org/resources/isaca-journal/issues/2021/volume-2/risk-assessment-and-analysis-methods.

IBM (2023) 'What is security information and event management (SIEM)?'. *IBM*. Available at: www.ibm.com/think/topics/siem.

IBM Quantum (2023) 'Welcome to the upgraded IBM Quantum Platform'. *IBM Quantum Platform*. Available at: https://quantum.cloud.ibm.com/.

IBM Quantum Learning (2025) 'Fundamentals of quantum algorithms'. *IBM Quantum Learning*. Available at: https://learning.quantum.ibm.com/course/fundamentals-of-quantum-algorithms/quantum-query-algorithms.

Lehman, N. (2024) 'Post-Quantum Cryptography Alliance launches to advance post-quantum cryptography'. *The Linux Foundation*. Available at: www.linuxfoundation.org/press/announcing-the-post-quantum-cryptography-alliance-pqca.

Main, D., Drmota, P., Nadlinger, D.P., Ainley, E.M., Agrawal, A., Nichol, B.C., Srinivas, R., Araneda, G. and Lucas, D.M. (2025) 'Distributed quantum computing across an optical network link'. *Nature*, 638, 383–388. Available at: https://doi.org/10.1038/s41586-024-08404-x.

Matuschak, A. and Nielsen, M. (2019) 'Quantum computing for the very curious'. *Quantum Country*. Available at: https://quantum.country/qcvc.

Mitre (n.d.) 'ATT&CK matrix for enterprise'. *MITRE | ATT&CK*. Available at: https://attack.mitre.org/.

Open Security Architecture (n.d.) 'The OSA vision'. *OSA*. Available at: https://opensecurityarchitecture.org/cms/.

Palo Alto Networks (n.d.) 'What is security architecture?' *paloalto networks*. Available at: www.paloaltonetworks.co.uk/cyberpedia/what-is-security-architecture.

Pirandola, S., Eisert, J., Weedbrook, C., Furusawa, A. and Braunstein, S.L. (2015) 'Advances in quantum teleportation'. Available at: https://arxiv.org/pdf/1505.07831.

Q-CRTL (2024) 'Learn quantum computing'. *Q-CRTL*. Available at: https://q-ctrl.com/black-opal.

SABSA (n.d.) 'Home'. *SABSA, Enterprise Security Architecture*. Available at: https://sabsa.org/.

Schneier, B. (1999) 'Modeling security threats'. *Schneier on Security*. Available at: www.schneier.com/academic/archives/1999/12/attack_trees.html.

SecureOps (2022) 'How EDR solutions are bolstering cybersecurity defenses'. *SecureOps*. Available at: https://secureops.com/blog/what-is-edr/.

Sonar (n.d.) 'What is clean code?'. *Sonar*. Available at: www.sonarsource.com/solutions/clean-code/.

Steane, A.M. (2023) 'Notes on Dirac notation'. *Department of Physics, University of Oxford*. Available at: https://users.physics.ox.ac.uk/~Steane/teaching/Diracnote.pdf.

Vaideeswaran, N. (2025) 'Comprehensive guide to data loss prevention (DLP)'. *CrowdStrike*. Available at: www.crowdstrike.com/cybersecurity-101/data-loss-prevention-dlp/.

INDEX

Page numbers in italics refer to figures or tables.

www.ingramcontent.com/pod-product-compliance
Lightning Source LLC
Chambersburg PA
CBHW041007050326

40690CB00031B/5294